RAILWAY LINES
AND LEVERS

Other books by the same author

Boots & Saddle

RAILWAY LINES
AND LEVERS

Ron Bradshaw

UNICORN BOOKS

First published in 1993 by
UNICORN BOOKS,
16 Laxton Gardens,
Paddock Wood,
Kent TN12 6BB

© R. B. Bradshaw 1993

ISBN 1-85241-015-9

Typeset by Vitaset, Paddock Wood
Printed and Bound in Great Britain

To Dorothea, a long suffering wife who cheerfully bore the depressions and frustrations that beset the aspiring author; and to the Stationmaster's daughter, Freda Skey, whose conception of a signalman's memoirs taking book form now bears fruit.

Contents

Settle-Carlisle

Twixt Whernsides flanks and Arten Gill
A cry arose, no man could still,
Perchance an echo, Sharland's ghost,
We know the answer, so do most.

A piercing shrill, a Midland crew,
Steam and guts, Helm winds, they knew,
These are Fells of sleet and hail
Washing peat from Hudson's rails.

Batty Moss to Dandry Mire,
Wild Boar Fell and Hell Gill Beck,
Studley Garth and Mallerstang,
Names that deem a mind afire.

Signals wanted amber, green,
A shining red at Ais Gill seen,
Signalmen in lonely boxes,
Garsdale, Dent and Crosby Garrett.

No more shall trains drive block to block,
Double Headers, Freights and Troopers,
A savage curse shall now descend
On Carlisle-Settle. This the end?

R.W. Bradshaw

CHAPTER 1

To Fashion an Embryonic Signalman

Ramsbottom is perhaps not a place name to inspire the imagination of a would-be reader of this narrative but, despite being the butt of many a music hall joke, it was in 1932 a lively Lancashire cotton town with a large railway marshalling yard and it figures significantly in my railway destiny, for better or for worse. The aforementioned year is vividly outlined in my nostalgic memories. At the then tender age of 10, I was to stay for a week of my school holidays with cousins who lived in the inauspicious surroundings of Crow Lane. Unfortunately for my cousins, who had all attained the ripe old age of 14, they were busily employed in the local paper mill. With a little apprehension, I set out on my first morning to reconnoitre the town and, like all small boys of the day, I headed for the railway, guided by the clattering of wagons and constant rumble of the shunting engines. Architecturally, Ramsbottom Station was not in any way imposing but it was an extremely lively rail-head serving as the junction station for Accrington, Burnley and Skipton on the one hand, and the busy Bacup branch on the other. The signalbox alongside controlled main-line traffic, the entrance and exits of the goods marshalling yard, also the level-crossing gates. I was subconsciously drawn to this box, for what better vantage point could there be to observe all the wonders of train and road traffic control.

Travelling by train, seeing trains and realising that trains surrounded you everywhere in those times was commonplace, but who operated them, who pulled the strings, who steered them from one route to another, told them when to start and stop, allowed them to go fast or slow? These questions seemed almost insignificant, as we took the operation for granted, but how was it all done? However, with my ringside seat I was suddenly aware of what really happened. With what appeared to be phenomenal strength, the signalman was pulling and pushing levers over the frame, operating electrical block instruments and frequently dashing to one or other of the several telephones, and winding over a huge wheel to open or close the level-crossing gates. To me, it was like the operating of my Hornby train set on a really large scale, and without doubt I now needed abundantly more rolling stock, track and signals. So thrilling was this chance encounter that on the way home I contemplated further visits to my new-found Eldorado.

Over the nest few days I returned to the same location to view the signal-man at work, he who controlled the endless shunting and marshalling of freight trains, and the ceaseless passage of both express and stopping trains through the station. Sadly, the holiday very quickly came to an end, though on my return to my native town of Waterfoot in the Rossendale Valley I had an avid desire to hear, read and see more of railway operation. Though not positioned on a main line, Waterfoot itself had a great deal of local railway interest. The large goods station, to this day still standing – and used, ironically, as a road haulage depot – was a hive of activity and I made many visits there due to my father's position as a shipping clerk. The mysterious signalbox opposite drew my attention but was out of reach across several tracks which, little known to me then, would be crossed daily later in life when I became a signalman there myself. About this time Waterfoot goods depot was selected to experiment with the new articulated 'Karrier Kob' vehicles and all horse-drawn carts were discontinued. Often I was treated to rides with old Tom Smith when he was collecting and delivering goods to the local cotton and shoe and slipper mills. These rides were a source of never-ending pleasure as a child, but I was to miss the dray horses, seen thereafter only in the valley at Bacup and Rawtenstall depots. Perhaps the fact that I was born not in, but next to, their stables at Foundry Vale caused me to hold a significant affection for them. Alongside my birthplace, were the unusual three tunnels passing through the Glen to Baxters brewery. The first two, known as Newchurch Nos 1 and 2 were built in 1852 for the single line to Bacup; the third bore was taken in 1881 to make the double track and became known as Thrutch tunnel. The original line to Waterfoot was extended from Rawtenstall in 1848 and the station was known then as Newchurch. Prior to industry arrriving in Rossendale, Newchurch was the much more important of the two villages. However, in my day it was given the name of 'Waterfoot for Newchurch', thus placating the residents of the latter village.

On that station, I recall gripping my parents' hands amongst the crowds awaiting a Blackpool excursion in the mid-twenties. As the train burst out of the Thrutch tunnel the surge forward began, with everyone wishing to obtain a window seat. With a penny bar of Nestle's chocolate to nibble, one would soon become oblivious to the horsehair seats and the consequential stabbing in the nether regions. Shorts for little boys were the order of the day irrespective of weather and any other discomforts.

A further piece of luck came my way in 1934. The stationmaster's house became vacant and my father, then a head clerk, took the option and we moved in. Having lived the past 10 years in a council house on the bleak Edgside estate, but with nevertheless the comforts of electricity and flush toilet, it came as a shock to return to gas lights, an outside toilet and a pantry complete with its own complement of mice. These inconveniences were outweighed by the overwhelming fact that fate had now brought me to live virtually on the railway, in a place where my bedroom was a mere two metres from the nearest of four tracks, something I became aware of at five in the morning following the move, when the Brewery sidings (Manchester) to Bacup freight train arrived. Within seconds I was out of bed and gazing happily at the early morning shunting with its accompanied clattering of buffers and waving handlamps in the murky morning, and clouds of engine smoke endeavouring to hide my view. Needless to say, Mother was not amused!

Further treats occurred at Waterfoot Station with the school trip to Edinburgh when our train of ten coaches was headed by one of the new and already famous Stanier 'Black Fives', a sight not often observed on the Bacup branch. The following year's trip to North Wales not only surprised us because we found people in Britain who spoke a different language to English, but because we were served at a table in a dining coach which was truly the supreme wish of any schoolboy railway enthusiast. With a stretch of the imagination, one could almost compare this to a journey on the Orient Express!

An insatiable appetite for all things 'Railway' was now slowly pulsating through my veins, and all seemed to be happening, as I was given an opportunity to see King George V opening the Mersey tunnel and to take a journey on Liverpool's famous overhead railway which had an excellent panorama over the docks, the majestic estuary of the Mersey and the transatlantic liners in their berths. I often made trips to New Brighton via the Mersey ferry and to Heaton Park, as it was only a short journey from Bury by electric train. Another wonderful outing was when my father took me to London, which entailed changing to the Euston portion of the Skipton to Wilmslow train at Ramsbottom. On several occasions I pleaded with Mother to allow me to visit uncle Edwin Warwick at Stubbins, too. This gave me an excuse to stand for hours on Stubbins Station excited by both passenger and freight trains taking advantage of Helmshore bank and hurtling through the junction at what was certainly an unheard of speed in the Rossendale Valley.

These practical observations stimulated my desire for reading more and more of railway operations. Certainly in those years there was no shortage of material. Dominating all travel and commerce in this area of Lancashire was the London, Midland and Scottish Railway Company, formed in the big railway amalgamations of 1923 when many large and small companies were grouped together to become the largest single employer of labour in the world, also the world's largest transport system with close to 10,000 locomotives.

The Lancashire and Yorkshire system, on whose tracks I was virtually born, was taken over by the London and North Western Railway in 1922 and swallowed up into the LMS within twelve months, although all around there was evidence of its origins, also of the Rossendale connection with its builders, the East Lancashire Railway Company.

The LMS from its inauguration a decade ago had seen tremendous changes, from the squabbles between the Derby and Crewe schools of thought, to the new age of the thirties. This I was now conscious of at first hand. 1926 saw the general strike which dealt the railways a savage blow, and to shake up the young LMS from its apathy came Joshua Stamp, later to become Sir Joshua. Simultaneously with the updated cogitations of directors on the rival east coast LNER, Joshua Stamp requested a GWR Collett 'Castle' to be used for extensive trials on the West Coast Euston–Glasgow route to the north. This proved an excellent move and within six years not only had the LMS changed its whole strategy, but by subterfuge and prevarication made a legal kidnap of the Assistant Mechanical Engineer of the GWR 'Bill' Stanier. A revolutionary decision, no doubt, but within two years LMS motive power operations had become unified with engines of the Midland, Caledonian, North Western and L&Y, taking their rightful places in territory they were built for and the new Stanier taper boilered 'Pacifics' were put to work on the vital west coast main lines to Glasgow, Edinburgh, Liverpool and Manchester.

During this revolutionary period, 1930-39, train performances were in the public eye continuously and publicity was excellent, with named trains coming into their own. The *Irish Mail*, the oldest named train in the world; The *Cheltenham Flyer*, introduced in 1923 and now in 1932 carrying a headboard with the imposing slogan 'World's Fastest Train'; The *Royal Scot* and *Flying Scotsman*, battled for supremacy on the rival routes to Scotland; and, pride of the GWR, *The Cornish Riviera*, to name but a few. However, all attention focussed on the new *Coronation Scot* which in 1937 snatched the former LNER 1936 speed record with a 114mph run. The final all-time battle occurred the following year, 1938, with Sir Nigel Gresley's *Mallard* setting the seal and establishing a world steam record at 126mph.

The *Coronation Scot*, as much an LMS train as could be imagined, was immortalised by the music of Vivian Ellis, though the story goes that Ellis's theme was inspired by GWR trains passing his home, and was sold by his publishers encompassed in a music folder depicting an LNER 'Coronation' class engine of Gresley's A4 'Pacific' series, probably much to the disgust of William Stanier the founder of the *Coronation Scot*. Other interesting news in 1937 was that following this record-breaking run King Boris of Bulgaria, a great railway locomotive enthusiast, by invitation had been allowed to handle the controls of the *Coronation Scot* during a scheduled run in July. Next came news of the LNER's Coronation train beating the GWR *Cheltenham Flyer's* start-to-stop record, by a non-stop run from King's Cross to York at an average of 71.9mph over the 188¼ miles. News also leaked of the near mishap of the *Coronation Scot* when setting up the 114mph record on 29 June. Only two miles south of Crewe had the brakes been applied and the facing points before Crewe Station were taken at almost 60mph, well over the speed limit for entering the station. Crockery was sent flying and flames were seen shooting off the brake blocks, much to the consternation of the kitchen staff. The passengers and crew alike were thrilled by these high speeds normally reserved for passengers dropping down Shap or Beattock banks further north. The press, however, did not over-react. These were pro-railway days, after all, and it was Coronation year.

School-leaving age in the 1930s was 14, unless your parents were sufficiently wealthy to allow you to continue your education and you yourself desired to do so. My parents were not rich enough for that, nor did I have the inclination to continue. I was only too eager to be a wage earner. It is an immature age at which to be snatched from school and thrown into the hurly-burly of life, but so it was to be and, despite my father's entreaties, I had no heart for life in a railway office. With no interest in an academic career, my schooldays could not end quickly enough, much to my regret in later years – a view shared by many mature adults.

Jobs were hard to find due to the depression at that time, but at least it was a little easier for a junior. I was fortunate to obtain a vacancy as an apprentice mechanic in a local boot-and-shoe engineering workshop and, despite a tempting wage of 7s 6d (37½p) per week, was not very happy. Not being a mechanically minded person, I was pleased when, a year later, my father announced his promotion to Bury, nine miles south and in the Manchester area proper. This move was to set the seal on my job-seeking within a few months. A short spell as a grocer's boy, trundling an old tradesman's bike, with ½cwt of groceries piled up in the front basket, sliding about on cobblestones, tramlines and icy roads, for 10s (50p) per 60-hour-week, knocked all desires for an open-air career out of my mind. What next?

A journey to Manchester by electric train one evening put to rest forever these jumbled thoughts, doubts and generally miserable feelings that only teenagers know. Flooding back to mind on arrival at Victoria Station came all those childhood dreams and aspirations. Here was reality, staring me in the face was all the hustle and bustle of a station handling 355 workings per day, comprising of both electric and steam passenger trains in the bay platforms just feet from the huge hydraulic buffers. Further along towards platform 8 and 9 lay the through lines to platform 15 and the country's longest platform (nearly ½ mile long) which connected with Exchange Station. The whole complex pattern of the workings here sent the adrenaline racing through my veins as I constantly retraced my steps, inextricably galvanized to the bustle and noise of this huge terminus.

I recalled that Queen Victoria gave her name to this main terminal of the Manchester and Leeds railway in 1844, then the country's largest station. Here I was seeing again, though on a much larger scale, the operations I had witnessed five years earlier at Ramsbottom. Trains were approaching from all directions and arriving at various platforms, guided here and there as if by invisible hands. It was not immediately obvious to the public eye that the trains were directed by the unseen hands of some ten signalmen, seven signalboxes and a combination of some 400 points and signal levers. After three hours of bliss, I nearly forgot the object of my journey, namely to purchase photographic material for my father, but one factor was most clearly established in my mind – tomorrow I would seek my fortune on the railway.

As the reader will by now have concluded, the customary boyhood dreams of growing up to become an engine driver was not one of mine. Consequently, Bury shed, the ex-East Lancs locomotive works would not be my port of call. Rather I would go to the operating department offices, situated alongside Bury's Bolton Street Station. Fired by an enthusiasm that only an impressionable youth can perceive, I slept little that night, then found myself duly positioned outside the Stationmaster's office at 9am. When the massive Victorian brass-knobbed door was unlocked, I presented myself, cap in hand, at the enquiry desk. After a feeble 'I'm looking for work, please' had been sarcastically answered by a confident 'So are several hundred lads', I was given an 'L&Y application for work' form, told to fill it in and post it to Hunt's Bank Offices, Victoria Station, Manchester, but they doubted if I would have any luck. The wind taken completely out of my sails, I swallowed the lump in my throat, gazed forlornly at the East Lancs' symbol on these old headquarters of that railway, and wondered why I had an L&Y application form for a job on the LMS Railway which had been swallowed up by that concern some 14 years previously! Things evidently moved slower than my personal enthusiasm. Perhaps father could put a word in, he had worked for the concern for 35 years and was now amongst the hierarchy, albeit in a different department. With youthful optimism, faith in my father's powers, and an offer anyway of 4s (20p) per week extra wage by moving into a local factory, I settled back, took that job, and waited.

Perhaps only two months went by, then I received a letter, again on L&Y letter heading, demanding my presence in Manchester for a medical examination. The elation of realising that I must have made an enormous jump in the queue for work was suddenly dampened when memories of two medicals I had taken some six months previously for the Royal Navy had shown me to be partially colour blind, and caused my failure. However, though this next test was to prove pretty exacting, I was later informed it was successful and when a vacancy arose, I would be duly informed. Another hurdle was over.

What now seemed to be an endless period of waiting was merely a matter of weeks. In the early months of 1938 the official form arrived advising me to report for duty in seven days' time at Bury Bolton Street Station. I informed the 'Hat Shop', the local name for the Hornby Street factory of Adam Ashworths that I would be leaving and for seven more weary days of steam-brushing half-manufactured trilby hats, I contemplated what would be in store for me as the days slowly dragged by. No intimation had been given as to my duties. Seven long days, seven long nights, and in that week we moved unexpectedly three miles away to the other side of town, near to Tottington. How would I travel to work? Surely I would be starting at some ungodly hour when there was no public transport! A cycle had been taboo since I had run away from home to join the navy some 12 months previously, but perhaps father would now relent after a promise of his son's stability. This proved so, and a secondhand 'Saxon' was purchased from Aspinalls of Kay Gardens. The next two days were given to cleaning, polishing, and generally endeavouring to give the bike a new appearance.

So came the final day's countdown: polishing of shoes, a haircut and all the usual trimmings that were associated with one's presentation to an employer in those post-Victorian days. This was it, the day had arrived; no bike was needed today, however, as a 9am start warranted a journey by tram, and a polished and immaculate appearance, with no trouser creases disturbed by cycle clips, would surely be appreciated.

CHAPTER 2

To Mould A Signalbox Lad

The headquarters of the East Lancashire Railway Company was an imposing structure, built around 1845 which now housed the offices of the Permanent Way Inspector and Signalling and Traffic Manager (more often referred to as Inspector), the Stationmaster, Telegraph and Railway Exchange, along with many other minor offices. Despite being coated with nearly 100 years of Lancashire smoke and grime, its brass letter boxes, huge door knobs and office door numbers still shone to a brilliant unreproachability. These offices were situated down the 'Slope' which led from the massive iron gates in Bolton Street paved by large and heavily rounded 'Sets'.

With cap removed, and a firm but slightly trembling grip on the 'butty box', a small attaché case containing sandwiches and a bottle of cold tea, I made my arrival known to Mr Day, the Stationmaster. In a short time this very pleasant and imposing personage arrived, showed me into his office and asked me to sit down, relax and try to stop shaking and to listen to what he had to say to me. Apologies were made to the effect that he was unable to introduce me to the Traffic Inspector who would be my supervisor. That indicative statement set my mind to all sorts of wild conjectures as to what my job would be, but it seemed I was not yet to be enlightened. With humorous and twinkling but ever-commanding eyes, Mr Day held my attention avidly and proceeded to impress upon me that I was an extremely lucky lad, chosen from many applicants for a railway career, and that at all times I must remember courtesy to passengers, the LMS Railway's passion for 'On Time' and lastly but most important, the safety that railway companies prided themselves upon in regard to the transport of the public.

In those ten or fifteen minutes I was to realise the true reason why Mr Day was known as 'Daddy Day', a true Victorian gentleman and certainly a different person indeed to the many men in authority I was to meet in future years. After informing me that I would be given a fortnight to learn my job and prove myself satisfactory to all concerned before being further examined, he donned his imposing gold-braided hat and ordered me to follow him. Striding down the platform in the Manchester direction and placing myself a suitable half-step behind, we were soon at the ramp and my heart was beginning to leap in all directions. Until 9.30am the traffic was very heavy following the morning rush period, and electric trains – some passenger-laden and some empty stock – appeared to be all around.

Here I was to have my first serious lecture on what a few thousand volts could do to a human body and how, when crossing these lines one had to exert extreme care in striding over the live rail. Furthermore, due to the station workings in this very compact area, trains would be coming in any direction at any time, and eyes in the back of your head were needed. Then negotiating several lines, with strictures on facing traffic at all times if possible, noting also that electric trains approached in their 'stockinged feet', and the warnings of all descriptions in my own bodily interest, we approached Bury South Junction signalbox. Rather perplexed and becoming apprehensive by the direction we were taking towards Bury shed, or perhaps could it be Knowsley Street Station, I was amazed to find my escort leading me directly to the signalbox. Utterly taken aback, and rendered dumb, I trailed Mr Day up the heavy wooden steps, clinging to the hand-rail, and entered the box. Then I encountered what I think was the greatest of all shocks I had ever experienced. I was truly dumbfounded. Was this real, was I to work here? Standing in the doorway, staring in awe at a huge man with a white polo-necked sweater, virtually ripping levers across the frame, I noticed a boy sitting on a high stool at the far end of the box who appeared to be answering two or more telephones at once, and I could hear bells from six block instruments which seemed to be all ringing at once.

'This will be your job,' announced the Stationmaster after passing the time of day to the signalman and train register boy. Stunned and speechless, I was placed alongside the high desk and shown the train register book. My duties would be to record the precise time of all bell signals received and sent, the passage of every train, to receive and convey all telephone messages and, when time permitted during slack periods, to clean the signalbox windows, blacklead the stove, scrub the linoleum floor and polish all block bells, telephone bells and lever handles. A furtive glance at the amount of window panes in a box this size caused a sudden shudder and almost transmuted me into a shivering jelly. Even to this day, my wife has to offer many inducements before I clean the smallest window willingly. Furthermore, it would be necessary to improve my writing considerably as train register books were liable to be perused by very illustrious Colonels at any Court of Enquiry following a railway accident. One such tragedy had occurred four years earlier at Winwick Junction, Warrington, culminating in 12 deaths. The signalman's initial mistake was not correctly noted by the train register boy, nor was the signalman reminded by him that a train was already in section when he cleared his block. At the resultant enquiry, the signalman was dealt with comparatively leniently, but the booking lad with much more severity.

These factors were earnestly impressed upon me and then my hours of training were discussed. I was to be put on immediate shift rota, 6am-2pm and 2pm-10pm on alternate weeks and the Inspector of Signalmen, Mr MacNiel, would come to see how I was progressing in one week's time. With the departure of Mr Day, I was left with a tall, smart, white-shirted youth of some three or four years my senior who looked at me as if he could kill me, and a signalman whose 6ft frame and broken-nosed profile stared at me with a look of 'can I knock some sense into this thin weedy looking red head'! 'Keep from under the feet for the next half-hour, and just take note of what's going on, then we will see what we can do with you,' announced this percursor of all my inward misgivings. Take mental note I certainly did. The booking lad's apparent surliness was due to the fact that he was a redundant clerk from some other department who would become unemployed if and when I passed out for this job, hence the antagonism.

Ted Cox was the name of the signalman who, little did I realise during those traumatic first few weeks, would shape my whole way of life in the future. His stature, command, leadership and guidance were a source of admiration. During my first hours I did not detect that in any way. On the contrary, I was perceptively afraid of the man, yet he was fascinating, as he had an educated accent with an irresistible command in his tone, and handwriting, which I had noted on the train register book, that was superb in its flowing copperplate style. To mystify me further, he had a total physical fitness and the features of a fighting man. I later discovered that amateur boxing had been his teenage pastime.

After one hour had passed since my entry into the signalbox, and seeing three times as many trains as I imagined ever passed through Bury in a day, the first of many lectures was given to me by Ted Cox. First I had to learn the block bell code and all 60 rings had to be known by heart. Most were used every day and all day, but several were emergency calls and had never been known to be used during a signalman's career. Nevertheless, they had to be learned in readiness for any emergency. Ted's theory, and I believe it to be correct, was to write down a signal, for example '3--2'; 'Express freight, livestock, perishable or ballast train *not* fitted with automatic brake', and then read it; read it again carefully three times before tearing up the piece of paper and throwing it away! If the day after you cannot repeat it from memory you repeated the process until you could, even if it had to be repeated ten times. The same system was also applied to learning the block regulations, engine headlamp codes, and engine whistle code. The latter fact intrigued me immensely. It had never even occurred to me, nor any other laymen I felt sure, idly hearing engine whistles that one long blast and three short ones means water required, four shorts means a right-hand junction, three shorts a left-hand junction, and so on. So, with my pencil and paper, I unceremoniously sat upon my jacket on the far corner of the floor – the one seat at the desk being occupied by my non-cooperative 'staff boy'.

These next few hours obviously were extremely boring and the continual noise of crashing levers, the perpetual ringing of block and telephone bells and the rumbling by of both electric and steam trains made concentration difficult. No doubt a few hours' study at home would be of great benefit and maybe tomorrow I would be allowed to observe what my booking was to be. At 4pm I received a message informing me to report to the clothing office at the station. I was duly sent on my way after further warnings of live third-rail dangers and delays which would be caused to traffic by power having to be switched off at Radcliffe sub-station whilst dead bodies were removed! I found that uniforms were dispensed in prison or army fashion. A quick glance was made by the clothing officer, who presumably carried a built-in tape measure in his head, then a suggestion that I purchase a belt, or better still have a good meal as he had no trousers in stock to fit my miserably narrow waist.

Carrying this bundle of clothing, roughly tied with string, I proudly strutted through the ticket barriers with my allotted pass. I gave a cursory glance at the 'Palaise De Dance', but dancing, damsels of the day, or any pleasure of the flesh, were far from my mind as I boarded the tram for home. It rattled its weary way to Bury Bridge and the Dusty Miller to rumble into the terminus at the 'Hark to Towler'. Stupidly, I had paid my tram fare whilst in my pocket I was holding an employee's residential free pass which enabled me to travel to Tottington station on the Holcombe Brook branch line! Unquestionably, I was decidedly disorientated today!

So ended my first day as a railway employee. My father's words that evening, fifty years ago and still ringing clearly in my ears were: 'Son, you have a job for life, look after it, you're a lucky lad.' Indeed, I was extremely and without doubt an infinitely happy youth that day in 1938. These were eventful days to both railmen and public alike. Inspiration and dedication to the silver rails abounded. Almost as if to seal my indomitable faith in railway transport came the news of Sir Nigel Gresley's triumphant all-time world record. 126mph achieved with his LNER No 4468 *Mallard*: God! How could anyone foresee the impending doom of 20 years hence when, by a government's lack of foresight, we would witness the greatest rape a transport system could ever endure?

Next day I was allotted a 'mock' train register book and told to distinguish and write down the various bell signals. Primarily, this would appear a simple task but if the reader can imagine six block instruments, three absolute block and three permissive, all obviously with a different bell tone, six wall telephones with switches to adapt to eight, a total of 14 different ringing bell tones, almost 70 levers constantly crashing across the frame, a continuous rumble of passing trains as the rush period commenced at 7am and both signalman and booking lad shouting their protracted instructions over the phone, or to each other, perhaps he will comprehend the frustratingly difficult task I had before me. This, I realise now, is why one is allocated a fortnight to learn the work. The peak period at Bolton Street Station at that time saw departures of electric trains to Manchester every 10mins and, on many occasions, every 5mins, the same number of arrivals from Manchester, with steam passenger and freight services from the Bacup-Manchester line via Middleton Junction and the Skipton-Salford route via Clifton Junction, so there was a 3hr period of perpetual and pulsating activity. Bolton traffic, on the whole, was handled through Knowsley Street Station. Tuesdays and Fridays brought extra express trains from Skipton, Colne and Bacup and these were provided primarily for the cotton-mill directors and buyers who by tradition, if not always by necessity, visited Manchester cotton exchange on these two days.

A signalman normally commenced at the level of a Grade 1 porter or shunter and he would then progress through Class 5, Class 4, Class 3 and then 2, over a period of many years, probably 20, before he even gazed inside somewhere like Bury South signalbox. Later he would rise to Class 1, Special Class 'A' and then 'B'. I was virtually thrown into this situation straight from the street. Little wonder I had many misgivings on that second day. Anxiously meditating, with pen in hand, I scribbled down what I hoped was correct, wondering if I would ever sit confidently on the same stool as the youth now bellowing telephone information across to the signalman.

Over the ensuing days the situation seemed to deteriorate, as I delved more and more into block regulations and the rule book with its legal jargon such as unending references to perhaps clause number something not applying under the said circumstances, except in the case of another rule number which has been duly amended and does not apply during fog or snow except when regulation number something else is not in operation! Having religiously read this rule over and over again and duly comprehended it, one could well have a further complication on the next page, for example, this aforesaid rule will not apply on the East Lancashire section of the Lancashire and Yorkshire Railway now controlled by the London, Midland and Scottish Railway Company between mileposts Nos 10 and 11!

By the weekend I was reduced to a sobbing and whimpering wretch. I confess when Ted Cox told me I had better pull my socks up, as there were only another seven days to go before at least 95 percent proficiency was required, the tears did truly well up in my eyes. That night, at home and alone with my thoughts, I broke down and cried. This was not the romance and life I had imagined! I lay awake for hours, though the spectre of a hectic 18 months still vivid in my mind cast my worries away at last. I had been a schoolboy, an apprentice mechanic, a grocer's boy, a factory machine-operator, experienced several fights with bullying senior apprentices. I had been 'tarred and feathered' by a group of mill girls, clipped behind the ear by a police sergeant and thrown into a cell to cool off. I had also experienced several risky tumbles with girls of doubtful repute, and only a fortnight previously toured the red-light area of Manchester and dared to climb the steps of the notorious Listers Bar off Market Street where I had gone to purchase two Guinnesses, one for myself and one for the first 'Lady' in the queue who no doubt would, and indeed did, return a small favour in the rear alley exit. This introduction to 'Love for sale' at the tender age of 15, and its half-promise of an erotic future at least caused the wisp of a facetious smile to cross my brow.

So here I was, crying like a schoolboy and feeling incapable of tackling an inextricable but challenging job such as this. No doubt, brains and not brawn were required, something I had not exercised a great deal since leaving high school. Sunday's break helped considerably and gave me a renewed fighting spirit. My father was able to help me with rule book and block regulation questions from the books I had been given and by lunchtime on Monday, when preparing for the 2pm shift, I had rid myself of this lethargic and morose mood.

As in learning a foreign language, there is an elusive barrier to be reached. Once that barrier is overtaken there comes a sudden understanding and clarity. You are thinking in that language, suddenly finding the light in the dark and acquiring a burning desire to progress. And so it is with signalling regulations and bell codes. By the eighth day that hitherto impenetrable barrier had been conquered and Ted Cox's face broke into a satisfied smile. With a pat on the back he announced 'You'll make it lad. Now we'll show you how to write. Your script is appalling.' Giving me a few dozen sheets of lined paper and showing me the correct way to 'balance' a pen between thumb and forefinger, he proceeded to instruct me in writing a continuous line of figure noughts, exactly touching the top and bottom of the lines and continuing until a full sheet of foolscap had been covered. This was a monotonous and boring way of spending the railway company's time, I thought, as I dipped my pen in and out of the chipped and stained inkwell but, without doubt, three hours later, with a full wastepaper basket, a complete and amazing change was made to my use of pen and ink. A further smile broke out on the face of the enigmatic signalman Cox and I now began to realise this man was human. I was beginning to live again! Tomorrow could not come quickly enough. Half-an-hour into my ninth day I witnessed another side to this intrepid man. Up to then, I had secretly feared him; now I felt a conversion to almost hero worship.

On that day the booking lad wrongly interpreted a telephone message which was to cause a minor delay, although that mistake was not his biggest. He chose to 'answer back' when receiving a verbal rebuke and within a split second received a clip 'round the ear 'ole' which sent him sprawling along the floor as the high 'Dicken's stool' overbalanced. Remaining outwardly calm but indeed trembling violently within, I witnessed this lad's final humiliation when Ted, as I had now been allowed to address him, later admonished him severely for not co-operating in the slightest to help this new learner and, if anything, deliberately impeded him. He was then told to 'clear out' for two hours, go where the hell he wished, providing he kept clear of the district offices, and return in two hours promptly. Duly dismissed, he virtually fell down the steps and so far as I was concerned the vulpine and insidious ex-clerk could have fallen under a train!

'Sit on that stool now lad and listen to me,' was the next command from this indomitable and punctilious signalman. 'We have two hours before the rush period and I'm going to make a trainbooker out of you in that time. You are doing well, and trying hard no doubt and I can see you have a keen interest, but you are extremely frustrated because you think you are not learning quickly enough. In a busy box like this it is extremely difficult to learn in such a short period of time. There are many signalmen who become paralysed with fear at the mere thought of working a box like this. They become qualified in a small country box and are content to stay there for life, never having any desire for promotion. As they are not born to be professional traffic controllers, they merely have a job that pays them a little more than what they could earn on a station. It's a pity the company cannot see sense and send lads like yourself to learn the initial stages of train signalling at one of those boxes. Let me now tell you about the telephones; you are going to be using them from now. You say that you have used a telephone previously; that would be the public phone system and you would hear only normal English spoken. Here you will not. The information you receive will be in railway jargon and punctuated by adjectives not normally heard on the telephone. They will be descriptive and words not to be found in the dictionary! Of course, there are no females using these local lines.'

Incessantly Ted talked on whilst working the frame, attending to the phones and describing every entry he made in the train registry book and stressing the importance of having a complete mastery of emergency regulations and bell signals, which was interposed by a recounting of several major accidents caused by a signalman's lapse of concentration or even pure negligence. The fateful triple smash at Quintinshill, Gretna Green, in 1915 and the whole subsequent sequence of events, when viewed in retrospect, were the result of the 'blocking back inside home signal' not having been sent to the box in rear. Therefore, you must learn what you have to do, and *why* you are doing it. This holocaust had resulted in the death of some 227 passengers, the majority being troops of the 7th Bn, Royal Scots Regiment en route to Liverpool. Quoting the Hawes Junction incident of 1910, which on those bleak and barren North Yorkshire fells had resulted in the death of nine passengers, I was warned of the dangers of over confidence and told of the need for continual vigilance and concentration when under stress and the absolute necessity of having no hindrance whatsoever from unauthorised persons in the box. Should stationmasters or enginemen, who have need to enter the box to sign the train register book in compliance with the rules, make any attempt to remain and gossip idly, they must be ordered out without ceremony. Twenty-one passengers had been killed on the L&Y 'other' electric line at Liverpool caused by a signalman's frustration during a rush-hour period. At all times you had to work quickly in the interest of speed and efficiency, but never let your legs and arms race your head, and what is, hopefully, inside it.

Ted then gave me a humorous description of his own initiation as a trainbooker on the Manchester-Leeds line of the L&Y railway at Todmorden East box. Then he proudly showed me the L&YR badges and mementos he treasured so much. Certainly masterpieces compared to the miserable piece of metal provided by the LMS, and well worth the time taken with steel slide and metal polish provided to clean it.

At one juncture in this long discourse he told mè to quickly 'grab' the receiver from one of the long bank of telephones. Now that my ears were a little more keenly tuned I had noted a two pause one call and took it to be a 'circuit' message. Not fully comprehending what was meant by a 'circuit', I merely took off the receiver and in meek semi-soprano voice replied 'Bury South Junction'! Several voices answered, accompanied by mild guffaws and comments including 'have we got a girl on the line now?', and the only clear words I deciphered from the message before all receivers were replaced was 'Accrington Oldham Road 46 and Castleton'. I repeated the message to Ted who explained its meaning. The Accrington-Manchester 'Oldham Road' freight train was passing Ramsbottom Station box and his load was 46 wagons, the next traffic stop being Castleton marshalling yard. As we were the next junction, it would be our job to route the train via Bury West and onto the Rochdale line, and we could now expect him to be approaching our section in about 15mins. According to Ted, one of the characters who had expressed the ribald comments over the phone would no doubt be the red-haired Yorkshireman, Walter Holgate at Bury West.

Bury West Junction signalman had now got advance warning of the precise position of this particular train, amongst many others, and would be able to make suitable calculations of how to fit this pawn into the chess-board web of traffic complexity. I was then allowed to take two more messages, and I felt a new confidence growing quickly. 'Bacup Moston 50, banker Bury' and 'Skipton express one up Clifton'. The former was interpreted as 'Bacup-Manchester (Moston) express freight with a load of 50 wagons, which was making no other stop but required a banker at Bury Loop Junction for the Broadfield Incline (1 in 86). The latter message I interpreted as the Salford-Skipton express running one minute before time at Clifton Junction. Now I followed the next one. 'Colne Camden full load London', and so on. A little sunlight seemed to be appearing now through this mental fog. Train signalling and traffic control were evidently a most necessary and flexible fusion. This man Cox was beginning to give a new and most interesting insight into its complexities. No longer was he a big man to be feared, but a big man to respect. Slowly he was beginning to exercise a tangible influence and a moral guidance over me which was to dictate my whole life from that point. I was transformed almost overnight into an insatiable student of train signalling and operation. During the next four days I sought and found all the answers I trusted would be necessary for the forthcoming examination.

When, on the final day allotted, the approach of District Inspector MacNiel was seen along the station ramp, I was totally and assuredly composed. Mr MacNiel was small in stature and carried the then customary non-committal frown of authority and, of course, the regulation bowler hat which at that time had replaced the 'topper' as the symbol of the Railway Supervisor. He greeted us civilly and, without wasting any time, went straight to the point. 'Is the lad ready for questioning?' 'Yes,' announced Ted, and without much fuss I was conducted from the box and onto the 'triangle' sidings at the junction of the EL and LY lines. I was not only questioned on bell signals and block regulation, but was asked general and practical questions such as: How would I remove a dead dog from the live rail? What would be meant if a driver passing the box was to be holding, up high, one open palm of one hand while hitting it hard with the clenched fist of the other? That meant he required a bank engine behind his train at Bury Loop Junction, and I must inform that box quickly.

Half-an-hour later we returned to the box, and a satisfied supervisor informed Ted of the result. I was told to take over on Monday at 2pm as a fully qualified train register boy. Sighs of relief and ultimate satisfaction could not adequately describe my feelings at that time, rather I felt an aura of total bliss. In this virtual dream-world I left work that evening fully elated, with a wave of inner satisfaction sweeping through me. Again my father's words were ringing in my ears: 'You have now got a good job for life. Your future is secure.'

CHAPTER 3

The Ecstacy of a Teenager

At 15½ years of age, I was quickly to learn the meaning of maturity and manhood, for here I was, a lone teenager thrown into a world of adult working men, without a single person of my own age group for companionship or consolation. During the following week I was to report for duty at 2pm on the afternoon of Monday and would be trainbooker to Bill Rockliffe, of whom I had heard some dreadful stories. Nevertheless, I would meet that hazard when it came. Tomorrow was a rest day and I would at least have that time in which to savour the victory over apathy.

Bill Rockliffe, generally known as 'Rocky', was a man of very few words and with an outwardly appearance of strict Victorian severity. He was immaculately adorned in a smart civilian check cap, black overcoat, highly polished black shoes and well-creased trousers, carrying his archaic leather Gladstone bag, and he wasted no time whatsovever on trivialities during changeover. He was every inch an unyielding and indomitable Edwardian. His 'Ow do' was curt and clear when taking over duty from another signalman and no time was wasted when advising the current traffic situation to his relief on finishing his term of duty. This seemed to confirm stories of his harsh treatment of signalbox lads who were neither efficient or courteous to him. Consequently, it was with some trepidation that I sat up to my desk on that faraway afternoon.

Signalman Griffiths and his trainbooker had left promptly at 2pm and Rocky curtly informed me to ignore the phones for the first hour and to concentrate merely on the train register book. He told me I had to be extremely neat with my figures, also that he would check my work after an hour had passed. Something in his brusque manner, starched white collar and rather Victorian approach sent a little shiver down my spine. That first hour seemed endless and only words of consequential relevance to signalling came from this Dickensian character. He was surprised when he came to peer over my shoulder to scan the work some precise 60mins later to find my hands trembling uncontrollably. 'What's the matter with you lad, your work's alright! I suppose "they've" been telling you what a little bastard I am. Well, so I am to folks I don't like, passenger guards in particular and relief signalmen who don't appreciate the shine on our lever handles and block bells when they work here! You do as I say, no cheek, keep the lever handles, bells, windows and floor spotlessly clean and we'll get on well. Now you can take the telephone messages and if you are not sure what's said, don't invent anything, ring back to the box concerned and say *Rocky* wishes to know!' A faint smile crossed his face and that was the only crack in his granite features I witnessed all day.

Two weeks with Rocky was then followed by a further two weeks with Llewellyn Griffiths an ex-GWR signalman from Ludlow, every bit an ex-countryman with an 'Old Bill' drooping moustache and pipe to match. He was certainly an unbelievable contrast to both Bill Rockliffe and Ted Cox. Unable to pronounce the Welsh 'Llewellyn' we local Anglo-Saxons were content to address him as 'Lew' and his long drawn out vowels and constant 'Aigh, aigh' for yes, his clay pipe and roll of Condor twist, his drooping 'Bruce Bairnsfather' walrus moustache and pronounced mid-Wales accent gave an unusual colour to this predominant Lancashire stronghold. As with Bill Rockliffe, I soon found myself at ease after the initial few days, but nevertheless was thrilled to be back with Ted Cox after four weeks, and surely 'fully qualified'. Now I could demonstrate my prowess!

Over a period of six weeks I had learned quickly that the contrast in working of the three signalmen during a similar specific time of the day was significantly marked. During the time of stress, information passed to them from the many sources, including Manchester control-room was vital. I could now give this accurately, and without fuss, when most needed. Truly I saw what a fusion of brain and brawn was necessary for the smooth running of traffic during the 4pm-8pm period. With one train running only one minute out of schedule, the consequential upheaval could last for hours unless counteracted by quick thinking. A split-second decision to re-route a train from say, platform two to platform one, or from one bay platform to another, may be disconcerting to passengers and station staff alike, but could be in the long term a well-judged and dextrous move. An animal electrocuted on the live rail, or a brake pin hanging from the end of its short chain unceremoniously obliterated by 1,200 volts, would knock out the breakers at Radcliffe sub-station, consequently bringing all electric trains to a standstill. After a quick appraisal of such a situation, and perhaps the removal of the animal by special tools, the message would be relayed to Radcliffe, the circuit breakers replaced and normal workings would be resumed. Albeit, 12 trains could have been brought to a standstill with a possible total 3mins delay to each, the subsequent 'chain' reaction spreading delays over a 20 mile radius of a closely-knit web of suburban railway, and perhaps taking three or four hours to bring under control. Such was the density of pre-war traffic in a pre-motor age.

It was in these situations that I regretted the unfortunate inability or opportunity of the general public to have access to control points to see what happens behind the scenes. Not to merely see the glamour of the railway engine but to observe the men at work controlling these monsters. The unseen eyes and hands that tell the driver when to brake, when to accelerate, which route he will take, when to start and when to stop. The mystery of the unseen power one holds when working a busy station or junction box was endearing me to this fascinating life at an early age. Within six months of my training I was able to 'unofficially' work Bury South and 'signal box mania' had set in.

In turn I made many visits when off duty to local boxes, Bury Loco Junction, West Junction, East, North, Loop and Tottington Junctions, were among all eleven with which I was reasonably familiar by the year end. When not working I spent many hours reading through railway statistics. Historical facts are of as much interest to the enthusiast of today as they were to a working enthusiast in July 1938, when the world's steam record was set up by the *Mallard* at 126mph. 'Yes, 138 he would be clocking at maximum,' declared Charlie Spillman, Bury's 'Ace' driver. Charlie was the only man who could leave Bury 5mins late with a six-coach train and L&Y tank engine, and arrive at Bacup on time after eight stops, much to the fireman's disgust.

From my reading of signalling and general railway operating many interesting facts emerged; for example, one of the highest and most lonely signalboxes in Britain was at Torpantau in the Brecon Beacons of Wales, at 1,312ft above sea level. The most claustrophobic signalbox in the world must surely have been the one 6 miles inside, in the middle of the Simplon Tunnel in the Alps. The most rain-lashed and bleakest in Britain surely was Hawes Junction, now Garsdale, on the Settle-Carlisle route of the Midland Anglo-Scottish line. Of stations, the highest in the world was Condor in Bolivia at 15,705ft above sea level. The largest was in New York and the busiest in Moscow. Of tunnels, the oldest was in the United Kingdom, the Talyllyn Tunnel, on the Brecon-Merthyr railway in South Wales, which was built in 1816, at first for the Brecon to Hay-on-Wye Tramway but later widened for the railway in 1860. The longest tunnel in the world was the Simplon, 12¼ miles. The highest in the United Kingdom was at Torpantau in the Brecon Beacons, again on the Brecon-Merthyr line at 1,312ft. The longest in the United Kingdom was the Severn Tunnel, 4⅓ miles.

The LMS railway did not have a long history. On the contrary, it had only been in existence for a mere 15 years. The section on which I was employed, however, had a very long and interesting past. 'Lancashire and Yorkshire' was a term associated not only with the battleground of the Wars of the Roses, cricket encounters, or jocular banters. It was also a name synonymous with the busiest railway in the world. Prior to amalgamation with the London and North Western in 1922, the L&Y had four times as many signals per mile as the Great Western and on a route-mileage-to-receipts basis was the busiest of the pre-grouping railways. It was formed in 1847 by the unification of several companies, including the Manchester-Leeds, the Manchester-Liverpool, and East Lancashire railways, and formed a key link in the industrial north from eastern to western seaports, and through the vast complex of cotton and wool towns of the two counties. Victoria Station, Manchester, opened in 1844, which took the Queen's name and was then the country's largest station handling 355 trains per day and it became the headquarters of the L&Y. This company later was to lead the way with electrification, and in 1904 the Liverpool-Southport route became the first operational electric system in the UK, followed by the Bury-Manchester line in 1916. It could be said the L&Y existed for three major reasons, and that if at the turn of the century that particular railway company had come to a standstill the country would have been bankrupted within a week. It's three basic functions were to move coal from the vast Yorkshire coalfields to the thousands of factories within the two counties, and to Liverpool docks to feed the liners and to export it in massive quantities. Secondly, its role was to transport the raw cotton and wool from Liverpool to the thousands of mills in Lancashire and Yorkshire; there were 250 in Oldham alone. Then the railway had to return the vast majority of finished goods to Manchester and Liverpool again, for export. Thirdly, and to a millworker the most important fact, the railway was used to take them and the family to Blackpool for the annual seven days' Wakes Week. All this, in addition to the daily commuting between towns and cities, led to the L&Y's just claim to retain its own 'unofficial' Administration across the complex network when sandwiched between the opposing policies of the Midland and North Western railways following the 1923 Amalgamation.

The new title LMS Railway, was in my opinion, a tragic mistake. Had the L&NW or the Midland decided to sink their pride, as did the Caledonian, and adopt one of the former two names, a pride and prestige similar to that of the GWR would have shone forever. As a neutral, my own choice would have been L&NWR and what better accolade for the company whose origins were nurtured in the first intercity railway in the world, the Liverpool and Manchester. Perhaps I was a little biased due to childhood memories of 1927. Thrust into an early and precursory adulation of all 'named' trains my Uncle had taken me onto Lancaster station to see the *Royal Scot* making its inaugural run. Seeing it pounding through the station at high speed, its screaming whistle so shrill and alien to the low throated L&Y sounds heard in my valley, here at the gateway to Shap Fell and the distant north, I felt railway history was truly in the making. Had it not always been so on this west-coast Anglo-Scottish trail; Euston, Rugby, Crewe, Shap, Carlisle and Beattock were all magical names to a railway romantic.

So that is how a carefree and very happy young railway employee saw events in 1939. It was a year which was, in retrospect, the beginning of the end so far as railway domination of transport in the UK was concerned, but nevertheless it brought a tranquil and optimistic beginning to a 17-year-old teenager.

In February, the LMS *Duchess of Abercorn* took the British record as the most powerful locomotive when it hauled a load of 610 tons on the Euston-Glasgow run, which included the two notorious climbs and all railmen and public anticipated more to come. Would perhaps the Great Western pull something out of the bag? Little had been heard from 'God's Wonderful Railway' of late, not since the inauguration of the *Bristolian* in 1935, which rattled off the 118 miles from London to Bristol in 105mins at a little under

70mph. Also in that year the famous *Cornish Riviera Express* from London to Plymouth established the world's longest run. Since these feats had now been surpassed by the LMS and LNER, perhaps something staggering would emerge again from that quarter. Nothing transpired, however. It was as if the winds of war had infiltrated the tightly sealed doors of Paddington and Swindon's propaganda departments, and no further challenges were to come as yet. These doubts and pessimisms were far from my mind as I completed my first year in Bury South Box. On recollection, it was a period of time that I consider to be the happiest working days of my whole life. I had found utter and complete fulfilment in my work. I achieved a true and remarkable rapport with any signalman or relief signalman I encountered in my work. Some relief men were surly, while others were quite sociable and garrulous, but they all appreciated an experienced signalbox lad, willing to co-operate and give help, and I prided myself on having achieved that.

On one occasion, however, when working with reliefman Joe Rodgers, a most likeable man and prolific raconteur, I made my first but most hair-raising mistake. In addition to the usual semaphore signals, Bury South also had a gantry of electric multiple aspect signals on the city-side entry to Bolton Street Station. These electric aspect signals were of an unusual type, operated by the normal semaphore signal lever and consequently had none of the counterbalancing weights beneath the frame. They merely needed sliding across the frame, rather than using the strenuous pull that was necessary to reverse a pair of points, operate a locking bar, or raise a distant signal. Joe was taking a 'breather' and mug of tea whilst I worked the box for 10mins and it was during this break that I signalled through the 4.25pm Salford-Skipton Express. With a clear road through and all distant signals 'off', the express was approaching at some 70mph. Passing under the footbridge a mere 200yds away, he saw our colour light signal at 'red'. In all my years I have never seen a fully laden train of eight coaches and a Stanier 'Black Five' come to a stop in so short a distance. Only drivers who have experienced a red light thrown in their faces at that speed with a fully-loaded passenger train behind them can know that sickly and hollow feeling in the pit of the stomach. Within split seconds the regulator was swept down, the brake applied at full, the reverse wheel frantically wound back and the sanders were blown. The Fireman, if not alert, could well finish up an inert bundle across the footplate. For my part, a terrible cold sweat broke out across my forehead and my hands trembled uncontrollably as I stood completely mystified as to the cause of the emergency stop. As I swung round I saw all levers were in the correct 'off' position in the frame, but after a quick re-check the obvious reason was quickly apparent. The repeater dial, a device used to denote the position of unseen signals showed 'wrong adjust' on No 8 down home signal. With an electric colour-light signal there can be no half-and-half position as with semaphore arm, it is either red or green. So the answer was clear. The driver had seen a semaphore distant at green and a colour light home red, and due to the short section workings of only a

¼ mile apart, they were interslotted with the box ahead. The driver could see *all* the signals through to Bury North box at the clear position and after a quick 'right away, driver' shouted hurriedly from the window, brake blocks were blown off savagely and the train was in motion again within seconds. Many angry faces peered from the lowered windows, including the guard with his inevitable notebook taking down the box name and prominently holding out his regulation watch. I thanked my lucky stars this train did not carry a restaurant car. Nothing further was heard of the episode. I assume to this day that the driver took for granted he had mistaken the signal, then made up the lost time before Skipton, and the guard with the inevitable notebook was 'squared'. Joe, rather than chastise me after the visible shaking-up, was feeling sympathy but repeated the importance of observing a constant vigilance and the importance of signal arm response and track circuit indicators. He quoted the Castlecary (Scotland) accident of 18 months ago when 35 people were killed. During the ensuing enquiry a signalman was held partially to blame for incorrect observation of the indicator of a distant signal.

This little episode had a sobering effect on my possible over self-confidence and was to remain a constant reminder when working busy boxes later, a truly graphic illustration of 'more haste, less speed'!

I found myself cycling to work more often, in preference to using the train as on many occasions it was more convenient, although since running away from home in the immediate post-schooldays, cycling had not been a serious pastime. An abortive night's sleep in a telephone kiosk at Otley in West Yorkshire on a freezing cold night had cooled my ardour somewhat. I was lost near Hull with no money, and the consequential return home with my tail between my legs to receive a severe rebuke from the harassed local police and my parents, who had spent many hours searching for almost two days, had temporarily halted my wanderlust. Ted Cox, however, with his daily bike ride from Ashton-under-Lyne displayed extreme fitness and his views on the joys of cycling renewed my latent enthusiasm.

The six-day week of post-war years left one very useful day to me, so I decided to use it to the best advantage. After a little training, a 100 mile day's ride now brought many areas of railway interest within a comfortable cycling distance. Supplied with a bottle of cold tea, and a liberal amount of sandwiches, I visited Carnforth, Settle Junction, Ribblehead Viaduct, Crewe, Preston, Manchester, Lancaster, Liverpool, Leeds and the trans-Pennine routes.

A friend had suggested I joined the recently founded Youth Hostels Association and this idea fostered a great interest, as long weekends away meant further distances to cover. Six months later, I became a keen cycle tourist and youth hosteller and celebrated my first annual holiday with a six-day trip to the Scottish Highlands, as I now had the availability of one free pass to anywhere on the LMS system. With the aid of this pass and membership of the YHA, I took this memorable week's holiday. The pass and a 'privilege' rate cycle ticket were used to Oban in the Western

Highlands and then the return trip was made by cycle, using youth hostels for overnight accommodation, and cooking by roadside during the day.

One of the highlights of this trip was the train journey from Wigan to Oban. The train was an overnight Euston-Inverness Limited Stop Express hauled by No 6228 *Duchess of Rutland*, one of 15 'Coronation' class engines streamlined by Stanier in the 1930s, which later had their additional 3-ton cladding removed. The sight of this sleek silver 'Pacific' pulling into Wigan Station in the murky light of midnight with its sleeping coaches, mail vans, first-class coaches and third-class corridor stock for the likes of me was truly impressive. Soon the cycle was stowed into a parcels van amongst a multitude of mail sacks and later my saddle-bag stuffed under my head for a pillow, and I was lying on the corridor floor. It was impossible to sleep. The clattering and shrill whistles as we thundered through Preston and Lancaster, the slowing down and the urgent engine calls as bankers touched and then opened up at the rear on the two major inclines over Shap Fell, all kept me awake. Oxenholme to Gayrigg, then Tebay to the summit, what a story these Fells could recount. One hundred years ago this famous 70-mile stretch, from Lancaster to Carlisle had cost the lives of 75 of the 10,000 men who laboured here earning the astonishing wage of 3s (15p) per day. Also put to work in this cruel terrain were 1,100 horses. This 1-in-75 gradient over the Fells saved an extremely long tunnel.

From the summit we proceeded towards Penrith where soldiers and police had on several occasions been called out to quell riots amongst these wild navvies of that bygone age. After Carlisle, came the second north-western climb over Beattock Fell and another fast descent into Lanarkshire and Carstairs Junction, where I afterwards dozed off until someone put their army boot into my backside to say we were pulling into Perth.

Changing from a fast long-distance main-line train to the Highland Railway and its comparative tranquility was a marked and sharp contrast. It was now daytime and quickly I shook the sleepiness away to enjoy the journey through mountains and along lochs. This indeed was something I had only read about in travel books. The compelling beauty and overall serenity of this part of Britain I had never truly visualised. It was far removed from the cotton mills, tall smoke-belching chimneys, grime and ceaseless noise. For me, without doubt, the solitude and immeasurable beauty of the mountains was ecstatic.

Oban was reached very quickly and my cycle tour commenced. It brought with it a further dimension. The YHA had succeeded in providing a new aspect to travel for young folk as it gave one the chance to meet people of all nationalities, to find new friends from all walks of life and to seek a broadening of one's outlook on life. All this was available for the cost of 1 shilling per night!

Windswept, sunburned and not a little saddle-sore, I returned much the wiser a week later with some 400 miles chalked up and a vision of Scotland and its compelling scenery that will forever be imprinted on my memory.

CHAPTER 4

A Poignant Farewell

Within a few weeks of my return from this, the first of many future ventures I hoped would take place, came the terrible news of war. On Friday, 1 September 1939, the four railway companies were put under government control. They would be operated from the disued low-level tube station at Down Street, London. On 3 September Britain and France declared war on Germany.

The authorities, in their debatable wisdom, put a plan into action which was to prove the biggest mass movement of people in the whole history of railway operation or, indeed, any other form of transport. It turned out to be a panic decision due to the collapse of the British Intelligence Network in Germany and the forecasted heavy bombing raids which did not materialise. In the first four days of the 'phoney' war 3,833 special trains moved 1,300,000 women and children from 18 major cities of the UK to less populated towns and rural areas. By the time the bombing of our cities by the Luftwaffe commenced in 1940, a large number had returned!

Nevertheless, the railways had proved what they could do when the occasion arose. 600,000 privately-owned wagons were immediately and compulsorily confiscated to add to the companies own 600,000. The majority of these were the property of coal merchants, collieries and other large concerns. They then became known as 'Pool' wagons. This was a major stroke for economy and commonsense, and saved the continual about-turn of empties, which had to be returned to their respective owners in coal and goods yards far and wide.

Very soon blackout precautions were introduced, with the consequent frustration and aggravation to train signalling, and to shunting in the large marshalling yards where the majority of work took place during the night-time. A signalman must be able to see every movement clearly and unimpeded from his strategically placed position. The windows, which in many cases surround the whole box are kept clear and clean for this purpose, and as much interior light as possible must be provided to enable him to see his levers, block instruments, phones and train register book. How could one tackle this inextricable problem? Initially no official method of light shielding was suggested and invariably an old newspaper surrounding a battered gas mantle was the practice, much to the consternation of air-raid wardens on their nightly patrols. 'Arcking' on the electric third rail was a continual and unavoidable hazard, along with open fire-box doors on the footplate, but a fireman had to do his stoking. Soon, however, these punctilious officials, somewhat akin to our present-day traffic wardens, were led to despair and diverted their attentions to the easier targets such as shops and private houses. Nevertheless, as any wartime pilot was aware, from a height of 1-2,000ft there was no way of hiding a railway four times as large and busy as it is today.

A most amusing and equally inappropriate item supplied to all boxes was a so-called air-raid shelter. It was a metal box resembling a portaloo or watchman's hut, and placed in the signalbox along with a bucket of sand, bucket of water and stirrup pump. The purpose of this shelter was questionable as no instruction to stop work and shelter during an air-raid was ever given. Indeed, on the contrary, many instructions and new regulations were issued as how best to operate the railway whilst under attack! In my experience the most practical uses given to this object were to have an urgent pee, sometimes held back for hours in a busy box, or to hide an unauthorised young lady in a quiet country box when officialdom approached! The closest encounter I personally had with an aerial attack at Bury South was some months later a little after 10pm when a string of bombs, no doubt intended for Bury loco shed, dropped wide and scattered cinders and ballast over a wide area. A couple of scratches were all I received and a bruised and cut knee after pitching down on the lineside.

I found the early months of the war quite eventful. Regulations regarding a maximum 48hr working week for youths under the age of 18 were scrapped as men were called up for the Forces. Overtime was abundant and a 12hr working day became almost perpetual for the next few years. During 1940 I found myself covering the regular 8hr shift in Bury South box and then having to take a turn of four hours in the telegraph office which was an interesting job, with training in the use of the unusual two-bell morse-code system which eliminated the long dash, and substituted all dots, thus making all messages some 50 percent more speedy both to receive and send. The best part of all was the telephone switchboard operation. When I was not too busy there was time to 'chat up' the girl operators at Rochdale, which included an attractive blonde who later in life became my sister-in-law!

On another day, perhaps the four hours' overtime would be allotted to Bolton Street or Knowsley Street Stations, carrying out a variety of duties. An amusing, though at the time embarrassing, incident I recall well happened at Bolton Street Station when working under a Station Inspector whose name I cannot remember, no doubt because he was commonly known as 'Mussolini' and certainly raved, shouted and swore at his men like some great dictator. Among many other items a full milk churn had been off-loaded from a train and left for removal over the crossing to another platform. Eager to show my initiative and zest, I took a two-wheeled sack truck, swung the churn neatly onto the bottom rest and then proceeded with the right foot on the axle to pull the truck forward in what appeared to be the professional manner adopted by the regular porters. Professional it certainly was not! As I pulled it forward towards me, both my feet shot under the truck and I found myself flat on my back with 20galls of milk gushing over me and the churn rolling quickly away and over the platform edge, to crash on the line. Soon up again, but saturated with milk, I scrambled down the track almost into the path of an oncoming goods train to rescue the battered churn. Within minutes 'Mussolini' was at my side, screaming abuse and letting me know in no uncertain terms the difference in the uses of two-wheeled and four-wheeled trucks. I then had the indignity of being made to follow him to his office, past a vast array of amused passengers, milk dripping from every stitch of my uniform and told to sit down whilst he made out a report for me to sign. I do not recall what I signed but I heard no more of it. Needless to say, the half-dozen station cats had a field day!

Following a 10pm finish at the box, there were many occasions when overtime would be forthcoming, working until midnight on the station ticket barriers. Here one was taught the noble art of pushing out one's foot quickly to arrest the hasty passage of some drunk or 'clever dick' without a ticket, and then remaining cool and calm whilst the railway policeman who had 'not noticed' the neat footwork, picked up the bruised and surprised offender and took the usual statements. Tactful dealings with local prostitutes returning from Manchester on the last passenger train was an eye-opener. If one had an insatiable sexual appetite and wished to turn a blind eye to the one penny platform ticket purchased on Victoria Station, then there was on offer a quite exhilarating but exhausting night ahead!

The war itself was not progressing well at all for the allies at this time and by early summer the British Army, along with the remnants of the French forces, were to receive their most shattering defeat at Dunkirk in northern France, the worst in their gallant history. Between the end of May and early June some 40 troop trains a day were leaving Dover with disillusioned but indomitable fighting men of the British Expeditionary Force, for nine consecutive days. These troops, evacuated from across the channel, were removed at all possible speed from Dover Harbour in order to escape the expected aerial bombardment by the Luftwaffe. Most fortunately it did not materialise and to this day remains one of Hitler's unexplained paradoxical decisions. The peace overtures of Rudolph Hess and the Nazis that followed were ignored and the country prepared rapidly for an invasion.

Among the many deterrents to an invader was the formation of the Local Defence Volunteers, the LDV. This was organised quickly by the army, and all youths and men of reasonable fitness drafted together in local church halls or similar suitable points. They were issued with khaki armbands and the letters LDV suitably emblazoned, and given rifle training. The arms situation and incredulous state of unreadiness was unbelievable and, if it were not so serious, could have been described as a pure farce. The Germans would never have believed it! For every 20 men, only one gun was available for at least three weeks. Then our transatlantic cousins kindly lent us the money to purchase some from them. If we were unable to repay the loan, perhaps a naval base or two would be acceptable! And so on several occasions I found myself, along with many other youths keen enough to repel the enemy, parading down Bury's 'Rock' and through the town centre with a broomstick at the regimental slope, headed by an East Lancs Regimental Band.

Thus the Home Guard was born, and within a few weeks we got our issue of guns and uniforms. The LDV tag held and we were commonly alluded to as the 'Look, Duck and Vanish' brigade.

A railway division was set up and I was drafted into a platoon stationed within the railway buildings at Bolton Street. Home Guard duties were compulsory and after a 12hr day shift in signalbox and telegraph office, an 8hr night-guard duty did not come easily. One might be called to tunnel or bridge guarding, patrolling marshalling yards or perhaps to first-aid or weapon training in a makeshift lecture room.

There were many lighter moments however, such as the practice sessions of a nameless quartet, with the author on harmonica; Bobby Duckworth on concertina; Fred Brown on fiddle; and Joe Earnshaw on drums. The rendition of Franz Suppé's *Light Cavalry* would have turned the composer in his grave.

A further light-hearted moment was when I foolishly volunteered to be bandaged to a stretcher and lowered vertically from a third-storey window in order to demonstrate the sergeant's hopefully correct bandaging techniques to the first-aid squad. In that 10min hair-raising operation, I vowed some ten thousand times I would never become a paratrooper or an Alpine rock-climber. I also prayed heartily that the supporting bandage intertwined between my upper thighs and genitals would not impair my eventual contribution to world population!

Another incident caused a great deal of mirth to the platoon, but not at the time to myself. It was an experience I do not recommend to be put to the test. The night was a particularly black and stormy one, with torrential rain and a high wind. Our platoon was on indoor standby and very lucky we were. When a call to nature was required, officers used the indoor toilets but we, as 'other ranks', were obliged to go out onto the platform and walk 100yds to the outside urinals. At 2am no passengers were about on this totally unlit station, the electric power to the live rails was disconnected and no freight trains were in sight. That was the situation when I crept out from the rain-lashed door, crossed the rain-soaked platform to the edge and opened my trouser-front to relieve myself as quickly as possible. Within a split second I knew my mistake. Without a great deal of electrical knowledge I think the reader will appreciate what can happen when a continuous flow of water shot from a human being hits a rain-soaked 1,400volt live-rail cover. With penis in hand, I was flung a full 15ft back to the station wall and was extremely fortunate to suffer only a severe shock, a cut ear and a pair of urine-soaked trousers. Much amusement and ribald comments later greeted my recounting of the episode. It was my first but not last encounter with the dreaded live rail. Some wit suggested I was now 'well charged' in the right place, though the gloomy ones gave the opinion that I was now probably sterilised and impotent! The first prophesy proved correct, and the latter not so, and I was to lead a perfectly normal sex life!

Two-and-a-half years had gone by now and I became almost a part of the fittings in South box. On my eighteenth birthday my call-up for the forces came and, having volunteered for RAF flying duties I was duly sent to Padgate near Warrington for a three-day test. This resulted in a partial failure, and aspirations for pilot, navigator or observer/bomb-aimer were dashed, but I was accepted as a trainee wireless operator/rear gunner, otherwise known as 'tail end charlie', the first one to be shot up!

After returning home and resuming work in the signalbox I waited patiently for my call up to the RAF; I am still waiting today, 51 years later! Behind the scenes, of course, a tug of war existed between various government departments, and essential work such as railway operation was deemed a reserved occupation. Indeed I was examined two years later by the Army, given the usual A1 certificate and told, at least a year before the Normandy landings, that I would be kept in Britain and then drafted into the ROD division of the Royal Engineers for army occupation when we had beaten the Nazis. Such was the optimism and overall confidence to win this war and a mere two years after Great Britain had been reduced from the strongest power and largest empire the world had ever known to a humble island, for the second time begging help from its former colony, the USA.

The compelling reality of signalbox work returned with a jolt one evening at around 9pm during the late shift. At this time the Aintree (Liverpool)-Healey Mills (Yorkshire) Express freight, partially vacuum fitted, was due through Bury Knowsley Street. Through the infamous 'Bury hollow', the lowest point of the descent to the Irwell Valley and viaduct, between gas sidings box and Bury West box it was necessary for all goods guards to be especially adept at rear-braking control because of the quick snatch as the driver opened up for the sudden rise through the L&Y station. Though this was of no concern to me in South box, from my stool by the window I could see clearly the line crossing under our EL line and the trains passing West box. I always thrilled to see the heavier coal trains, and the passage of any express freight trains always gave me an additional stimulation. On this particular evening the West signalman had refused acceptance of a train from us and that signified to me that, as usual, at this time he was 'all off' for the Aintree-Healey Mills. Almost at once the customary shrill NW whistle was heard as the driver blew his approach warning, but this was followed immediately by a nasty snatch as couplings snapped and the dreaded 'train divided' situation arose in seconds. The complete train of about fifty wagons passed West box with a six-wagon length break in between the two portions. The train divided signal 5-5 was forwarded to Bury East and all of the other usual emergency movements put into operation.

The use of Regulation 20 in dealing with a divided train however, is highly complex, particularly in such a situation as existed at Bury East, with six main lines and short section workings. The first and sometimes regrettable reaction of a signalman receiving an emergency signal is to throw all signals in the clear position back to danger as quickly as possible. This is quite a natural response. On this occasion the situation allowed the first portion of the divided train to proceed at least to the next box, Bury Loop Junction, thereby giving the guard a good chance of bringing the second portion to a stand without mishap. The signals at East Box, however, were prematurely and unnecessarily thrown to danger. The driver applied full braking power and within seconds the up fast line through the station was strewn with wreckage as the looselinked rear portion smashed into the fast-braking vacuum fitted front portion. Fortunately, no other train occupied the station at that time and only the guard paid the tragic and fatal price of that emergency signalling error.

The year of 1940 saw the only major accident of the whole war period, a total of six years, with the exception of damage caused by enemy action. The long, major accident-free run of the GWR came to an abrupt end on 4 November of that year at Norton Fitzwarren in Somerset, by a fateful coincidence at the very place where 50 years earlier, the GWR had suffered a major smash to the *Cape Mail*. On this occasion now, in the height of the black-out, eight passengers were killed, and the resulting enquiry showed that the driver of the Paddington-Penzance night-sleeper was to blame. Inadvertently, he had taken the signals cleared on the adjoining fast line as applying to his train, which was travelling on the slow line, and consequently he was derailed at the protective catch points where the two lines converged. With a 'King' Class engine and some ten coaches travelling at 60mph, wreckage was then strewn across the four tracks and only seconds had saved a far more tragic situation. Had the overtaking newspaper train, moving at a very high speed on the adjoining line, been travelling but thirty seconds later a smash of gigantic proportions would have occurred. This situation was to be brought home to me some years later when working in a similarly situated box.

More and more, after having witnessed one tragedy and immediately afterwards hearing full details of the second, I was reminded of all the caution and vigilance instilled into us by our supervisors. An element of responsibility for the safety of the travelling public rests with all railwaymen, but without a doubt the highest burden lies in the hands of the signalman and driver. Whatever mechanical or electrical safeguards are provided they cannot be proof against their own actions or bad judgement. Block system working, made compulsory in 1889, with its many variations, absolute, permissive, station yard working, its consequential emergency regulations and wrong line working, take many months of careful study before proficiency is attained and many a signalman has spent a lifetime without having had to put into use certain of the emergency procedures for which he has been trained. He is examined annually and must always have the right answers as to what procedure to take if and when such emergencies arise.

During my 25 years' experience and the working of 24 boxes in the north and west country, only once have I used Regulation 20 and forwarded the dreaded 5-5 signal, 'train divided', and again only once have I sent the 2-5-5 signal 'train running away in wrong direction'. Certainly not conducive to maintaining a normal level of blood pressure, the receiving of an emergency bell signal occasionally keeps a signalman on his toes and is excellent exercise for reactive response. The most frequently used is the seven beats, 'stop and examine train', more often than not for a hot axle box on a freight train or a carriage door open on a passenger train. Signals are flung to danger against the approaching train and for any train in the opposite direction on an adjoining line. On a foggy night, should a tail lamp be missed on a passenger train the signals are 'nine' to the box in advance and 'four five' to the box in rear, the appropriate emergency actions then being taken at the two latter boxes. These, and many more bell signals have to be studied regularly and a local examination is given annually by the local inspector and at head office level when changing boxes or districts. What has been proved is that however well a man is trained in theoretical and practical signalling, no one can anticipate his vital reactions to a crisis until that situation arises. It is also unfortunate that many a tragic accident has been caused by a signalman's own bad judgement or even his own gross negligence. No matter how many track circuits and safety gadgets are provided, in the end human error will still be a dominant force to be reckoned with.

A few days later, armed with a small parcel and a large amount of trepidation, I was despatched from South box early in the afternoon to visit Arthur Baily in North box, situated at the far side of Bolton Street tunnel. Despite the fascination and interest for reading about tunnel construction, it gave me no consolation as I approached the tunnel mouth and I secretly prayed no train would appear before I had passed through. It was merely a 400yd tunnel, but it gave me an instinctively anxious foreboding. I had fears of some fool opening a carriage door and severing my head from my body, being scalded by escaping steam or perhaps electrocuted by blinding flashes that came as an electric train took the crossover at the entrance! My fears were well founded when I saw North's distant signal 'off' and by the time I was only halfway through, an up coal train entered. Flattened against the tunnel stonework, it seemed a lifetime before the last of those sixty coal wagons passed, leaving me trembling, coughing, choking and wiping soot and ash from my eyes. This was the first of many tunnel journeys which I had to take on foot and something I never acquired a liking for. The return, however, proved much more pleasant as I was given a lift on an EL yard shunting engine returning to shed, and it was my very first ride on a footplate.

Three years had now passed since first I stepped inside South box and I had grown to love my work dearly, enjoying every new day which never ceased to bring changes in routine, caused by troop movements, air-raids, diversions and the inevitable breakdowns which occurred more often during wartime due to lack of maintenance.

Two years into the war and at nearly 19 years of age, I was not at all surprised to be called to the District Supervisor's office and told the news that I was to be taken from the box and sent to one of the many marshalling yards around Manchester to take up duty as a goods shunter until I was of age to return as a signalman. The experience would be good for me, I was assured, but not very convincingly. To supersede my once eager anticipation of flying in a Lancaster or Blenheim over Germany, came visions of being plastered by Luftwaffe bombs in a prime air-raid target with no protection other than a shunter's pole and a handlamp. I was instructed to take two days' leave which were due to me the following week and then report, as a temporary measure, to Bradley Fold Station near Bolton where I would work as a junior porter. My ultimate destination would be notified in due course. It was to be a sad farewell to a period of my life which will forever hold cherished memories. I had been extremely happy working during the last four years in this box, but the parting with Ted Cox was like losing a parent, and I can never forget those poignant moments when we said our farewells.

CHAPTER 5

Across the Pennines

The two-day break gave me the chance to do something I had promised myself for a long time – a visit to the two railway centres of Crewe and Horwich, both having featured so prominently in L&Y, LMS and LNWR history. They could easily be accomplished by cycle, staying overnight at one of the convenient Cheshire youth hostels.

Crewe itself was not quite the town I had expected but, like Swindon in Wiltshire, its growth was attributed to its strategically placed position at the junction of two or more main-line routes.

In 1837 the inhabitants of the hamlet of Crewe numbered a mere 20. The LNWR chose to build their works in that parish and 80 years later the population had grown to 40,000.

From second-in-command at Swindon GWR works, William Stanier came here in 1932 as chief, and revolutionised the locomotive policies of the new LMS. In 1933 came his first 'Pacific', the *Princess Royal* 4-6-2 No 6200. It took to the rails at 104½ tons without tender, its GWR style taper boiler stamping on a new and distinctive style for the LMS. The famous 'Black Fives' followed in 1935 and in that year alone, the production of 179 set the seal, and they proved his best all-round locomotive ever. In 1952, 842 of these incredulous 'man of all tasks' were in service. His heavy freight class 8F, 2-8-0 was another masterpiece. Of the 'Jubilee' class 4-6-0 of 1935, 191 of these were built. Stanier had been greatly influenced by Churchward of the GWR and, although a 'defector' from that company, it is most consoling to note that Swindon Town honoured this man, together with its other famous locomotive builders, by naming one of its streets after him. Stanier Street is as well known to a Swindonian as is Dean Street, Gough Street and Churchward or Collett Avenues.

It was Crewe Station, however, along with its signalling system that drew my overall attention and I spent many hours wandering the platforms, kicking myself for not having had the foresight to request a pass to visit at least one of the big boxes. It was here that in 1898 the first electric signals and points were introduced by the L&NW and I would have been thrilled to see into at least one of these bastions of traffic control. It was consolation, nevertheless, to see many Anglo-Scottish Expresses passing through, their gleaming coachwork now dulled somewhat by wartime grime and lack of maintenance. A fleeting glimpse of the *Irish Mail* steaming hard for Holyhead. Shortly it would be taking on water from the troughs near Bangor on the North Wales coast. These troughs were the first in the world and had helped the LNWR to make claim to a faster service to Holyhead and thus on to Dublin. It proved a superior route to the challenge that the GWR could provide via Fishguard.

Some of the comparatively new and varied coaching stock I noted on these Anglo-Scottish trains, along with what I had previously seen on the two Midland long-distance routes, gave sure credibility to the adage of the twenties and thirties: 'the most comfortable ride on a railway train is in a Midland coach on a length of Great Western Track'. Though sadly in need of polish and paint, these main-line trains never ceased to give an extremely impressive sight when roaring through the station or drawing alongside a platform.

After spending a pleasant night in the Delamere youth hostel, I returned to Lancashire, by way of Warrington and Wigan to Horwich, the following day.

Everyone was familiar with Crewe, Swindon, Derby and Doncaster works, but here under the shadow of Winter Hill and Rivington Pike spread this small and neatly arranged town, again having sprung from nothing in 1885 to boast, within ten years, of a railway workshop employing a 5,000 workforce. The factory was built for the Lancashire and Yorkshire Railway Company by John Ramsbottom of Crewe and Barton Wright, ex-Swindon, and in 1896 the great John Aspinall took charge. By closure of the East Lancs works at Bury, and the Manchester and Leeds Works at Miles Platting, the resulting economies and bold planning were to be proved here in an excellently organised works, virtually a totally independent unit. Excellent staff facilities were provided and, as I was later to observe at Swindon, a care and well-being for a mass group of employees far superior to that known by any of the railway operating staff. It appeared to me, and I later found my views confirmed, that employees in railway factories are not basically motivated by railway folklore or by the pioneering of distant railroads, but are akin to the cotton workers of my locality, purely factory workers following in father's footsteps. Their mass strength appeared to have provided them with working conditions which certainly put to shame those of staff on the line. I left Horwich perhaps a little jealous but certainly impressed, and was pleased at least to have seen the birthplace of the majority of the engines operating in my area. Anyway, I consoled myself that, despite superior conditions, I could never be happy shut away within the confines of huge stone-walls and wideglass roofs. My sights were set on impressive signalboxes, complex junctions, big stations and the overall independence and latent thrill of traffic control.

These far-sighted visions were soon shattered when I reported for duty at Bradley Fold Station the following day. Why I was sent there I shall never know, probably it was simply a short waiting period for some poor rain-soaked shunter to be flattened by one of Hitler's bombs or to be squashed to pulp between the buffers of a 20-ton wagon in an unlit marshalling yard not far away! Whatever the reason, the Stationmaster, ex-Sergeant Major

Wheatcroft, with suitable military bearing and regimental moustache seemed intent on keeping barrack-room discipline, and between assisting with station duties and pushing a huge hand-cart around Little Lever loaded with parcels, the only light entertainment and relaxation came during the allotted 10min break at 5pm. Then the quick 'brew up' and a sandwich was followed by an electrifying few minutes with the newspaper girl behind the porter's room. This was a perk not available to other members of the staff, or so she told me!

Apart from that light relief I was not at all happy there. The only big activity of the day seemed to be when the local ammunitions factory, Dobson and Barlows, spilled out its workforce and within a few moments the station was packed to capacity.

A sixpenny piece, handed to me after helping an elderly gentleman with his suitcase, was the first time I had ever been tipped and I felt grossly insulted. I handed it back to him in disgust, deeply hurt, as no thought of remuneration had entered my head. I had a lot to learn as the years went by!

Sunday work was not part of my rostered work here and I took any opportunity for cycling to unexplored areas. The wilds of the north-west Yorkshire dales had long fascinated me, both because of my readings in the *Dalesman* magazine and also the epic stories heard of that great Settle-Carlisle railway line across the roof of the Pennines. Recently, I had made friends with YHA groups both in Bolton and Rochdale and when I suggested they keep me a bed in Askrigg youth hostel, where a weekend trip had been organised, they willingly agreed.

Finishing work at 10pm on a Saturday evening and starting out on an 80-mile bike-ride I did not find unusual. As a keen cyclist now, and accepting irregular working hours, I took no exception to changing from railway uniform into shorts and cycling shoes, stuffing the former into my locker and setting out on a brilliant moonlight night such as it was that night.

By midnight I had shaken off the industrial smut of north-east Lancashire, ridden by the imposing Whalley Viaduct with Flanagan's famous 32 brick arches, and was approaching Settle Junction. I braked here almost automatically. Could I not tear myself away from my work!

Sitting there on the indigenous limestone wall with an aluminium bottle of cold tea and an ample supply of peanut-butter sandwiches, I stared longingly into Settle Junction box whilst a north-bound freight rattled over the facing points to start the 'long drag' over Ais Gill summit to Carlisle. It was pure ecstacy and only the chill frost now descending shook off the grand illusions. Merely 15mins stop I allowed myself here, but in that 15mins what a kaleidoscope of bygone feats and oft-recounted legends crossed my mind. The detailed surveying of the route, 75 miles from Carlisle to this spot, was accomplished by the sagacious Tasmanian engineer Sharland in only ten days, despite a three-week delay whilst snowbound at the Gearstones Inn 11 miles north of Settle. This 75 miles of stone, timber and steel provides the most romantic of British railway factual stories ever written. The building of

19 viaducts and two major tunnels at over 1,000ft above sea level, the track lying over thousands of acres of tenacious slime and bog. The laying of water troughs at Garsdale 1,000ft above sea level, the highest in the world, to feed thirsty locomotives after their 25-mile climb at an average gradient of 1 in 100. These troughs were later to be steam-heated to prevent the danger of an ice build-up.

Work had commenced on this Midland venture, a dangerous challenge to both the North-Western and North-Eastern routes to Scotland in 1869, and was completed in 1875. The aftermath resulted in many dead, including a few women and children, mostly from the effect of blizzards and illnesses experienced during the construction of Ribblehead Viaduct. Finally, the five contractors were all but bankrupted.

Compensation came to the Midland Railway swiftly, however. In a short time it was realised that due to the terrain, what the company would lose in speed over this route to the two major cities of Glasgow and Edinburgh, they would gain by the luxury provided for their first-class passengers. The astute George Hudson, son of a Leeds cloth merchant, with the co-operation of American George Pullman, had introduced Pullman cars to Britain two years previously and with them, on this St Pancras-Scotland line, the Midland were to introduce a mode of travelling comfort to a long-distance passenger which was unknown at that time. It paid handsomely, and likewise within a short period freight traffic increased enormously, much to the consternation of the L&NW who made life not a little difficult for the Midland in Carlisle joint station.

Back in the saddle, I found myself very much alone on the slow and lonely road climbing to Stainforth and Horton, winding along with an infant Ribble far from its industrial estuary at Preston Docks. Taking the sharp bend and facing directly to Horton in Ribblesdale Station with its five miles of sidings, I took in the impressive sight of a 'Night Scotsman' really making the best of this long drop from Ais Gill summit. At some 80-90mph I doubted the fireman was resting easily on that dancing footplate after his mammoth stoking job on the 48-mile climb from Carlisle. The thought of these locomotives consuming around 1cwt of coal every three miles at high speed was daunting.

Within five miles the true grandeur of this wild area was brought vividly to its stunning eminence at Ribblehead Viaduct, known also as Batty Moss. The forbidding north-eastern slopes of Whernside, the rise of Blea Moor and the infant Ribble, with the stark flanks of Pen-y-Ghent, all glistened in the brilliant moonlight. Had there not been a chill breeze, certainly I could have lingered here for hours. 'What is this life, if full of care, we have no time to stand and stare.' So wrote William Henry Davies, the tramp poet, and no more apt words were needed here.

A distant rumble shattered the peace as a heavy freight burst through the grim portals of the 2,629yd Blea Moor tunnel. A mournful whistle echoed over the mossy plateau and I remained a few minutes longer, long enough to see that truly magnificent and impressive sight which only the railway builders could give us. The passing of a long heavy express freight over this most famous of all British viaducts with its 24 high arches on such a night as this is perhaps a once-in-a-lifetime sight, and a priceless experience.

And so I veered away from the railway to take the wild road to Newby Head and then the long and exhilarating plunge to Hawes in the upper reaches of Wensleydale, and on to claim my bed in the youth hostel at Askrigg. The time, I recall, was about 2am. My friends had decided upon a visit to Ripon and York for their Sunday return trip but the call of the wild had bitten deeply into me and, following the customary toast and porridge breakfast, I made my apologies, turned my wheels westwards again and headed for Hawes Junction, now better known as Garsdale.

Lying eight miles west of the town, Hawes Junction perhaps stirs no emotion in the hearts of the general travelling public, but to a youth now instilled in railway history and with a highly charged romantic drive, everything encompassed in this 15-20-mile radius was the ultimate in outdoor enjoyment. The sheer solitude of the barren slopes of Batty Moss, Black Moss, Mossdale Moor and Wild Boar Fell cast a magical and impressive spell. This lonely signalbox, station and junction with a stockade surrounded turntable over 1,000ft above sea level, and to the south the forbidding and sinister tunnels of Rise Hill and Blea Moor. Northwards, the final drag over the Lunds and Dandry Mire to Ais Gill summit, 1,169ft above sea level. Encompassed in this wild expanse of fell and moorland are the watersheds of some five or six rivers which include the Dee, Wharfe, Ure, Eden, Air and Ribble, the invisible boundary of Westmorland and the North and West Ridings of Yorkshire, Britain's largest county.

With a crisp easterly wind blowing, accompanied by a clear sunny sky it was a perfect day for my quest and I sat at lunchtime contemplating the many moods of these rain-lashed Fells and gazed at the silvery rails which could tell so many fascinating stories. From my sheltered grassy seat of moorland turf I watched the junction signalman going about his work and was so vividly reminded of the grim but true facts that pertain to this desolate and beautiful, albeit in inclement weather, sombre and sometimes cruel and hostile stretch of main-line track. It was here on that fateful Christmas Eve in the year 1910 that nine people were killed. Signalman's error was the prime factor but part of the blame was shared by a fireman of the two light engines standing at the down advanced starting signal. Thirteen minutes had elapsed and Rule 55 had not been carried out.

Traffic was heavy that night, as it was now when my idle thoughts shifted to watch a double-headed troop train making heavy work of an undoubtedly overloaded train of mixed stock. A tightening of the stomach muscles and a dry throat brought back the circumstances of the 1910 disaster. No doubt my sensitive nature, coupled with the continual instilling of circumstances which precipitate a potential accident, caused me these ponderings. I knew only too well that a lack of concentration, a tired mind or an inability to co-ordinate one's planning when under heavy pressure, was the prime cause of this and many other railway disasters. Sitting amongst these gaunt fells little imagination is necessary to visualise a pitch black night with rain and sleet sweeping across the signalbox windows, and at 5am the night signalman tired, bleary-eyed and more than ready for his 6am relief. The pressure that night would have been great, with five engines awaiting 'a road' to either Carlisle or Skipton, between heavy freight and passenger traffic; all and sundry pressing for the return of pilot engines to be speeded up.

A fine margin occurred between a down express and the midnight sleeping car train, the London St Pancras-Glasgow Express. As is customary in a tight margin, the two coupled engines for Carlisle were dropped forward to the advanced starting signal to await clearance from Ais Gill box of the express. When clearance came minutes later the down *Scotsman* sleeper which had been accepted from Dent box was forwarded on to Ais Gill. 'Line clear' was received and all signals lowered. The scene was then set for disaster. The 'forgotten' two coupled engines now rightly moved ahead, but their speed was no match for the double-headed *Scotsman* making up time with both regulators wide open. Bursting out of Moorcock tunnel at almost 70mph, the inevitable happened. The two coupled engines were swiftly overtaken and the pile-up of four engines and the following twelve coaches resulted in nine deaths and a multitude of injuries. The classic two-trains-in-one-section situation was distressingly demonstrated yet again.

To the reader who asks how can such a simple mistake occur, I can simply suggest experiencing the situation. Only when one has worked under the intense pressure at a busy junction or a large stationbox can this answer be found. It's simultaneous telephone work, the sheer physical strain of constantly running along and operating an 80-lever frame, dashing back and forth to murky windows to 'catch' tail lamps, observing the passage of trains for open doors, hot axle boxes or anything else amiss. Ears are tuned for engine whistles, all of which have many meanings, working the block instruments, checking headlight codes against the description of the train signalled, cocking half-an-ear to some angry goods guard or footplateman outside who, with an unprintable stream of adjectives, informs you his train has now been waiting ¾hr for a margin. An uninitiated control clerk sits in a centrally heated office 'buzzing' you for information regarding some freight train which passed you ¾hr previously! A broken signal wire which is causing delays. You have been on duty now six hours without the least chance of a cup of tea or a sandwich, and to cap it all you are bursting for a pee! There hasn't been even time to tie a knot on the end! You cannot stop the railway in order to indulge in either of the latter two pastimes. Only by experiencing these conditions is it possible to ascertain how one can make the most minor, but often tragic and terrible, errors. I know, because I have made more than one error in my time. Like many thousands made during any given 12 months, a contra move is often made and a recipe for disaster averted.

Two other incidents in the near vicinity to where I now sat were instrumental in the installation by the Midland Railway of the Rotary Block system with its track circuits and 'Lock and Block' aids to counteract a signalman's mistakes. A little to the south on 19 August 1880, a signalman's error at Blea Moor sidings box caused a smash ½ mile inside the Blea Moor tunnel. To the north, just beyond Ais Gill box at 1,167ft above sea level, 14 people died in 1913 when the up Inverness-London night express ran into the rear of the Stranraer-London boat train during another typical black and storm-ridden Pennine night. This time it was driver error. All signals at Mallerstang box, a little north of the summit, were overrun at danger and the southbound express rammed into the back of the stationary Boat Train which had stopped for steam.

Truly, if these fells could only talk they would have endless tales of great pioneering feats, and both romantic and hair-raising stories of this undisputably greatest route to the north.

It was time to move. My reminiscing had caused me to become oblivious of a wet behind – this was, after all, a watershed. Leaving this ultimate shrine of railway romance, I turned my bike westwards again towards Sedburgh and, later, again eastwards into Dent Dale. Many stops had to be made for map consultation as at that time all signposts had been removed due to the impending threat of invasion. This did give more opportunity to appreciate one's surroundings, and at the same time taught many uninitiated road-users the art of map reading. A Bartholomew's half-inch was the cyclist's favourite, whilst a hiker would prefer the Ordnance one-inch.

Five miles on, at the head of Dent Dale, I was parallel to the railway again after a long detour by road. Dent Station I viewed with awe. At 1,145ft above sea level, England's highest and loneliest station, where express trains on the down gradient swept out of the grim portals of Rise Hill tunnel at 80mph, whilst on the northbound incline 40mph was hard to achieve with a heavily loaded freight. No bank engines were to be seen in this vicinity, double heading, as with the GWR, being the Midland policy for this line. Here in 1885 steam sanding equipment for a slipping locomotive was successfully carried out and later became an international standard piece of engine equipment. Following the road south, and within three miles, are the two equally impressive viaducts of Arten Gill and Dent Head, to be followed by the awesome sight of the northern portal of Blea Moor tunnel. To view this notorious bore, I left my bike at the roadside and walked some ½ mile along the 1,500ft contour.

By now it was late afternoon and, with a wind that had veered from east to north-west during the course of the day, also a bank of cloud that had appeared in a remarkably short time, it seemed prudent to apply a little more pedal power. The unseen powers that be, had decreed, 'enough of this mighty railway across the backbone of England; and was this the notorious Helm Wind' that I was now facing? By the time I had retraced my steps to the road, snow was falling and I was extremely glad to have the wind on my back as I climbed over to Newby Head and then took the long downhill road to Settle and home. Another day I would return to the church of St Leonard at Chapel le Dale where some 100 of the shanty-town dwellers of Batty Moss were buried after their almost inhuman existence over a period of six years. Indeed Ribblehead Viaduct and Blea Moor tunnel, coupled with the terrible elements experienced at that time, extorted a very high price for man's intrusion into this sacred wilderness.

If any impetus had been needed to spur on my ambitions and utmost longing to become a fully fledged and competent signalman, then that journey would have provided it.

CHAPTER 6

Between the Buffers

A message came instructing me to report to Inspector MacNiel's office which shook me out of a rather lethargic and pessimistic mood and sent great hopes surging through my veins. Was it goodbye to lugging heavy parcels to Ladyshore Colliery; goodbye to platform sweeping, polishing toilet-door brasswork; goodbye to shutting carriage doors and being treated with contempt by officious passenger guards? Was it, sadly, a farewell to the newspaper girl who had given me the only exciting ten minutes in every boring day of my three months' stay at this now long-forgotten station. Reporting to Inspector MacNiel the following day, I found it was goodbye, but unfortunately not to take up any signalbox appointment. The necessary qualifying age for a signalman at that time was 21 but it had been lowered to 20 due to the wartime emergency. I was then 19, so it would be compulsory for me to be employed as a goods shunter for the next 12 months.

What of my qualifications for air-crew training given during the short spell with the RAF, I enquired, feeling that it would be more interesting to drop bombs on Germany than to be stuck in some highly vulnerable marshalling yard in Manchester or Liverpool whilst Field-Marshal Goering's protégés dropped them onto me. No such luck, I was informed. The RAF had ample men now, and I was to have further outside railway operating experience in preparation for possible service in the Railway Operating Division, Royal Engineers. Nevertheless, the Inspector was pleased, as he was sure I would be also, that I was to be stationed here in Bury at the East Lancs and L&Y yards. I would be allocated the 'mean' rate of pay, that is a figure midway between youth and adult weekly pay.

Tomorrow I was to report to the Yard Inspector's office for training and have with me food to last for 12hrs, this being the usual length of a daily shift worked now due to excessive staff shortages. In addition, a pair of stout boots or preferably clogs, would be essential and I was to call at the stores to collect a new macintosh, handlamp and shunting pole. On collecting these items, the following day and signing the company's receipt, I was wished Good Luck and told 'Watch your fingers,' by the smiling clerk. When I asked for elucidation of the latter comment this jovial official informed me that very few shunters could count up to ten fingers, and within the next few days I was to find the reason for this.

Four years of signalbox work and a little station experience had done nothing whatsoever to prepare me for the shock treatment I discovered now as a trainee shunter. This was without doubt a far different and dangerous life. When staring down from a signalbox window, a 15 or 30-ton wagon may appear forbidding as it rolls by, but it in no way compares to standing between them or running alongside at perhaps 10mph in pouring rain, feet tripping on sleeper ends and rough ballast while you try to pin down a brake or couple up these monsters. Buffers smash into each other with an alarming impact as they are linked together into the formation of a train.

Within a few days I learned the advantages of wearing clogs with their wooden soles and 'rubber' irons. During a day or night's perpetual running over ground that would soon rip to shreds any conventional footwear, the men's preference was soon apparent. Rubber soles in place of the conventional irons were most essential on this busy East Lancashire section owing to the presence of the ever-sinister live rail. A sou'wester, too was far more practical than the official uniform cap during heavy rain. Like a sailor at sea you may be working hours without break in torrential wind and rain, then the use of a handkerchief tied around the neck and a sou'wester pulled well down had a tremendous advantage.

Many dealings with passenger guards had not endeared me to the species, as they were usually unfavourable people in my eyes, but now working constantly with goods guards, I found these men to be a different breed of people altogether. Like their serge uniforms, their manner was perhaps a little coarse, and with a flat cap replacing the official uniform headwear they presented a far different picture than I had visualised. Not for them the smooth-cut jacket and trousers, nor the gold-braided cap of a passenger guard, the highly polished shoes and their never-to-be soiled hands. These goods guards were alive, they were real, rough speaking, rough working, yet extremely efficient and intelligent when marshalling a train. Once an understanding with them had been established they were a pleasure to work for. Their knowledge of the geographical situation of tranship yards over a wide area of the network was extraordinary. A mixed freight train of 80 wagons may be carrying traffic for twelve different tranship points en route and must be marshalled in the correct order, each set-down being taken from the locomotive forward.

Since that time I have experienced work in a post-office sorting office, also a railway-parcels dispatch office and, together with my marshalling-yard experience, I found it an extremely interesting method of learning the geography of Great Britain. Practical experience in whatever shape certainly has a considerable advantage over the classroom blackboard.

The first duties of a trainee shunter are to learn the 'roads' or sidings, this being most essential during nightwork as all yards were now without their floodlighting for the duration of the war. Then we had to learn to 'hook up' the loose-linked wagons, which at that time comprised 95 percent of the freight rolling stock. After learning this 'knack', and how not to be 'knackered' in the process, one then proceeded to put this dangerous move into practice. Holding both the shunting pole and handlamp at the same time in one hand and directing the beam onto the draw bar of the approaching wagon is the first move. If the wagon you are about to hook up is stationary, and the approaching one is travelling at excessive speed, the move had to be extremely well-timed. After the link-up the wagons momentarily squeeze buffers then snatch violently following the shock of impact. If your shunting pole-hook was inadvertently trapped under a link, then the sure thing to do was to let go fast and 'duck', for within two seconds the pole would swing round at a devastating speed and probably sever your head from your shoulders.

People living within ½ mile of a large marshalling yard in those days of bustling rail activity frequently complained of the incessant noise during the night, but to be alongside these wagons continuously for hours on end, with the perpetual clamour and forceful thrust of shunting engines, the sudden brake application, consequential skidding and blowing of steam and crashing of buffers, was to be something one accustomed oneself to. Loud and earsplitting, at least it drowned the incessant sound of Junkers, Condors and Dorniers flying overhead on their cross-country raids to Liverpool and other Lancashire industrial towns.

Soon I learned that your best friend in this job was your handlamp, and religiously when starting duty, 5mins was spent topping up the paraffin oil and polishing the reflector and bulls-eye glass. Smearing axle-box fat on the upper rim was most important as a very quick spin of the lamp interior to change a light from green or white to red was often required. The final priority was to leave your personal pint mug at the ready, suitably charged with a spoonful of tea, in preparation for the 10min break which came between the fourth and fifth hour. The time chosen was at the head shunter's discretion and was always more than welcome. It was a brief space for rest, never afforded to a signalman working an extremely busy box who could be required to work non-stop for 8 or perhaps 12hrs. This 10min break was always a mad scramble between shunters, engine crew and guards, and God help the yard foreman if the tea urn was not boiling when this evil gang arrived either bathed in sweat, or wet and shivering.

With what to dress a sandwich was a continual problem during these wartime days of austerity, and no works' canteens and suchlike were available to railway operating staff. Butter, jam, cheese, meat, bacon and bread were rationed and the allowance certainly did not satisfy the ravenous appetites of a rugged outside worker employed on a 12hr shift. Most days, sitting back on the wooden forms, someone would offer a new suggestion and it emerged that peanut butter, sprinkled dried egg, sweetened condensed milk, dried fruit and other non-rationed foods were passable when you were lucky enough to obtain them.

Where to purchase cigarettes was an eternal problem and a perpetual subject for discussion. Where was anything obtainable other than the infamous 'Pasha' with its repugnant and overpowering Turkish odour. I never met anyone who liked it. Dried tea leaves and 'dog-ends' helped stretch out a hand-rolled fag, providing you had been fortunate enough to buy ½oz tobacco to mix in. The other main topic during this all too short a break was man's everlasting subject when females are absent: that of wishing they were present, and then suggesting what delights and exotic antics they could expect from so virile a group of would be Casanovas.

The undeniable advantages and mortal disadvantages of a beautiful clear moonlight night were ever-present. It was sheer delight to be working on a night shift when you could see clearly the ground you tramped over, the lethal rows of signal wires and point rods, the treacherously icy sleepers and those ever-sinister and invisible volts shimmering along the live rail. But against the obvious advantages that the most welcome beacon of the night sky provided could be the realisation of your relentless vulnerability from the air. Yes, you are a bomb-aimer's delight as he lies on his belly, with the silver lines of railway track and river invitingly gleaming up at him from below. It was a far easier target to find than a blacked out airfield. At Bury, however, though a mere six miles from the city centres of both Manchester and Salford, we were extremely lucky throughout the bombing in comparison to some of our neighbouring towns.

Before long, I was passed out as a capable shunter and three months later was to be swinging a shunting pole and handlamp like the rest, or riding the steps of an engine, and holding the brake of a fast-moving loaded wagon with suitable agility. Like any 19-year-old youth of today, fresh from passing his driving test and setting out alone, I was just as cocky and over-confident, and shortly paid the ignoble penalty.

I prided myself on being able to match the speed of any head shunter and pilot driver; shunting engines were known hereabouts as pilots. Although 'fly shunting' was strictly against the rules it was widely practised and railway companies turned a convenient blind eye, so long as everything went well. Hours of tedious drawing forward, pinning down brakes and carrying out other time consuming moves were saved, and marshalling a train or 'shunting a yard' speeded up tremendously by these unofficial workings. Blatantly dangerous it was, but nevertheless a train load of mixed freight wagons dispatched into their various 'roads' in a goods yard would be one hour's work by normal methods, whereas by using 'fly shunting' and other unorthodox moves, and rule 'bending', it could be condensed into a 20min operation.

So this was the situation one black and foggy night when I was working with 'young bloods', both on the footplate and on the ground. My head shunter had called for number six, eight and five roads, and with three batches of four or five wagons coming at me swiftly, with barely a 10-wagon gap between them, quick movement was the essence of the game. Dashing from one to the other lever, there is no time to check the correct return of these spring-operated facing points and the consequences of a blade, a mere ½in out of line, can easily be imagined. Sand blown from the engines during wet weather is the shunter's worst enemy, but he always trusts that the daily application of oil has been carried out and will be sufficient to make the points function correctly. The rule book states otherwise in its inextricable legal jargon, thus preventing any blame or responsibility on the part of the company for all accidents due to the employees' failure to carry out the set rules.

Now the wagons were dispersing into their respective roads really fast and then, suddenly, with my hands firmly gripping spring lever number five, I was petrified at the ugly sight of five wagons ploughing through the sleepers and grinding to an earsplitting halt at facing point number eight. I was stunned, the leading wagon was slewed at 90 degrees across the track and the following four were leaning precariously over to one side. I was so paralysed that I failed to chase the loaded wagons along number eight road and they pounded into the warehouse buffers with a sickening thud. I gulped as the sudden realisation of what I had done hit me, and I went cold and stupified.

The resulting chaos, for I had virtually sealed the yard entrance, took some four hours to clear. Bury 'tool van' was incapable owing to the bufferlocking, and Newton Heath steam crane was required. This was my first close experience of what a smash-up was all about, even on a comparatively small scale, and the consequent excitement contributed little to my normal equanimity. Several days later the realisation came of how lucky I had been in not being flung beneath this tangled mess, as only a matter of two yards were between myself and the wreckage. Instead of the severe reprimand I expected to receive with possible suspension or worse, a caution and advice conveying 'non-recording' of a first offence was beyond my wildest hopes.

This little episode did a lot to dispel youthful overzealousness, and from then onwards there was a more cautious note in my hitherto rapid calls to head shunters or guards who attempted to make me move faster than was safe. Tragically, it never rains but what it pours! In two weeks I was on the rampage again. After taking over the head shunter's job for only the second time, I 'hashed it up'. The guard or head shunter determines the speed of the shunting engine as it pounds into the wagons before he hooks off the load for their intended sidings, and that night this was my job. Two short sidings with buffer stops adjacent to Peel Mill was the usual refuge for timber wagons and on this occasion I was shunting three double bogie bolster flat fully-loaded with tree trunks. The tremendous weight can be imagined, and when I shouted 'hit 'em up driver' and swung the white light swiftly side to side, he really did. Hooking off neatly at speed and giving the driver a 'red' these bogie bolsters were probably then moving at 15mph on a falling gradient, which was too fast by far. A man running furiously with his pole hard down under the wagon cross beam and over the brake lever could not hold this weight, even lying across the pole whilst struggling to pin down the brake. This I couldn't see as I drew the pilot forward for his next shunt; then I heard it, as there was a deafening thud, followed by the ominous cracks and splitting of timber and grinding of twisting metal. The head shunter was miraculously unhurt, but the buffer stops had been shifted a good 12ft.

Timber was hanging precariously from the wagon where the securing chains had snapped and, in the light of our handlamps, the scene was frightful. My luck was in, however – indeed, it was never better. An air-raid was in progress and the night a black one. The head shunter's uncompromising and nonchalant words were 'we knows nowt, Ron'. And with that we got on with the rest of the night's work. Enquiries the following day failed to ascertain the reason for this mysterious incident and I am afraid when the Yard Inspector's report was received in Manchester, the German Air Force took the blame.

Looking back, I find it difficult after 50 years to recall the names of the men I worked with at that time but one name stands out vividly, that of George Lawless, goods guard. George was a gentleman of the first order and a very keen first-aid worker. He instructed our platoon of the Home Guard in first-aid and put his knowledge to excellent use when, without any doubt he saved the life of a passenger shunter who had had both his legs severed in an accident behind Bury South Junction box. George used his expertise well and gave much needed reassurance to me during my experience of being 'bandaged' to a stretcher at Bolton Street Station offices, already recounted in Chapter 4. George, who did not 'bat an eyelid' when I threw two fog detonators into the brake-van stove of a Midland guards van to clear a sooty chimney, but simply lifted me by the scruff of the neck out onto the verandah of the van and then slammed the door before the deafening explosion all but split the flue pipe into pieces. When the smoke had cleared we returned to find my tin of cooked cheese scattered across the floor and soot and ashes smothering my sandwiches. He calmly retorted 'I don't think you'll do that again in a hurry, lad!'

After several minor scrapes and bumps I was thinking how lucky I was to have retained not only my ten fingers but also my ten toes. Then, along with the rest of my limbs and arms they all but disappeared forever one extremely wet winter's evening. 'Riding the steps' of your shunting engine was common practice. Don't walk if you can ride was the logical routine. When bringing an engine and perhaps 20 wagons along one of the loop lines it was habitual to climb up onto the first or second step of the engine, handlamp in left hand, shunting-pole in right hand and holding onto the vertical handrail of the engine at the same time. The live rail, carrying 1,200 volts and protected by its wooden side shields, stood almost at the height of the lowest step on these L&Y saddle tank 0-6-0s so with rain dripping fast from a saturated raincoat and sodden clogs, a contact with the live rail, although partially screened, is next to fatal.

That was the situation on this particular stormy evening. Grabbing the handrail as the engine came by, I mistook the boxed live rail for the bottom step and immediately my wet clogs made contact I was flung into oblivion. What happened I shall never know. I was revived a few minutes later on the footplate where apparently the shock had lifted me, but my handlamp and pole were smashed under the engine, and all I recall was the sensation of a sledgehammer hitting me at the top of my spine. As if that was not enough, I made a quick recovery in readiness for the next potential meeting with my maker when pinning a slack brake at Woolfold two weeks later. Whilst pressing hard down on a pole streaming with rain and with the steel hook touching the live rail, this, again, was not conducive to longevity. I was 'brought round' ten minutes later in the weighbridge office, having been knocked unconscious when the shunting pole smashed into my forehead. Needless to say, I nowadays treat electricity with great respect and, apart from wiring a plug or fitting an electric light bulb, my association with this form of power has since been purely academic.

Twelve-hour shifts and a predominance of night work was all to be expected in war-torn Britain at that time. If you were not working you were expected to take Home Guard duties, but on occasions you may have a 10pm duty shift and, following your daytime sleep, an hour or two may be free in the evening. Many dens of iniquity were to hand nearby in the city but Bury itself remained tranquil and comparatively respectable. A little 'light entertainment' could be found, however, before starting work in the L&Y yard at Knowsley Street in the late evening. Following a 'jar' in the Two Tubs, a quick walk around the corner past the Derby and Atheneum took us to Rayners Vaults by Kay Gardens for another 'gill'. Then along Princess Street to the Three Crowns, and if there was no life there, then we would have a jug of old ale and try Union Square as a last resort, keeping well clear of Johnson's Doss House. The despicable dregs of humanity that surrounded this establishment would almost demand a shilling from you, and that amount of money would then forfeit the purchase of two pints of beer, or two halves, and the company of a cheerful lady of ill repute, if only for half-an-hour.

Six months of this life in the open air, cheerfully accepting sun, wind, rain or intense cold had hardened me immensely. Despite sleeping irregular hours, I was never fitter. The absence of responsibility and stress, accompanied by the element of danger and bravado was a strong stimulant. Neither did I lack the energy nor the incessant craving to get out the bike and cycle endless miles.

Not every week in the continually changing rota was a permanent slog. Once in every ten weeks a shunter was required to accompany the guard on the two-nightly goods trains which served the Holcombe Brook branch from Bury, and this little trip was always something to look forward to as a temporary respite from the gruelling monotony of shunting in the two Bury yards. Without doubt, the Holcombe Brook branch was of unique interest. It was opened in 1882 for steam and later electrified by Dick Kerr and Co of Preston in 1913. It became a trial ground for an overhead wire system, subsequently to be used on the Brazilian Railways. The pioneer electric locomotive used on this line which climbed the final 1 in 40 gradient into the station was known locally as the 'Beetle'. After a short period the overhead electric scheme was changed to a third-rail system and thereby integrated with the new Bury-Manchester installation. The line was operated on a single line Tablet System and at night-time the signal boxes were switched out. The shunter was then in charge of the tablet and operated the ground frames at Woolfold and Tottington and the frame only of the Holcombe Brook box during the night-time.

It is now quite difficult to perceive all this nocturnal activity in the confines of Bury's premier residential area. Those two-nightly goods trains, six days a week, shunting wagons into position at the Holcombe Brook, Tottington and Woolfold yards in preparation for loading and offloading during daytime hours, have now gone. Even in the heyday of the railways I always found it inconceivable to comprehend how little the general public understood of the incessant movement of the vast volume of freight traffic during the night-time over our system; the heavy freight trains rolling along almost 'block to block', the banking on numerous Pennine inclines and the continual clatter of night shunting, which at six in the morning gave way to passenger train movements with an air of more orderly and methodical functioning.

Looking back after almost 50 years, many vivid memories and nostalgic moments come to mind, indelibly stamped there forever – Dick Critchley at Tottington junction, was always ready to fill up your 'tommy can' with hot water during a cold night; Fernhill Sidings and the corporation yard where pick-ups were made daily which included at least one wagon-load of maggott-ridden bones which stunk to high heaven and oozed their vile mass over the side when buffered up a little too sharply; stewed tea on the brake van stove and someone's black puddings found at the bottom of the tea urn; unwanted items flung from a fast moving, blacked out passenger train, including empty beer bottles and used condoms which could bombard your head if you were not wary; a 56lb tarpaulin wagon-sheet, saturated in storm water and broken loose from its cleats, flapping wildly 3ft from the wagon-side as an express freight thunders by; endeavouring to hook up wagons with a gale force wind on your back and being thrown within inches of a grisly end as the pitiless buffers came into violent contact; toilet facilities, virtually non-existent, with results that could fill many an 'embarrassing moment' collector's handbook twice over; 'springing' buffer-locked wagons apart, which had to be seen to be believed and would make a safety officer's hair stand on end.

My most vivid memory, which I am now free to relate was that of the Bury Drill Hall fire fiasco during the winter of 1941-2. Was it sabotage, was it an accident or was it enemy action? The answer, if it was ever made clear, was never given to the public. Looking back, I recall that night to have been a particularly busy and disorderly one. I was working the 12hr night shift and, as finishing time approached at 6am, I prepared to cross from the down sidings, over the main line to reach the Yard Inspector's office. From this angle the rear of the Drill Hall was clearly visible during daytime. Today, however, it was a dark and miserable morning and as I started to cross I was quickly roused from my stupified exhaustion by the sound of splintering glass and the sight of flames shooting from a rear window of the building. This came from a few yards above me, overlooking the up side wood yard sidings. Apparently, I was the first to see this and, unfortunately, our railway telephone system, although extremely large and efficient, had no direct link with the GPO National Service, excepting specific points such as telegraph offices with their own switchboards. After giving a quick message to the Yard Inspector, I ran at full pelt through Bolton Street tunnel, up the station approach and was calling the fire brigade from the GPO kiosk within three minutes. Still clutching my handlamp, I crossed to the Drill Hall and was hammering hard on the heavy studded doors, when to my amazement two fire engines hurtled down the 'Rock' into Bolton Street and disappeared out of earshot. I heard afterwards that they arrived at Wellington Barracks, one mile away on Bolton Road and quickly realised their mistake. It took some five minutes to wake the guard – regulars I hasten to add, and not the Home Guard. By this time the fire brigade had returned but the rear of the building was well and truly ablaze.

We were now to see British disorganisation at its pinnacle, with firemen running round not knowing where water hydrants were, and a railway goods shunter helping to find these with the only light available. This he had removed from railway property without written permission, and would pay the price later! The same railway employee informed the resident military that the building they were supposed to be guarding was on fire and was close to the armoury. To cap it all, for at least five minutes, no water was coming through the hosepipes as no one seemed to have the necessary key to turn the valves.

Within twenty minutes, it appeared that control of the fire-fighting had overtaken the initial chaos, and with a perfectly clear conscience, and feeling I had done my bit, I suppose I should have made an inconspicuous return to the Yard Inspector's office, signed off and gone home to bed. That would have been a very sensible thing to do, had I been an individual of normal intelligence! But, oh no! I was but 19 years of age, the adrenalin was now flowing fast and there was an evident shortage of firemen. The sight of a hosepipe lying unmanned on the balcony above the armoury proved too much of a temptation for me and within seconds I had bounded up the steps, snatched up the hose and joined a regular fireman into directing water down through the burned-out ceiling and onto the blazing inferno below. By now the main hall was dense with smoke and our breathing was fast becoming laboured. Small arms were exploding below and there were shouts from somewhere for all men to withdraw. Two far bigger explosions which rocked the balcony convinced me, and I came down post-haste. Then passing the front of the lethal armoury with a solitary fireman working in direct line, a massive explosion rent the empty hall and I was thrown six or eight feet across the floor and the blast almost drained my lungs completely. Clenching my hands together to protect my head as best I could I surprisingly remained conscious and when glass, bricks and other debris ceased falling I stood up, only to sprawl immediately headlong across the body of the fireman who had been in direct line with the blast. At this stage, I was obviously very dazed but managed to get my bleeding hands under his armpits and drag the man out through the main entrance and into the care of the ambulance men who had now arrived. At this point, I passed out completely and only regained consciousness some time later in one of the wartime first-aid posts in Haymarket Street. There I was informed that the man I had dragged out from the blaze was dead; he was killed outright along with the other fireman I had worked with for a short time on the balcony. There were many other injuries, including one to the goods guard I had been working with during the night. He sustained a broken arm when bricks showered the timber sidings. As for myself, I received a none too serious head injury which required only a few stitches and I was back at work within a week. Excepting the obvious tragic deaths of the two firemen, there were the usual and almost hilarious consequences. I myself was interviewed at length by the press, my photograph taken whilst covered in bandages, then told of the glowing reports that would appear in the northern editions of the *Daily Express* and all local newspapers. But, of course, this was wartime and the censor soon put his blue pencil to use on any reports of that nature.

The local coroner's inquest was held on the two dead firemen, as a matter of course, but the 'buck' passed to the Army. The military enquiry followed in full style and I was sworn to secrecy before enduring a long and tedious questioning by an imposing array of officers headed by a Brigadier. I was requested most emphatically to attend this enquiry in Home Guard, and certainly not in railway, uniform as from 6am on the day concerned I had, on their authority, signed on 'Voluntarily' for Home Guard duties. Who was I to argue, as already from the LMS Railway Company I had received a letter of reprimand for leaving duty five minutes early on the said morning, not having signed off duty, lost a cap and handlamp, the property of the railway company and, furthermore, the said company could under no circumstances be held responsible for injuries caused to employees on public land! So much for service to the community!

At that point, I made a mental note, that if in the future I should have occasion to observe a fire on or alongside the company's property, I would stand and unhesitatingly watch it burn. Thereby, I would be protecting the company's clothing I was wearing, and protecting the body within for further duties on the morrow. The outcome of the military tribunal was, of course, secret and not imparted to the public, but at least one very high-ranking regional army officer was prematurely retired to my knowledge. Apparently the fire authorities had not been warned that cases of hand grenades were stored in the drill hall armoury or, no doubt, more care would have been taken by the fire officers working in that vicinity.

At least I had seven days at home and received a week's pay from the Army Pay Corps and a verbal commendation from a Lieutenant-Colonel.

Maybe with two days' service with the Royal Navy, three days with the Royal Air Force and now seven days with the Army, I could make claim to some shortest time ever service record.

A year had now passed since I first sampled this unexpected working life in the open air and although I did not dislike the work I always held a secret yearning to be back in the signalbox. Only one more mishap was to occur before my ambitions were fulfilled. Coal-wagon doors, basically a 2cwt 'flap', were a common curse to us. These doors were supposed to be put back in position by the merchants when they had scraped clean the wagon, but invariably they conveniently 'forgot' and rather than leave the wagons behind when it was essential to return empties quickly to the coalfields, we did the job ourselves, cursing every coalman from Land's End to John O'Groats. Often when ice and snow clung to these wood or metal doors they would prove a bad fit and come crashing down. Doing this particular chore one very frosty evening, I all but lost the fingers I had previously been warned about but, fortunately, I suffered only a badly bruised hand and the shedding of practically all the skin from one arm. Still nursing my sores and feeling a little dejected some days later, I was handed a note during the morning asking me to report to Inspector MacNiel's office immediately, and my duties were taken over by a relief shunter who accompanied the messenger.

Wild speculations, alternated by forebodings, dominated my thoughts as I rushed along to the office of my ex-supervisor. Was it a notification for call up? Only two weeks ago I had faced an army selection board in Bolton and qualified for service in the Royal Engineers. Again, it could be a transfer to one of the larger marshalling yards which were taking such a hammering from the Luftwaffe, or perhaps a signalbox posting! All these relatively aimless ruminations were quickly dispelled when I stood facing Mr MacNiel, trying desperately to regain my breath.

'I've got good news for you, lad,' was his greeting. New regulations were agreed between the railway companies and the War Office he informed me. The result was the lowering of the age of a signalman's eligibility for duties from the age of 21 to 20 and the job came under the category of a reserved occupation. He also had news of something which he knew I had been patiently awaiting, namely a vacancy which had arisen in the box at Summerseat, a little to the north of Bury and I was to report there the following day for training.

To say I was flabbergasted would be a mild statement. I was utterly speechless. It was the culmination and zenith of all my wildest dreams. For five years I had waited for this day. If one looks back when approaching old age at the trials and tribulations, the good times, the bad times and, in particular, to the time when you can honestly say: 'that was the happiest day of my life', then I can say this was mine.

Eureka!

CHAPTER 7

The Proudest Day

The shunting pole and handlamp were handed in, the clogs sold, the locker cleared, and I said goodbye to a surprisingly happy period of my life.

Situated on the northern ramp of Summerseat down platform the Class 4 box to which I was now allocated had a neat and typical layout where one learned and applied block working in a very orthodox manner. There were no permissive block workings, no terminal station working, no loop lines. It simply had a crossover road, two sets of sidings, two small goods yards and the usual up and down distant signals, outer and inner homes and starter signals. In the box were two detonator placing levers for emergencies, two 'absolute' block instruments, two telephones, a desk, stove, metal air-raid shelter, a loaded rifle placed high on one wall, and the 30-lever frame completed the situation I found in Autumn 1942.

Its location, midway between Bury and Ramsbottom on the old 'East Lancs' Manchester-Bury-Accrington-Colne, and Bacup branch lines made it, apart from the daily visit of the local 'goods', a vital block post between Fernhill Sidings and Ramsbottom Station box. Traffic had increased at this time to 50 percent above the 1938 figures, mainly due to troop movements, increased factory output, petrol rationing and the general deployment of the populace employed in war-work. Rarely was there a 'clear block' on either the up or down lines.

An unusual feature of this box, was the casting of 'L & N.W. Ry Co HORWICH' on the frame backboard. The L&NW Railway Company had swallowed the L&Y into its ever-increasing territory in 1922, only one year before itself becoming amalgamated into the LMS Railway Company, and I doubt if many of these frames were ever manufactured bearing that auspicious title.

The tunnel on the Ramsbottom side was the cause of many a problem, with the up distant signal situated on the north tunnel entrance. The signal wire ran through the whole length of the tunnel and was beyond the normal pulling distance. Very heavy weights were used under the frame for lever-pulling assistance and should a wire have broken, before or during the heavy pull required, the consequences were disastrous. Steel ramps were bolted to the frame for a man to place his foot on in order to gain extra leverage, and should the wire snap on starting the pull, one had the alternative choice of being ruthlessly castrated or breaking one's back. Experiencing this catastrophe, and being thrown across the box onto the stove and into the wall, came my way on several occasions but I hasten to add, I have since raised a family and did not suffer the former indignity.

The problem of signal wires passing through tunnels was quite common. Pulleys carrying the wires needed weekly oiling and maintenance by the signal and telegraph department men, and no one enjoyed working in a tunnel. Consequently, this most important task was constantly shirked and resulted in bitter arguments between signalmen and the S&T gangs.

No bus service was available at that time to the residents of Summerseat and cars very few. Passenger traffic was therefore quite brisk and the return of passengers on the last train from Bury on a Saturday night was something reminiscent of the pre-motor car age.

The Stationmaster was a typical product of the LMS supervisory staff policy: very smart, very official and very ex-army major, but unfortunately lacking railway operating knowledge when called upon to leave his station duties. I hasten to add, however, he was a perfect gentleman.

Having worked 12hr shifts around the clock, the two resident signalmen were not overkeen to welcome the appearance of a young trainee. The 12hr duty in a box of this class was not overdemanding and the overtime pay was most welcome. Income tax problems had not worried the man in the street up to then, but very soon that situation would change.

I found the frame very straightforward, along with the local station working regulations and, after seven days, appeared again before Inspector MacNiel. I was given a test on the frame and traffic working, and a rigorous grilling on block regulations, with particular attention to the emergency situations and finally questions on the rule book. The Inspector omitted the block-bell code, locomotive-head codes and whistles and miscellaneous details, knowing well that, with several years spent as a booking boy, I was unlikely to have forgotten those.

Two days later I was appearing in the Hunts Bank Offices at Manchester Victoria, facing a Chief Inspector who must have given me just about every possible emergency situation to deal with. He included every bell code there was, and let me know in no uncertain terms that I was the youngest trainee signalman he had ever examined; also stressing that, up to the present time, a man had been extremely fortunate if he was able to become a signalman under the age of 30, let alone 20! He didn't know what things were coming to and had no doubt that the consequences of 'boys' of this age being given command of a signalbox would be responsible for many grave accidents in the future. After kindly informing me I had now qualified to become a signalman, the remainder of the Chief Inspector's chat with me was devoted to a lecture on the avoidance of accidents which were purely and simply due to human error or misjudgement.

A crash after a runaway accident, not far distant from the box I would be working, had killed 11 people. This was on Helmshore Bank in September 1860. Signalmen's errors had caused a grave smash in 1890 on the GWR at Norton Fitzwarren, killing 10 people; in 1892 on the NER at Thirsk, killing 8. In 1915, again on the NER at St Bead's Junction, killing 19; at Hull

Paragon in 1927 killing 12; and as recently as 1935 on the LNER at Welwyn Garden City, killing 13. Articulately and emphatically, the Chief Inspector recounted the signalman's terrible mistakes at Quintinshill near Carlisle, with the resulting loss of 227 lives, which proved to be Britain's biggest ever rail tragedy. Applying this as a useful illustration, he again plugged the necessity of using the 'blocking back in section' regulation at all times, and the importance of lever collars and ever-constant vigilance.

The Chief Inspector then rose from a massive oak desk and proudly informed me I could boast of being a fully qualified signalman, working for a company that was the largest employer in the world. Its work force was larger than the British Army, with 20,000 miles of track and was operating in 32 of the 40 counties of England alone, and furthermore, deep into the shires of Scotland, Wales and Ireland. With a friendly handshake, a rather unusual gesture from a north-country boss of Victorian vintage, he bade me farewell and good luck, with the accompanying words that 'Ahrons stated it was a feature of the Lancashire and Yorkshire Railway Company to employ a large percentage of red-headed individuals' – obviously this was meant to convey something; I certainly had a mop of red hair and the accompanying Celtic freckles, but I never did understand these parting and perplexing words.

I virtually ran out of this oppressive building, my white starched collar and company's black necktie almost choking me. It was time to celebrate. I had three spare hours of the company's time at my disposal before returning to Bury. Following a now accustomed route, I crossed Victoria station, walked the entire length of the connecting platform to Exchange Station, which was the longest in the United Kingdom, and saw Deansgate behind, and decided to enter briefly into the seamy side of city life.

I roused myself at the civilised time of 7am and prepared to report for training. Well fortified in both mind and body, following a carefree evening out, 'signalman' Bradshaw rode off to work the happiest man in Lancashire.

Although not the easiest of places to reach by road, it was nevertheless one of the nearest boxes to home I was destined to work. Summerseat was a pleasant village nestling in the Irwell valley under the slopes of Holcombe Hill and Knowl Moor, each proudly boasting a Victorian tower. Transport to and from work was by cycle, not simply because cycling was my pastime but, apart from walking, there was no other method. Rarely could I ever get to and from work by bus or rail, owing to the very early start or late finish. Possession of a car was beyond the wildest hopes of the average worker in those days and often, due to the long distance involved, walking was out of the question. At one point in time, some years later, I was cycling 20 miles to work and 20 miles home, six and sometimes seven days a week. Today, the average motorist would be amazed to learn that over one year in the late 1940s I clocked up 26,480 miles of cycling, 6,000 of those riding to and from work alone.

I arrived 10mins before the 2pm signing-on time, a proud and eager signalman with a wealth of confidence starting his very first day alone. I was given the usual information regarding traffic movements and trains already in section, general information of trains 'circuited', that is, any trains following out of course or not in the normal timetable scheduling. Perhaps it would be an additional freight, a light engine returning to either Newton Heath, Bury, Bacup or Accrington sheds, or an empty stock train returning to Lightbourne carriage sidings following a troop movement.

With an additional flourish, I signed 'R.W. Bradshaw on duty at 2.00pm' in the train register book, swallowed hard to clear the feeling of latent excitement which burned the throat and lungs, and gave the laconic 'cheerio, see you tomorrow' farewell to the departing signalman. Suddenly alone and in full charge of a box for the first time gave me an acute sense of superiority, but at the same time I recall the awful realisation that should something drastic happen, I no longer had an adult in charge to turn to. There was not long to wait for excitement, as 3hrs later, just as the hollow pit at the bottom of my stomach had disappeared and I was beginning to relax, and 10secs after receiving 'train on line' for a down Skipton Express, the block bell clattered out seven beats, 'stop and examine'. My training served me well. When all signals had rapidly been returned to danger, the explanatory telephone message was taken from Fernhill box. An axle box was smoking badly, and though serious, it was not grave enough to warrant holding traffic on the adjoining line. I drew the Express forward slowly after it had checked at my outer home, and informed the guard who then examined the problem. It was decided to allow the train forward at a reduced speed to Ramsbottom where it would be met by a carriage-and-wagon department man and the coach would then be taken off.

Hot axle boxes were a common cause of delays because of inadequate maintenance during wartime. Although fires were more common on coal wagons with their fat or grease boxes, there were nevertheless a large amount of oil-box fires. As with any delay, even the most minor, the tight timetable schedules on those highly congested main and branch lines were thrown drastically awry following such an incident, and this evening was no exception. It was 9pm before traffic was flowing normally once more. On the whole, however, when the night signalman arrived I had a profound feeling of satisfaction. Certainly, I missed the big box atmosphere, but I knew it would not be many years before I would again ascend the steps of perhaps a Class 2 box in Bury, and later one of the Class 1 or 'specials' of Manchester, Rochdale, or Bolton.

After my farewell to the nightman, I regrettably decided to try a short-cut home by way of the AA Battery on Longsite Road. With an air-raid in progress, I was extremely lucky to escape the shrapnel fall-out and arrived home safely, despite my obvious stupidity. Army issue helmets were provided to all workers whose duties kept them outside during an air-raid, and who were unable to avail themselves of the shelters. Mine was usually to be found strapped uselessly over my saddle-bag. Riding a racing bike adorned in a tin hat did nothing for my ego, and perhaps a gash on the head from a vicious piece of jagged shrapnel would have taught me a lesson.

I soon settled into this pleasant box but, as winter approached, I quickly realised its isolation. Though only a few miles outside Bury, the northernmost suburb of the twin cities of Manchester and Salford, it was a very typical country box. Before long I found several differences between work here and in the big towns. There was no immediate call upon standby men during snow, gales or fog. Here you were on your own, and had to do something quickly about outside problems yourself until assistance arrived. This box, along with Fernhill Sidings, was switched out on Sundays when traffic was lighter and a long block section was used from Ramsbottom-Tottington Junction at Bury. Arriving at 5am on Monday, after this 24hr shut-down, with all main line signals in the 'off' position and no movement of points and signal wires having been made during that length of time, could well be daunting. Probably the worst situation to meet with would be a layer of snow which, having thawed during the daytime, had subsequently frozen hard during the night. On opening the box and switching in, the fun would commence when attempting to return signals to danger. Quite possibly, the nearby stop signals would drop back after a few slams of the levers back and forth across the frame, but the distant signals ½ or ¾ mile away could persistently and obstinately remain off. Should this fact be unobserved on the signal indicator provided in the box, the result could be disastrous. Even the points may be frozen solid. Facing points and locking bars, which all signalmen know to be evil to reverse in such conditions, could well have been packed tight with ice and snow and then it would be necessary to clip or scotch them. After an hour of dashing in and out of the box with kettles of boiling water, brushing snow off from point and locking bar rods, kicking and cajoling the signal wire pulleys, the men you had called out would arrive, rubbing their hands fiercely and calmly asking if the kettle was boiling for a 'brew up'!

Another chore I had not previously experienced, and never took a particular liking to, was the replacing of a signal lamp which had somehow become extinguished. Apart from the very few electric signals, the lamps were illuminated by paraffin oil, as were the engine headlamps, train taillights, and shunters and guards handlamps. It was a marvellous piece of equipment, and far more reliable and less prone to failure than its electrical counterpart. If cared for and serviced as intended, it would rarely fail and, as in the case of a signal lamp, burn continuously for seven days. The official lampman, who could well cover a very long stretch of track dependent on the amount of signals, had a full weekly task servicing these lamps. A failure at night-time was a rarity. Perhaps an extremely strong gale-force wind, or rain water impregnating the oil, would extinguish the lamp and on these occasions, if no other member of staff was available, a signalman would be unofficially expected to get out and do something about it. Climbing a tall signal post and leaning precariously backwards on the metal half-ring or clambering along a slippery signal gantry, swaying dangerously in a Force 10 storm appalled me. I had no head for heights even in a far more pleasant environment. I was always pleased to feel my feet on the ballast again and to regain my sense of balance. Whatever prompted me to volunteer for the Royal Navy those five years ago I know not, as the sight of a ship's mast and a crow's nest would surely have brought on a heart attack!

These minor discomforts were surely well and truly compensated by the unbelievable sights that were to be enjoyed by a close observation of activities in many a passing compartment of non-corridor stock. These were sights which, if photographed, would have filled a pornographic connoisseur's album to capacity. At this time the blackout was almost total, though carriage compartments were fitted with a low consumption bulb. However, blinds along with the leather window straps had mysteriously disappeared; the latter were taken for 'stropping' a cut-throat razor as these items were unobtainable now in a shop. Carriage blinds were stolen for use over a small toilet window or some such purpose in an effort to beat the ARP warden. Inside a dimly lit compartment, a virile and wildly abandoned couple have little care or interest in what may be observed from the outside. They were not on a public road and nothing presumably would be seen of their passionate pastimes as long as they were suitably composed and had rearranged their dress when entering the next station. Signalboxes situated on the lineside were an insignificant and casual hazard, so they carried on regardless. Over the telephone, the message 'second coach, third compartment' warranted special attention to the regulation that stated a signalman must carefully observe the passage of all trains! This book is not intended to be either sex educational nor to provide pornographic entertainment, so I will allow the reader to let loose his or her imagination on the captivating and pleasant spectacles that were afforded to a lonely signalman.

About this time, many valid and logical scares were circulating with regard to Hitler making a desperate 'now or never' invasion attempt, and security was tightened rigidly for the second time. Extra precautions were put in with regard to blackout arrangements and over the rail system new regulations were issued for emergency action in the event of a determined paratroop drop. Signalboxes, radio stations, telephone exchanges and any non-military guarded key installation was particularly vulnerable. Indeed, many boxes in the larger towns did have a night-time military protection. Summerseat was not one of those chosen, however, and the only defence in the case of enemy action was the Lee Enfield rifle, hung out of sight on a wall with five rounds of ammunition ready loaded. This was permitted only because the three resident signalmen were Home Guard members and had taken rifle drill and fired their course on the Holcombe range. I mention these few facts in a little detail on account of what happened on a particularly black night in early 1943, when I all but shot and killed my best friend and future brother-in-law! An air-raid alert had been sounded before midnight and by 1am there was a heavy droning above from the sound of the

Luftwaffe's heavy bombers, but no bombs were exploding within earshot. Over the telephone, between the passage of trains, the idle chatter was 'is Liverpool catching it again?' Searchlights were raking the skies and ack-ack was bursting high up as far as the eye could see. 'Perhaps this is going to be the paratroop drop tonight,' suggested my colleague in Fernhill box. 'Maybe,' I agreed. 'There are no bombs dropping anywhere that I can hear.' A night goods train rumbled by, the fireman struggling to feed a hungry engine and trying hard to shield the firebox glare as he shovelled furiously. Hardly had the freight cleared my up starter when I heard a spurious movement on the outside steps. Never on the night shift here had any person, not even the local policeman, been near to this box whilst I had been on night duty. Who was it? About ten more slow steps, trodden undoubtedly by army boots, or probably jack boots, and then the glimpse of a uniform, decidedly not railway, filtered through the cursed ever-revealing glass that surrounded a signalbox walls. The vision stood there, not speaking, not moving, a sardonic, or was it a facetious, grin on its face. No doubt he couldn't speak English and he was covering me, cold and maliciously, with a sub-machine gun; any second now would come a shout of *'Sieg Heil'* and then he would gently squeeze the trigger. With a stupid lump in my throat, and a sickening sensation in the pit of the stomach, I casually strolled along the frame, threw back down signals to danger to stop an oncoming train, and sent the obstruction danger signal in both directions as we had been instructed. I had no option now but to cross to the door. A cold perspiration was streaming down my forehead as I approached it and my eyes were shifting to the loaded rifle. It was out of sight to anyone standing at the door, so my right hand eased onto the butt as my left hand extended to open the door. I wondered what the hell to do next, I was almost paralysed with indecision when the apparition finally moved its lips and blurted out in broad Lancashire tones 'Arn't ti benna opent' door Ron?' The constricted breath in my lungs burst out as I released my grip on the gun. The perspiration turned lukewarm and my pent-up tension dissolved as my trembling hand turned the key of the door lock. A Forces uniform it certainly was, that of a British naval officer and the man a very close friend of mine, Fred Rees of Waterfoot, in the Rossendale Valley.

He dropped his kit bag on the floor and gave me an explanation as I slowly regained my composure. He had been given a seven days' leave prior to sailing for overseas duties and had unhesitatingly taken the first available trains from Chatham to the north. Arriving in Bury on the last passenger train at night, he found himself marooned there for the next six hours, awaiting the first morning train to the Bacup branch, so he took a chance that I might be on night duty and it paid off. After a weary 4-mile trek he was well compensated by a far more comfortable stay than he would have had on a blacked-out and cheerless station platform. At the time it was a traumatic experience and on reflection, I often wonder whether in those next few seconds, had my friend not spoken, would I have shot first or issued the official challenge: 'Halt, who goes there?' and given the enemy the chance to shoot first! Fred caught the first morning passenger train, however, and all ended well.

Breaking, or rather bending rules and regulations is a common occurrence in any industry. With railway transport, the protection of the travelling public, the protection of the railway company and, lastly, the care and interest of the employee were the order of priorities in the application of company legislation. When employees decide to work strictly to the rules instituted by the employer, many times at governmental direction, they are accused by the media as operating a 'go slow strike'. On many occasions this is far exaggerated and a gross distortion of the facts. To a signalman, block regulations are primarily in force for the protection of the travelling public and to implement safe operations in the movement of traffic from block section to block section. Any violations are usually made with the express desire of speeding up traffic movement in the interests of everyone concerned and never are these regulations broken when risk to the safety of the travelling public would be a consequence. On only exceptionally few occasions has a signalman been convicted of manslaughter caused by negligence or by a flagrant disregard to the signalling regulations. These numerous block regulations, rules, and their sometimes inconsistent variations adjusting to local circumstances, are too technical for explanation in detail here. Suffice it for me to relate a few instances where incorrect procedures have caused, or have narrowly missed causing, a serious accident.

One such 'scrape', my first as a fully qualified signalman, occurred whilst at Summerseat and I duly took a verbal reprimand from the operating superintendent. For the second time I was fortunate in not having the misdemeanour recorded against me. Tottington Junction's up distant signal had become stuck in the off (clear) position due to a minor fault and I was informed subsequently over the telephone. The procedure then is to slow down all trains at both the outer and inner home signals, draw the train forward to the box and stop it. The driver would then be informed of the circumstances and it would be emphasised that he must treat the signal concerned as being in the danger position and on leaving the station must pass the faulty signal with caution. This was all very simple and clear-cut, but the circumstances on this particular evening were not at their best. On such a rainswept and dark night, with a complete blackout of the station, it was inevitable that when a train was stopped within a short distance of the platform, one or more passengers would open a carriage door, step down and promptly fall some 6ft onto the trackside. This happened many times during the wartime blackout and had caused more than a few broken limbs far and wide across the country. To avoid this situation occurring, a simple but nevertheless gross disregard of the appropriate rule was operated, merely to ask the station staff to inform the driver and give him the signalman's instructions. This was an easy task, but after three trains had proceeded without problem, the porter inadvertently forgot to pass instructions to the next driver. This fourth train, although checked at the advanced starter, went away merrily with the driver unaware of any problem ahead and eager to make up lost time. The distant signal approaching Tottington Junction was obviously showing green and he let his 'Black Five' have full rein, only to round the next corner and find the home and starter signals both at danger, and to see an ominous sight, ¼ mile ahead of three red lights on the rear of a goods train rolling slowly by Bury North box. With brake hard on, sanders blowing wildly and driving wheels thrown into reverse, he overshot the outer home signal by some 200yds and was visibly shaken and in no mood for compromise. Certain that he had seen a green distant, he raced up to the signalbox steps, gave vent to his anger at the innocent signalman and stated in no uncertain terms that he would report the matter. That, he certainly did on arrival in Manchester!

Had this driver not been as attentive, and had taken for granted that the next two stop signals would be showing clear, as the 'Off' position of a distant signal implies, the result could have been catastrophic in the short section between these two boxes. Doubtless this would not be my last error and I felt at the time that at least it served a purpose in jolting one's senses of responsibility and acted as a remedy to any signs of complacency.

Semaphore signals sticking in the 'Off' position was not as frequent a hazard as in the past, now that the LMS system had replaced lower quadrants with upper quadrant arms. This policy had been adopted many years ago after an accident enquiry's recommendations had advised this procedure. It came then as a surprise when traversing the GWR system to find lower quadrant arms still in wide use.

Rather than use my annual free pass to travel out and return to any given destination I had adopted a habit of travelling as far across the country as possible and cycling home by the most interesting route. That was how I came to be using the GWR. At that time, the one free pass allowed me to travel only on the LMS railway, or over other companies where the LMS shared running powers. Such was the case on the Manchester-Newport (Wales) line via Shrewsbury and Hereford. The pass permitted me to use the GWR as far as Pontypool Road Station on the ex-LNWR route in South Wales and with the annual holiday at that time being seven days, it gave me six days to cycle the return journey following the Wye Valley to its source in mid-Wales and then through Snowdonia, to Chester and home. I would stay once more in the very pleasant Youth Hostels which I had been assured were to be found in the Cumbrian mountains. I crossed my fingers for good weather.

On arrival at Pontypool Station, a fascinating and bustling junction at that time, I noted it had truly been given the GWR 'treatment' during its past 10 years of new parentage. The overall smartness of the station restaurant, the waiting-rooms and staff, gave me a jolt. No thick serge cloth uniforms and cheap cap badges were to be found here at all. Smooth cloth uniforms and classically moulded GWR cap badges were in much evidence and I envied them and their superior conditions, giving little thought, at that time, to ten years hence when it would be my everlasting pleasure to become a proud 'Western' man. Nor, in my wildest dreams, did I ever imagine when cycling alongside the Hereford, Brecon and Swansea line two days later, that 30 years on I would be purchasing a house on that same Cumbrian length of track near Llangorse Lake.

This particular line was greedily and spuriously acquired by the Midland Railway Company after several devious moves in the battle for rail supremacy during the railway mania period of the last century. Following acquisition of the Hereford-Brecon stretch and the Brecon-Neath, the Midland obtained a through, though somewhat hazardous link from its central and northern spheres of operation to the west Wales port of Swansea and the ever-intrepid George Hudson was casting his eyes further west to the Atlantic.

Indubitably it was an astute tactical move, and with more capital available, given time, this route could have achieved the everlasting fame of Hudson's parallel creation, the Settle-Carlisle line. Unhappily, it was not to be and the sheep again graze peacefully across the barren slopes of Fan Gihirich and Cefn Cul, the western outposts of the impressive Brecon Beacons. At 1,200ft above sea level, passengers from the industrial Midlands undoubtedly had spectacular and exquisite views of the forbidding upper reaches of the Usk and Tawe rivers as well as over the ostensibly unyielding face of Bannau Brycheiniog and the remote watershed of Llyn-y-Fan Fawr.

And what of that totally contrasting land, a mere seven miles south of the summit. There, a scene utterly incomparable to the tranquility of mid-Wales would have met the eye in the early railway age and, indeed, over the preceding 90 years. A town, then in its embryonic state was to rise to world fame. Its population in the year 1800 was 700. At the end of that century, it was 80,000. A town whose significance in Britain's meteoric rise to world industrial domination in the 1800s claims little recognition in today's modern history teachings. That township is Merthyr Tydfil, at one time one of our largest industrial centres, and the greatest iron and steel pioneering town in the world.

The early exploitations had been ore, then came coal, initially to fire the furnaces and replace charcoal. From 1759 onwards, and in quick succession, four ironworks were founded. By 1803 the Cyfarthfa ironworks had six furnaces in blast and was the largest in the world, but again the fact paled into total insignificance when statistics show us that by 1845, in the phenomenal grip of railway mania, Dowlais was operating 18 blast furnaces, Cyfarthfa 11, Penydarren 6, and at the Plymouth, the astute metallurgist, Anthony Hill, held a permanently oversubscribed order book! The Dowlais works were at that time producing 1,700 tons of rails and bar iron weekly and employing 10,000 workers.

Coal mining followed. Not initially visualised as an exportable commodity, it was mined solely by the iron masters in 'works owned' pits in order to secure a regular flow to fire the now ravenous furnaces. It eventually fell to the enterprising Robert and Lucy Thomas to merchandise 'black gold' and they became the founders of a lucrative Welsh coal trade.

Iron and steel production was however, the over-riding source of Merthyr's power and dominance. In the midst of this tremendous surge, and the insatiable demand for 'rails', these were rolling out of Merthyr's works at an unprecedented volume. Firstly to lay the tracks of the Stockton and Darlington line from 1821, then to the Liverpool and Manchester in 1829, and subsequently they were to be exported to the USA and Imperial Russia among countless countries across the world anxious to follow Britain's lead in the field of revolutionary transportation.

With almost contemptuous ease our modern history teachings allow the dominance of coal and steel in the Merthyr district to overshadow the predominant fact, that it was here, along this Vale of Merthyr, that the very age of steam railways had its roots, and witnessed the first steam locomotive in the world running along a track.

On a recent visit to the town I had evidenced scant recognition of the intrepid Cornishman whose invention signalled the most profound impact in transport since the invention of the wheel itself. Richard Trevithick was this individual, and his contribution was to give us the world's very first steam locomotive. With modifications, Hedley's *Puffing Billie* and Stephenson's *Locomotion* were designed 10 and 20 years later but, as Doctor Stuart Owen-Jones of the National Museum of Wales aptly quotes in his publication *The Penydarren Locomotive*, rarely is appropriate recognition awarded to the happenings of that momentous day.

No one can dispute the importance of Trevithick's locomotive and the significance of its epochal journey in 1804, yet little is recorded in contemporary literature. It is persistently overshadowed by railway historians who deem the Stockton and Darlington, the Liverpool and Manchester, and the Baltimore and Ohio Railways hold a far deeper significance. With all due respect to Hedley, Stephenson and the aforementioned railways, it is illogical to ignore Trevithick's achievement, or the fact that over 20 years were to elapse before *Locomotion* took to the tracks.

Trevithick's locomotive, an invention which gave a privileged few the first glance of a steam engine mounted upon wheels and, in turn, onto rails, commenced its epic journey on the Merthyr-Abercynon Tramway on 21 February 1804 at Penydarren ironworks. To the Navigation House at Abercynon the distance was 9¾ miles, and with 5 wagons, 10 tons of iron and 70 men piled high, the journey was accomplished at about 5mph, despite several stops in order to remove rocks and cut down projecting trees. This Cornish engineer named his locomotive the *Tram Wagon*, and a replica can be seen in the National Museum of Wales in Cardiff.

Far from Trevithick's thoughts would be the vast network of railways that later encompassed Merthyr and circumvented the whole district. Dowlais

Top, almost 1,200ft above sea level, with its shanty town and 6 stations; the squalor of 1870 as hundreds of navvies slaved endless hours for a pittance and squandered the bulk of their hard-earned cash on liquor and the favours of an army of prostitutes that haunted these uplands.

I had walked the Taff Vale Tramway, trodden the stone blocks that carried the rails, and felt a deep emotion whilst seeking some form of recognition to Trevithick; there was nothing but a commemorative stone and concrete monolith, erected at the foot of Dowlais Hill where the Penydarren ironworks had once stood. In contrast, Crawshay, the intransigent and daunting, but equally famed ironmaster, had left behind his own memorial, Cyfarthfa Castle, built in the style favoured by a vast array of successful Victorian industrial barons. May I at least raise my glass to this great man Trevithick, and perhaps propose an old Cornishman's toast: 'fish, tin and copper!' and furthermore, salute the man who placed Newcomen's and Watt's original inventions onto wheels, and motivated a staggering revolution in world transportation. As the BR *Evening Star* achieves so great an acclaim as the last steam locomotive to be built in 1960, likewise *Tram Wagon* should take its rightful place alongside, as the very first to be built in 1804.

This became a truly memorable journey for me as the charm and welcome of mid-Wales came as a genuine surprise, perhaps because we northerners always seemed to assume the countryside of Wales south of Snowdonia was all coal mines. In fact, from the sea resorts and mountains of the north to the border of industrial South Wales lies some 2,000 square miles of unspoiled and idyllic countryside. Plynlimon's high grassy slopes spawn the source of the Severn, Britain's longest river, and the salmon-rich Wye, reputedly one of Britain's cleanest. West of Plynlimon lies Aberystwyth and from here I struck north to the Cader Idris mountain, Talyllyn lake and pass, and through the old towns of Machynlleth and Dolgellau. Then I cycled into rugged Snowdonia and along the climbs through Blaenau Ffestiniog and over the Clwydian Hills to reach Chester and the plains of England again. It was in Herefordshire that my wheels last turned on a level stretch of road; confirmation that the Anglo-Saxon invaders of fifteen hundred years ago had taken an instant dislike to any ground much above an altitude of 1,000ft.

Back home again, and despite intermittent pangs of nostalgia and wanderlust, I settled down to a further few months at Summerseat where nothing much out of the ordinary was to happen. Monotonously, the daily crashing of coal on the point rods as Charlie Spillman or some other friendly driver passed; the almost mocking gaze of a white owl habitually staring in through the window on its verandah-rail perch after darkness came; the daily innocuous but tantalising banter with the village girls who dared you to leave your box and seek more interesting pastimes in the woods beyond! Summerseat did not possess a cinema, a dance hall or any other form of entertainment and, with television not having arrived in the barbaric north, there was little else to occupy the youth of the village other than the age-old custom of chase me, catch me, and to hell with the consequences!

Later, a request from Inspector MacNiel to work Bury South during a flu epidemic, and the highly unofficial hiding of a girlfiend in the boxes' air-raid shelter, when a fireman came into the box to carry out Rule 55, served to break the monotony of working this quite busy but rather tedious post. On the whole I was becoming bored and looked forward to a move. Finally in winter a vacancy arose on the Bacup branch line at Hall Carr crossing box in Rawtenstall. Although this position was situated in the Rossendale Valley and close to my birthplace, I was in no way inspired by branch-line workings. The money, however, did attract me. Promotionally, it gave me no advantage whatsoever, but Sunday working and overtime was available so I took the plunge, applied for the post, was given it, and within two weeks was transferred.

I confidently assumed I had said goodbye to Summerseat, but no, it was merely au revoir, as time would show.

CHAPTER 8

A Return to the Irwell Valley

One distinct advantage of training at a new post is that the trainee is permitted to choose his own hours of duty, varying them to sample all workings throughout the hours the box is 'in circuit'. Some boxes are open continuously, whilst others may close during the night or on Sundays if traffic is light. The regular two shifts here at Hall Carr were from 5.15am to 2pm and from 2pm until the passage of the last train from Manchester, normally about 11pm. Given this option, on the first day of duty obviously the trainees chose the 'office hours' of 9am-5pm, arriving after the morning rush period and departing before the early evening traffic increase.

Suppressing a smile in front of the resident signalman, who had no doubt spent his entire railway career in a Class 5 or 4 post, I peered at the small 'Saxby and Farmer' frame and the crossing gate wheel, wondering how many days I dare stretch out my training period. Perhaps a week, with a bit of luck! But I underestimated the Superintendent's intentions and, due to staff shortages, I was examined four days later and found suitable to take over the following day.

As a result of seven years' experience pulling and pushing levers on an L&Y frame, the Saxby and Farmer proved extremely strange. No doubt it was one of the only few left in existence and I wondered whether this frame had been in the locality since the East Lancashire Railway Company had opened the line to Rawtenstall in 1846. Observing the wear and tear, it certainly appeared so. In addition, adapting oneself to branch line working following seven years on the main line was also very strange. The work in general was carried out at a much slower pace and obviously there were far fewer trains.

The reason that many of these branch line boxes were receiving relatively good pay was due to the abundance of level-crossing gates. Throughout the valley, branch lines crisscrossed the roads and rivers over and over again, and almost in every ½ mile would come a bridge, tunnel, level-crossing, cutting or embankment. 'Points' amassed in the continual operation of these gates, and the locking of pedestrian wicket-gates by lever substantially affected the boxes classification. They caused, however, a stream of constant abuse from impatient car drivers or cyclists and deaf ears had often to be turned by the operating signalmen. These were days when the revolutionary inventions of Trevethick and Stephenson took priority over those of Benz and Daimler.

Hall Carr box was situated on the down side of the track opposite to the 'wooden hut' café, at the foot of Hall Carr brow. On many occasions, when brakes failed to hold a car descending this 1 in 4 drop, and the driver found the crossing gates against him, it would be seen careering tortuously to the right and on to the cinder and cobblestone road that ran along the river bank, before skidding to an abrupt halt.

Rising directly from the bed of the River Irwell, massive timber supports sunk into metal shoes suspended this signal box aloft in its precarious position, and very little clearance was allowed for down passing trains.

At holiday breaks, the dozens of mills dotted alongside the river, from its source at Irwell Springs, opened up their mill lodge sluice gates in a pre-arranged form of rotation. For perhaps six hours the river would rise by 2-3ft and the stench was overpowering. It came from a deluge of rats, cats and dogs, most of them dead, some still alive, as they were swept along, together with a huge assortment of debris, much of which would become trapped under the base of the signal box. Shod in the ARP issue of wellington boots and carrying a fireman's shovel, quick visits were made through the trap door, down the iron steps and into the river, to assist this obnoxious medley on its swift passage to Manchester and The Ship Canal. 1880 had seen the double tracking at this point and, with little space between cotton mill, river, road and track, the decision to build over the river was the only sensible solution. It had become at that time essential to take a double track to the valley terminal at Bacup, linking up to the new Rochdale-Bacup line, thereby completing an efficient transport system in one of Lancashire's richest industrial valleys.

By now I had become accustomed to working odd hours but, looking back, I shudder to anticipate that ever again I would have to rise at 3.30am, set out at 4.15am to arrive on duty at 5am, and possibly after only two or three hours' sleep. In all probability, the previous evening I would have cycled to and from Oldham, a round trip of some 20 miles to visit my girlfriend and future wife, arriving home at 1am. The bike journey 2½hrs later and a hilly 9 miles with the cobblestones of Stubbins Brow thrown in, would not come easily. An occasional forced stop by police or Home Guard to show identity cards was customary during night-time, and hair-raising it certainly was to be free-wheeling at 40mph down Horncliffe Hill and to have a policeman come dashing out onto an unlit road bellowing to you to stop for identification.

Fate struck a blow within three weeks of my new posting when my alarm clock prematurely broke down. To purchase a new clock, one needed to visit the police station or labour exchange in the first place to obtain a permit application form. This you then took to your employer to obtain his authorisation that your hours of duty necessitated the use of an alarm clock. You then returned your application and waited several days before your permit was issued and then came the daunting task of carrying it round several of the local towns before you were lucky enough to find a shop with one in stock. Consequently, over the three weeks that elapsed before I replaced the clock, I came very close to being late for the 5am start on several occasions. The railway company was in no way sympathetic to staff arriving late on duty, as I was to find out to my cost and when a land mine, dropped by the Luftwaffe presumably to smash up Stubbin Junction, plummeted into the river bank in front of my Uncle Edwin Warwick's bungalow, I lost 10mins getting through the resulting confusion and debris. Only by one minute was the 5.10am Bacup-Manchester train delayed and the driver made that up before arrival at Bury. This mitigating news was given to me later in the morning by the guard of the train, Ted O'Shea, who informed me by phone from Manchester that he had not recorded the delay. Such was the insistence on good timekeeping even when 'Jerry' was up above. My relations had suffered only cuts and bruises and, despite a considerable amount of damage both to their home and in the village, no one was killed.

Intent on alleviating the worry of late arrival during inclement weather, I set out from home at 11pm on many such nights, and slept on the uncomfortable signalbox floor for 5hrs. Even rolled up in a company's overcoat, and with merely an old blanket between floorboards and hip bones, I slept with more mental, if not physical, comfort that at home where I had the constant subconscious reminder of having to make a long bike ride to work in the early hours of the morning. On occasions, whilst snoring merrily in front of a primitively 'blacked-out' fire, I would be disgruntedly awakened by an inquisitive policeman passing over the crossing, or quite often by Snip, an Alsatian dog owned by my friend, Douglas Taylor of Waterfoot.

Personal friends, I am sure, would never forgive me if I failed to write a few words about Snip. At this time he was approximately eight years of age and, from the time he was born, he was destined to be a roamer. Although my friend Douglas was his owner, he had always been in the company of our little gang of lads in Waterfoot during the pre-war years. He had hiked alongside us over Pennine paths and moors over a wide direction, and camped with us regularly on all our various sites on the Rooley Moors and in the Yorkshire Dales. To follow four young cyclists pedalling furiously in order in order to 'drop him' as far afield as Clitheroe, Preston, Burnley or Rochdale, gave him no problem at all; he revelled in it. When we arrived back at night, there he was, eagerly waiting to greet us. His sense of direction was phenomenal. Now, after an absence of several years, I had returned, and he had found a long-lost friend. I had found my way back to Rossendale Valley, so whilst his master, Douglas, was away in the Royal Marines, and his adopted master Fred Rees was in Ceylon, he would settle in with me. Sometimes arriving for the late shift I found him lying outside on the signalbox steps. He would spend 9hrs with me and later calmly wander back to Waterfoot at 11pm whilst I cycled home in the opposite direction. On the early shift, I would find him arriving at 8am, and on occasion he would follow me home to Tottington, running alongside for the 9 miles.

By now, and over the many years, we had all become accustomed to Snip and his eternal and nocturnal wanderings, and when I lost him in Bury one extremely foggy day, I did not worry unduly; after all, he had many times taken in his stride the 10 miles home to Waterfoot. This was, however, to be the one time when things went wrong.

Standing on Bury Bolton Streets down platform, Snip alongside and as usual not needing a lead, together we watched the approach of the Bacup train as it made its grinding way round the sharp check railed curve from Knowsley Street station. Halfway along the platform the train ran over the appropriate fog detonators under north boxes down distant signal. Under the canopied station roof the explosion echoed appallingly. Never have I seen Snip panic before; he bolted up the station steps like a bullet from a gun, and I chased madly to stop him bursting headlong into the rush-hour traffic on Bolton Street. From beyond an oncoming tram my first and last sighting of him was streaking away like a greyhound towards 'The Rock' but, at least to my satisfaction, northbound. Confident as ever that he would find his way home as usual within a few hours, I caught the next train to my own home and promptly forgot the matter. Very few people indeed possessed a domestic telephone at that time, and there was no way of confirming any possible doubts.

A surprise it was then, when on the following day a policeman arrived at my door with a message to say that an apparently savage-looking Alsatian dog had been found abandoned on a snow drift near Littleborough, five miles to the east of Rochdale. A very brave man had dared to approach it, had tempted it with food and managed eventually to read its name and address on the collar. The dog, he stated, would not take food or water, the police were sceptical about taking it into care, and they could find no one at home at the address shown. Neighbours however, had informed them of the mysterious railwayman 10 miles away who seemed to have a 'share' in the dog and subsequently the message arrived via five police forces: Littleborough, Rochdale, Rossendale, Bury and Tottington. Very worried now, I took the train to Littleborough and, armed with the street name, started my search. A two-mile trek brought me to a row of houses close to the entrance to Summit tunnel and there, behind the back streets, forlornly lying on a heap of snow was a very exhausted Snip. Had he been a Poodle, a Scotty, or perhaps a Corgi, each a breed by which I have been personally attacked, he may well have been cosily sprawled by someone's fireside! Regrettably, that is the lot of an Alsatian. For 14 years he lived, and was only once known to have bared his teeth, and that was to a tradesman attempting to kick him!

For a few seconds he portrayed a pitiful sight, then seeing me he quickly raised his head, succeeded in a flutter of his tail, and soon I had him eating the food previously thrown to him from a safe distance. How little people who have had few dealings with animals realise that if you yourself show fear of them they, in return, are consciously afraid of you.

Snip was tough and wiry and subsequently proved no worse for his experience. I soon had him in a warm railway carriage and back to Rossendale after his 25-mile detour. At the time of the fright, no doubt his mind was confused and this caused him to take the right fork at the northern end of Bury, and within yards he was striking eastwards to Rochdale. Several times in later years I would receive messages from various boxes on the line between Stubbins and Bacup: 'Ron, your dog's here'. The usual reply was 'Don't worry, send him off and he'll find me' and sure enough he did before the day was out.

Before the winter of 1943-44 was over I tired of travelling inconveniences, and took up lodgings locally a few months prior to my marriage. House-hunting has never been an easy pastime, and in wartime Britain it was virtually impossible to find vacant properties. Millions were being knocked down by our continental cousins, but none rebuilt. Whatever was offered was at least worth looking at. Only the fact that I was aware my future wife trusted my judgment – not always a correct surmise – gave me the courage to say yes to the offer of a rented house at 2s 6d (12½p) per week situated near to the 'Owd Betts' Inn, high on the barren stretch of road between Edenfield and Rochdale. Water was drawn from a communal outside hand-pump, and lighting was by paraffin oil. At 1,000ft above sea level on the edge of Knowl Moor, it was daunting to a mother-in-law, but a future haven of bliss to a love-torn youngster of 22. It would be my dream home! Two weeks later, however, I was given the option of a re-opened, but pre-war condemned slum at 3s 6d (17½p) per week in Crawshawbooth, a mere two miles from work. I took it without question.

I moved there after marrying later in the year. With an outside toilet, gas lighting and no electricity, plaster falling from the walls, a flagstone floor and rotting bedroom floorboards it nevertheless held no misgivings for me. I had no care at all when I ruminated over the crucial fact of its close proximity to my work. A mere two-mile bike journey, so who cared abut what time of the day or night one had to start or finish work. It would be eternal bliss.

Branch lines in the industrial valleys of Lancashire, Yorkshire and South Wales were notorious for their proneness to flash snowstorms and consequential blockages, particularly if the lines should be closed for a few hours during the night. The Bacup line was positively no exception and, during the winter of 1944, I soon accustomed myself to climbing into bed at perhaps 11pm, ready to be up at 4am, then being awakened two hours later by a shower of grit thrown at the bedroom window by a nonchalant local constable. Opening the window to ascertain the problem, the message was with regularity, 'report for duty immediately, the snow ploughs are to be run all night'. The compensation for this inglorious night-time interruption, was, of course, the overtime pay and this was always a most welcome bonus to a newlywed, possessing but a few meagre items of utility furniture.

No medals or bouquets were ever given for 'devotion to duty' or for inconvenience caused, not even a word of thanks from anyone in authority. But working for a big company, it is ever impersonal and one becomes accustomed to this form of obscurity, and to being regularly 'summoned', and not 'asked' to perform any extra duties. The treatment I received however, for arriving 10mins late only a few mornings after working an extra Sunday shift at short notice, still rankles considerably to this day. Setting out to work in good time at 4.45am, I skidded within ½ mile on black ice and took a nasty fall. Road conditions were particularly bad, and I received nasty cuts on hands and arms, and was all but concussed. Determined to get to work, I half ran, and dragged an unrideable bike in considerable pain, to find the early morning train waiting signals at Cloughfold and consequently delayed about 5-6mins. Admittedly, this caused a chain reaction of delays at further connecting points, but at least I had put the railway company's business before my personal needs, such as urgent application of bandages. Furthermore, I could easily have reported to a doctor and obtained a sick note.

For this gallant gesture, I later that week received a company's 'Form One'. To the uninitiated, this was certainly not a railway VC or anything of that nature. On the contrary, it was the prelude to anything from a one day's suspension to the ultimate sack! Upon this dreaded form, for the use of anyone who believes the issue of the notice of a decision to mete out disciplinary punishment is at all unfair, are provided a few blank lines for one to state one's objections, and to signify acceptance or refusal to the offer of a hearing at head office. The offer I certainly took, and on the appointed day, arrived at Manchester Hunts Bank offices, accompanied by a Union representative and a letter of confirmation from Rawtenstall Town Council transport department. Due to the atrocious weather conditions prevailing on the said day, the first bus to take the road I used, due out at 6am, had been unable to leave the depot until almost 9am. No 'trial by jury' was to be allowed. Merely one man appointed by the company, and my spokesman, the trade union representative, who along with myself, were the only ones present at the hearing. Following a long and tedious argument between these two men, I myself merely being addressed a couple of times, I was at last spoken to, or at least spoken *down* to, by the company's authoritarian arbiter of so-called justice and punishment. In his deep wisdom he suggested that should it be deemed by a company's committee on discipline that I be allowed to continue my duties, during all winter months I must allow walking, and not cycling, time to work, irrespective of distance, thus not contravening the wartime relaxation of the rule stating that any employee must reside within close proximity to his or her employment. With ideas suitably repressed in regard to asking this white-starched-collared autocrat how he would like to allow walking time of perhaps 3hrs for a 10-mile journey, often arising in the early hours of the morning, I accepted his verbal but incomprehensible reprimand and was dismissed forthwith. A week later, I received notice of one day's suspension without pay, and the recording against me of the grave disregard to the rules of prompt timekeeping! The one day's suspension did not worry me unduly, for to obtain a day's leave during the operation of the 'essential works order', normally required a doctor's certificate or the funeral of a close relative. It had taken two weeks of tedious and bureaucratic correspondence to succeed in obtaining a day's leave to get married! The recording of this so-called 'crime' however, did rankle, and always will.

Suppressing a feeling of discontent at ever coming to this branch line after enjoying the more varied and interesting work offered in the Manchester area, I plodded on, every week scanning the vacancy list and optimistically hoping for a Class 3 promotion away from this miserable crossing box which I was fast becoming to dislike intensely. Surely the Gods decided in the early summer of 1945 to help me on my way. It was an extremely hot, close and humid midday and, although no thunder was to be heard in the vicinity, there was an excess of heavy crackling coming over the box telephones and Snip, cowering under the desk, was trembling violently. Visibility had been reduced to that of almost late evening, and it was becoming difficult to see even the block instrument needles. Just a split second after stepping off the frame, having taken 'train on line' from Rawtenstall East box, there was an almighty crash directly overhead, a vicious bolt of lightening flashed from end to end of the signal levers, and smoke poured ominously from the two block instruments. Shaking like a leaf, I took off the telephone receivers and found the lines dead, then turned round to see all block needles at neutral with two trains in section. I had a total block failure! My first, and only one ever. The next two hours of operating the 'time interval system' gave a little unexpected variety and at least kept one in practical touch with the application of the emergency regulations. On reflection, I often wonder whether I would have been alive and writing this book now, had my feet been on the metal frame one second earlier.

Installation of new and more modern block instruments and telephones were a compensation, however, as normally complete breakages were the only sure way of replacing old and worn-out equipment. Further evidence of this fact was born out after an outside step broke away one early morning in the dark and I all but ended in the river below. A complete new flight of steps was hurriedly fitted to the side of the box and I was later fortunate in being able to purchase the old ones for the sum of 5s (25p). They duly went into the making of a strong and very substantial dog kennel, which, I regret to say, Snip did not appreciate. He expressed his contempt by hauling it ½ a mile down the road until the chain snapped. I sold it to a nearby resident for 10s and made a handsome profit with the surplus firewood.

In retrospect, this 12 months had been a distinctly uninteresting period with regard to my personal gratification in train signalling, but nevertheless there had been many both amusing and hair-raising incidents, particularly in the operation of the crossing gates. The few instances when a signalman had contact with the general public gave chance for a little banter with local girls, and many a flared skirt was 'accidentally' caught in the locking mechanism of the wicket-gate locks. A sure way to get into immediate and apologetic conversation with an unsuspecting young lady of mature age.

Not long after my fourth close encounter with the dangers of high voltage electricity, my wife presented us with our first child, and immediately following that happy occasion came a letter confirming my promotion to Class 3 signalman at Bacup junction, a post I had applied for with little expectations of receiving an appointment. I was overwhelmed and completely taken aback. At last, four years after leaving Bury South box I was again to see the inside of a truly functional signalbox. A satisfying and sobering thought. Satisfying to my aspirations, though sobering when I mused over the many shrouded legends I had heard recounted by the truly great raconteur, Joe Rogers of Bury.

CHAPTER 9

A Vision Achieved

To relate or adequately describe to anyone, railmen included, the complex working and sheer slogging at Bacup Junction Box, prior to its winding down in the late 1940s, is beyond the limited powers of an extremely unaccomplished writer such as myself. As a train register lad, I had heard many fearsome stories from Bury reliefmen of this 'Hell hole' and of their dread at spending only one day, let alone a week, at this uninviting terminal, miles away from civilisation. To any relief signalman from the Manchester and Bury area, to the right and beyond of Stubbins Junction was a snowswept and barren wilderness in winter, and in summer, a boundless area of smog-shrouded valleys which never saw the sun. Signalmen at this box had evidently screws loose in their heads to be working here at all, and for only 5s (25p) a week more than most other boxes anywhere along the line from Rochdale or Ramsbottom. Had it not been due to the industrial revolution and the ensuing arrival of 'King Cotton', the town of Bacup, nestling between the slopes of Deeplay Moor, Inchfield Moor, Carr and Crags Moor and Brandwood Moss, would surely only have remained a pretty and sleepy village alongside the upper reaches of the infant River Irwell.

The station itself I remembered well from childhood days. Arriving from Waterfoot, only a mile or two distant, although this seemed far afield to me then, I would jump off the train, brushing aside my parent's protecting hand and race to watch the fireman uncouple his engine for the run round. I would plead with father to be allowed to run down to the platform end to watch the engine take water at the column.

What a bustling station this was with people changing trains for the Rochdale line, or boarding a Manchester train, engines shunting carriages on the up side and at least two engines on the down side goods yard, working at full pressure and adding to the general noise and hubbub. Bowler-hatted businessmen from the city strode importantly off the platform to call their taxis and rush off to one of a multitude of cotton mills that embraced the whole area. Along with other kids, there was the mad rush up to the 'Rec' in an attempt to be the first to grab one of the rare 'swing boats'; or we would hurry along with other neighbours and their families to Stubbylee park, carrying the usual paper carrier-bag, sandwiches and thermos flask. In this park was a long row of large bushes where I could hide with my red-headed little girl friend, and rapturously explore the delights that nature offered, even at that early age.

To the subconscious senses, there was an ever-prevailing odour of spinning cotton, the eternal clattering of insatiable looms in Plantation Mill and, as ever, the ultimate treat of watching the black-faced and perspiring stokers as they hurled an endless supply of coal into the huge fire boxes of these mill furnaces. The whole scene is today incomprehensible, but those were my recollections of Bacup town and station as I cycled through the goods yard, crossed the tracks and reported for training duties at 10am that early summer's day in 1945. Being there as early as possible was an advantage, as when you were training in a box the first essential task was to learn the frame. From 5am until 10am the regular signalman there had no time whatsoever to assist a trainee. Indeed, during those hours, and again from 4pm until 8pm, he would be extremely lucky to find time to make a mug of tea, let alone converse with a learner. Of all the 39 frames I have worked at different times, this one proved to be the hardest. The layout of the entire junction had been re-designed when the L&Y line was brought in from Rochdale and a new station built in 1880, but its cramped siting led to endless problems. With the small area of land available, and considering the large volume of traffic it handled, the whole site was extremely congested and operationally inadequate.

Only from the signalman's position in the elevated box, or from the observation of the working diagram over the frame, could a clear picture of the criss-crossing of facing points, trailing points, diamond crossing and sidings be visibly identified. Immediately beyond the junction facing points, check rails were vital on the sharp sweep of the Rochdale lines as they took the 90 degree curve into the 1 in 37 climb to Britannia Station. Locking bars and facing points all but intermingled with each other and significantly, during snow and ice, when hard-worked 'snowmen' were salting and hammering to release a jammed set of points, it was only the tell-tale shaking of the lever in the frame that gave you an indication that the man was endeavouring to release the correct locking bar. Little of the point rodding and few of the signal wires ran in a direct line, and with other adverse factors such as the height above sea level, almost 1,000ft, and the vulnerability to hostile winter conditions, this frame was aptly named a 'bastard frame'. It was gratifying to me, nevertheless, that it was an L&Y frame and, after seven days of patient study and practise, I mastered it.

Familiarising myself suitably with the traffic workings was to take another week. Varying my training hours over the two or three notorious rush periods, and copying over and over again the printed standard workings and essential moves to counteract any variation, I eventually felt confident and was subsequently examined by Inspector Bull. He was satisfied and I took charge the following Monday at 5am.

On the morning I was totally confused when the alarm rang at 3.30am, but I arrived at work with a clear head, a 7-mile bike-ride having dispelled any perplexity. My luck that morning was assuredly out, however, in spite of all my careful preparations. Amongst the early morning queue of engines to come off the shed, there had been a mishap, and the consequence was that my carefully prepared sheet of workings was totally scrapped, and the element of luck and former experience had to be relied upon to get me through this impasse. Contrary to all my apprehensions, there were no delays caused, and when traffic eased at 10am, I was more than pleased with my efforts. A subtle and satisfactory exhilaration, motivated by the mastery of an unexpected and very awkward situation, made my blood flow warmer and when the time came to hand over to the late-turn man I had inwardly achieved a new perspective of responsibility and personal satisfaction. For the first time since being awarded a signalman's status two years earlier, here I was, in my early 20s a Class 3 man, probably by far the youngest over the area. I revelled in the position I had achieved and laughed now at the suggestions by the older brigade, 'He won't last there five minutes' or 'Youngsters of that age have no right to be working boxes in that category'.

Exceptionally few safety precautions such as track circuiting or lock and block were to be found in use here. Inside the home signals from both the Rochdale and Manchester directions, terminal station workings, known officially as 'station yard workings' were in operation. Within the station confines the whole area was subject to neither normal absolute block or permissive block workings. It was literally a 'free for all' and operated even now, just as it would have been immediately following the resignalling 65 years previously. A clear home signal gave a driver notice that the line was clear to the buffers at the end of the station, but a 'calling on' arm in the off position denoted that the line was clear only as far as the box and that, beyond, a train may be already standing in the station. Extreme vigilance was therefore necessary at all times and particularly in fog, for without an electrically operated diagram displaying the positions of trains in all the occupied areas of the station it was unbelievably easy to inadvertently overlook the presence of a set of carriages, an extra mail or parcels van, or even an engine which had been stood at a crossover road for a considerable time awaiting your next move. This may seem difficult to comprehend, but given a long enough period of continual pressure during a particularly busy few hours I have known a signalman to become completely mesmerised and to sit down for a few minutes and virtually 'stop the job', or 'put the block on', as the phenomenon was commonly referred to.

The actual work load at Bacup Junction was equal to that of a high category Class 2 box, or a low Class 1, but due to a most unusual twist it was much lower rated. To ascertain the rating of a box, points were allocated for the work involved over a 24hr period. Whereas all other boxes on the branches feeding out from Bacup were closed during the period from the passage of the last train at night and the first of the morning, normally 11pm-5am, the station box here was kept open irrespective of there being no traffic operation. Due to the extenuating circumstances which prevailed, it was considered both prudent and economical to pay a man to do nothing other than operate his points and signals during snow and ice, and at least be there.

The unthinkable failure of a signalman appearing at 5am at Bacup in those days would have the drastic effect of virtually 'sewing up' the whole of the Rossendale Valley.

In consequence the night duty shift between 11pm and 5am every third week was something to look forward to. Ever intent on expanding my literary education, books from passion to porn and from Shakespeare to Sholokhov passed through my eager hands. During the day shifts, however, I never remember a dull moment as no two days were alike. The blissful manner that Jack Nathan took a train from the station onto the Brittania incline, compared to the skidding and spluttering attempts on a wet rail, and eventual failure by a less experienced driver, was a joy to watch. Steam and sand scattered everywhere and in particular into the facing points when blown too early on the bank by an inconsiderate or inexperienced man. 'Wrong line orders' were issued with regularity to guards authorising their trains back into the station for a second and even third attempt over this notorious curve. 'Mad Harry Taylor', the unpredictable was the one and only Bacup driver I ever knew to stick on the curve, yet one of the few men who could, if he felt inclined, make up 5mins of lost time over the 12 miles between Bury and Bacup. It was no mean feat when taking into consideration the very tight scheduling of these branch-line steam services. Granville, a station foreman with whom it was a great pleasure to work and liaise, was profound when telepathic and co-ordinated operation was the essence of efficiency. With no train at all registering 'in section' on block instruments to either shed box or Holt Mill sidings, one could well be involved working with two goods trains either marshalling or shunting in the yard, two passenger trains piecing up in the platforms and a couple of engines taking on water or shunting carriages and mail vans. Assuredly, among this ceaseless activity and overall preoccupation I had never been so happy since leaving Bury South box. Ted Cox had indelibly stamped his spell on me.

Fog working was extremely difficult here and fraught with danger. In early November, I came extremely close to making my first, and what could have been fatal blunder. Having no track circuits was a major drawback and when shunting stock across the junction or running engines round a train, the code of whistles and their audibility is extremely important. Beyond a distance of only 5yds a signalman may be completely blind and his ears then become his only guide to the position of any train under these circumstances. The various codes inform a signalman in which direction a driver wishes to move, if he requires water or a banker or if he is 'inside clear' of a particular set of points, among many other indications.

On this occasion, a notoriously awkward driver was working the local Rail Motor, push and pull, or 'Little Billie' as it was locally known. After returning from Bury on one of the afternoon runs it was booked to be shunted into the Stubbylee sidings alongside the up main line, a move which required it to cross directly over the intricate junction, passing some four or five ground signals, and then through the siding facing points, a distance of perhaps 400yds. A few minutes after lowering my signals for the move, the empty train crawled by the box and was obliterated by the fog within seconds. On the down main I had a passenger train approaching, and was waiting patiently for the rail motor driver to whistle 'inside clear', which was the correct procedure. This was something he rarely did in daylight, or even in dark and clear weather, but at least I expected to hear it under these conditions. After several minutes had passed and nothing was heard, I used the signalman's old dodge and eased the lever of the trailing points out of its notch in the frame. No train stood on them and I assumed it to be inside clear. Then seconds after swiftly reversing the entire junction and pulling off the down home signal for the approaching train, I heard the ominous creaking as wheels began to turn and brake blocks were blown off. Suddenly, I realised the rail motor had stopped for some unknown reason and then restarted towards the sidings. Its very short length standing between the various points had fooled me when using the old dodge. I threw my down main home signal back to danger and instantly reversed the junction. The trailing point lever was almost snatched out of my hands as the empty train took the points, but the down passenger train had already passed the signal before it was thrown to danger and missed smashing into the rail motor by only a foot. It subsequently finished in the wrong platform but no damage was done. It was a miracle, and with fog so dense, I don't believe either driver knew what really had happened.

I shook steadily and perspired for quite a while before the reality struck home, and a mental picture of what really could have transpired stared me in the face. As was customary, the fog had descended with no warning whatsoever, the fogmen had been called out but arrived only as it was thinning out. This was merely a taste of what was to come. Without doubt, during that winter, after a few months of heaving and pulling at frozen and snow-filled points I had no reason to disagree with the relief signalman who deemed this as the hardest box in the east Lancashire district of the 'Lancs and Yorks' system. The most vulnerable points to freeze up were obviously those on either side of the water column and I feel no shame whatsoever at the expressive language imparted to any fireman who waved about the flexible dripping column pipe after filling his tender in sub-zero temperatures.

A fogman stationed in the box, in addition to the usual outside men, was a priority here, and in these vile conditions I soon learned the full meaning of this additional rule. After my recent close encounter with tragedy, I recalled the recounting of events at Hull Paragon Station in 1927 which resulted in the death of 12 passengers.

Not having been prone to any major illness since childhood it took me by surprise when, after a short bout of overtime working, I was taken seriously ill early in the winter of 1946. During my own bedridden six weeks our first child became suddenly ill and tragically died with only a two-hour warning.

This was a great blow to both my wife and myself and at the time we took little joy from a misunderstanding which arose and caused much embarrassment to several of the railway staff in Rawtenstall, Bacup and Bury. When a misinterpreted message arrived at Bacup to the effect that I myself, and not my son, had died, a collection was immediately started in order to purchase me a wreath. Inspector Bull, the Area Traffic Manager, penned a most sincere and considerate letter to my wife, commiserating with her on her bereavement and expressing his deep sorrow at the passing of a truly conscientious and hard-working railwayman who would be sadly missed by all!

Two days later, and after several letters had been exchanged, the misunderstanding was rectified, though I never did ascertain the total amount which had been contributed for my funeral flowers! It was decidedly not amusing at the time, but on reflection, I often ponder over the question of how many people have had the cost of a wreath collected for them whilst still alive.

Reluctant to return immediately to work, and intent on getting away for convalescence following my illness and our combined shock, I was granted a week's special leave with the usual forfeiture of some pay. By now it had become less difficult to obtain even one day's leave. The war was over and the essential works order had been all but nullified.

My wife had an uncle who lived at Apsley near Hemel Hempstead in Hertfordshire, just a stone's throw from the main line from London-Crewe, and we were invited to stay with his family for a week. Needless to say, much of my time was spent vigilantly watching both north and south bound expresses hurtling along this 'race course', from the steps of a footbridge near Apsley Station. This was, and indeed still is, one of the busiest of all main lines in the world, with only minutes between trains during the entire 24hrs of every single day. As a spectator of these majestic 12-coach loads at high speed, sometimes double-headed with a couple of 'Stanier' Class 7Ps, it made me realise the magnitude of any potential collision this overall tonnage and combined speed could bring. It had happened only four months previously and a mere four miles from this point, a little north at Bourne End. Forty-three people had been victims to this disaster, following the accident to a heavily loaded Perth-London night sleeping car express when it was derailed on a crossover road. It had been unexplained why the driver, who was killed in the smash, took the facing points at 50mph when he was perfectly aware of the 20mph restriction due to engineering works at that point. It was just one of the questions never answered, and a parallel situation was to repeat itself at Steventon, near Didcot Junction, on the GWR in the mid-1950s.

In order to give a little more interest to the journey home following a very pleasant week's rest, I cajoled my wife into a hasty visit into London and then spuriously arranged to board the *Mancunian* for the return from Euston-Manchester. It was a suitable finale. After the customary one-and-only stop at Wilmslow to shed its large complement of predominantly first-class passengers into the Cheshire 'Rolls Royce' belt, the train later pulled into London Road Station with a comfortable 50secs to spare.

Rarely have I ever been so pleased to return to my work. The events of the past eight weeks had been traumatic, but gloom and depression were incongruous to my nature and I was happy to be once again in the saddle and inhaling the grit, smoke and sulphur that belched from the endless factory chimneys on my 7-mile ride through the valley.

Rossendale's annual 'Wakes' week came in the last week of July, and that was an annual event dreaded by all concerned at Bacup terminal. Supervisory staff tabulators, expert as they are in compiling a timetable of the movements of all extra trains within the framework of the regular time-table, leave no gap whatsoever in their calculations for unexpected eventualities that surely will arise. After studying the 'fortnightly notice' and its accompanying weekly supplementary notice, the man who was to operate this complicated and chronologically arranged masterpiece, namely the signalman, knew it could not possibly work to any degree of satisfaction.

On the appointed Saturday, the correct timekeeping of regular service trains was of foremost concern and the marshalling and despatch of the many specials to Scarborough, Morecambe, Windermere and, in overall priority, Blackpool, was undertaken as efficiently and punctiliously as possible. A situation of great amusement, but nevertheless paramount pride in one's traffic working ability, was to see the Area Traffic Supervisor sitting at the desk acting as a train register boy, and being wholly content to pass on telephone messages, whilst leaving the signalman completely free to work the traffic as he thought fit.

Peacetime had returned, and many extra excursions and holiday specials were reintroduced with a view to a return to the pre-war holiday atmosphere. The Saturday following brought the return of an even greater situation of organised chaos, as you attempted to 'run round' empty stock trains and return them speedily to Lightbourne sidings, praying that the driver would not 'blow' for water. Long tender engines would foul the crossover roads whilst taking water and could consequently block the junction for 10mins. Under these conditions another signalman's fervent prayer was that a driver would not insist on running on to the shed to reverse his engine, but would return the 20 miles *tender first* to Manchester.

In company with Oldham holidaymakers, known in jocular fashion as 'Owdam ruf yeds', I believe Rossendalians were picked out to enjoy, or otherwise, the largest array of ancient locomotives and primitive coaching stock ever to be assembled since pre-grouping days. The variety seen at Bacup during these carefree days was to confirm the saying that 'mill workers don't care tuppence on *how* you get them to Blackpool, but how *quickly* you can do it'! The utter chaos on the return of the populace was pitiful at the time, but laughable now on reflection. To relate the ultimate in pathetic organisation, I recall more than one occasion when a 10 or 12-coach double-headed train pulled tight up to the station buffers and in consequence of the short platform, left several coaches well outside the station limits. Some brilliant inspector at Blackpool had marshalled non-corridor stock for the unfortunate return holidaymakers and the result was a 20mins hold-up whilst passengers in the rear coaches were assisted down short ladders and across the tracks. A tail-back of trains then ensued block to block from Ramsbottom on one side, and from Whitworth on the other. Those were the situations the little bowler-hatted men, sat in their dingy offices juggling with their statistical charts, never did visualise.

Toilet facilities in most boxes I worked were reasonably good, but here the situation was extremely primitive. Including South Junction at Bury, this was the fourth I had worked in, but I had visited many others, some near stations where the facilities provided would be a water closet, and others in the country where a signalman would be provided with a chemical closet. Despite being within 300yds of the station and with connections to the main drainage system a bucket in a hut at the bottom of the steps was all that existed here at Bacup Junction. The railway companies were not subject to the jurisdictions of the twentieth century 'Factory Acts', and deemed that a hole be dug in the grass embankment and the contents be emptied therein and suitably covered by earth. This none-too-pleasant task would take far too long for a busy signalman and without doubt would cause delay to some train. So a disgusting habit of emptying the bucket into the river which ran close by the box was initiated. This practice appalled me. I had seen, smelt and reeled from the stinking filth which polluted this same river when working immediately above it some five miles west at Hall Carr Box.

A curt answer in the negative was the reply to a request for a chemical closet which I forwarded to head office, jointly signed by my fellow signalmen, Cyril Jones and Wilf Lomas, coupled with those of Jim and Charlie Quarterman, whose S&T cabin was situated virtually over the river. Indignant and feeling a little 'bolshie', I replied to the refusal by suggesting the practice may come to the ears of the local council health inspectors. It did the trick, and within two days a brand new chemical closet had arrived.

Studying the fortnightly area vacancy list with an insatiable desire for promotion, I eagerly awaited news. Whilst extremely happy at this box, the quest for additional remuneration was continually uppermost in the mind of a young married man and, in any case, I still had that inward yearning to get closer to the environs of Manchester or Salford, or out on to the main express lines further afield.

Returning from a fortnight's cycling tour in the West Country, I scanned the vacancy list with renewed zest and noted a Class 2 position advertised at Broadfield, midway between Bury and Rochdale on the L&Y section of the Liverpool-Leeds and West Yorkshire line. As a matter of course, and as I had done with every other Class 2 vacancy which had arisen, I forwarded my application. I did not expect to have any luck. After all, I was only in my mid-20s and would probably set up some kind of record as the youngest Class 2 man ever, if it should come my way. The utter surprise on receiving confirmation of appointment to this post, which I was given two weeks later, jolted me somewhat, and I wondered if I had done the right thing in my haste. Time would tell.

Broadfield box was 13 miles from my home and would necessitate a 26-mile bike ride every day, as there would be no suitable train or bus service to fit in with the hours of duty. I was a fanatically keen cyclist, however, and now on the point of engaging in serious cycle racing with the West Pennine Road Club of Bury. Emphatically, this would be ideal training. As if fate had decreed it to be, I had only two weeks earlier purchased a new racing bike with the proceeds of the money saved during a 12-month lapse of smoking. Surely this would be a supreme opportunity to attain full fitness. These were brave words in October, but to be deeply regretted and swallowed hard at 4.30am during the uncompromising and remorseless winter of 1946-47.

CHAPTER 10

Step Up, Then Step Down

Broadfield box was situated a little beyond the summit of the 2-mile incline from Bury Loop Junction, with Heap Bridge box, primarily a block post to the west, and Heywood Station Crossing box to the east, in the direction of Castleton Junction and Rochdale. Here little respite existed between the passage of trains on this highly industrialised trans-Pennine route. With the exception of Sunday's traffic, it was virtually non-stop. When linked throughout in the mid-1880s, this busy line served a very vital purpose in diverting through cross-country traffic away from the congestion of Manchester and Salford. In particular, it was invaluable to the innumerable heavy trains from the Yorkshire coalfields bound for Liverpool, and for the returning empty wagon trains.

Coal contributed immensely to the large volume of traffic dealt with here and, along with other mixed goods traffic, it probably accounted for 75 percent of the work load. Passenger traffic was comparatively light, although during holiday periods, and in particular whilst Blackpool Illuminations were in progress during the autumn, heavy excursions and special trains would steam through well into the early hours of the morning. Coal trains heading westwards invariably had a marshalling of 40 wagons, a loading of approximately 600 tons and were hauled usually by one of the old L&Y 0-6-0s or an 0-8-0. Heavy freights with loads of up to 80 wagons trundled along with an Austerity WD 2-8-0, or a Stanier 8F 2-8-0 at the head. The sleek and probably most versatile locomotive ever built, the Stanier 'Black Fives', were a familiar sight on the customary 10-coach Yorkshire to Blackpool expresses and specials. 'Ironclads', 'Crabs' and the ever-faithful L&Y Aspinall 2F 0-6-0 were commonplace, and perhaps a Midland 'Compound' would occasionally trespass and cause a second glance. 'Jack of all trades' hereabouts, however, was the Aspinall 0-6-0, seen working mixed freights, local pick-ups, shunting, banking or, during a 'Wakes' week often hauling double-headed a Blackpool excursion train.

Here at Broadfield, they were constantly to be seen covering duties as Nos. 1 and 2 bankers, assisting from Bury Loop Junction and then racing back there at all possible speed. It was not as familiar to the public as the well-known Lickey Bank, south of Birmingham, though Broadfield bank was in effect a somewhat similar incline both in gradient and length. Permanent bank engines Nos 1. and 2 were employed only at night-time when freight traffic was at its heaviest. Should a bank engine be unavoidably needed during the daytime, one of the shunting engines from the L&Y yard could be called on quickly.

Arriving for training, my initial surprise was to find a 'Midland' frame, now known as a 'standard', in use. Its base was raised a foot above floor level, and the low angle of the projecting levers appeared positively evil. Apparently, this signalbox was comparatively new, in railway terms that is. The L&Y frame had been broken up during the demolition of the old box and since the regrouping and amalgamation of the old companies in 1923, only Midland type frames were being manufactured for the LMS at the Derby works. In the first hour I was to learn, not without a little pain, the completely different 'swing' required on this raised frame where levers, after being pulled forward, finish at a far lower angle than that on the L&Y frame. The immediate frontal pull must be avoided at all cost, and a swing to one side of the body adopted, otherwise the devastating result could well be an injury of deep significance to one's manhood. Having only a few days previously made a decision with my wife to attempt raising a family once more, I pondered on this hitherto delightful task, wondering if it would now be at all possible, following my first day on this sinister frame.

At first sight, this deceptively 'ordinary' box, with its very simple layout and lack of visual importance, did not appear to warrant a Class 2 status, but what it lacked in traffic regulation and junction operations, it gained in telephone work and the continual heavy nightwork involved in bank engines activities.

As had been the case throughout the war, and still remained the overriding factor contributing to the excessive banking, was the gross overloading of trains, and locomotives were fast succumbing to the lack of maintenance and the pressures put upon them over the past six years. This dire situation caused banking to be far more frequent than ever on this incline. A driver, confident in his locomotive classification and its power to haul the given load, would often find by the time he was passing Heap Bridge box his power had diminished drastically and he was fast losing steam. His loud and clear whistling for assistance then came as no surprise to the Bury Loop Junction signalman, who was as ever with his ears attuned by constant habit, and at the ready for the instant moves required. Barely would his ground disc signal have been lowered, before the vigilant banker driver would be on the move, endeavouring to make quick contact before the train was at a stand.

Here at Broadfield, telephone work was extremely complicated as the box was a 'circuit' end. On average, up to 10 boxes would comprise a basic box-to-box 'circuit', and the far one, more often than not a junction, would pass on the indispensable details of traffic requirements to the next 'circuit' when appropriate. Block instruments and their accompanying code of bell signals adequately describe to a signalman what type of train he is signalling through, but do not inform him of their ultimate destinations, their loads, and their traffic stops, plus other vital details necessary for efficient operation. This information, and much more, is passed along well in advance of the actual signalling of a train over the block system, and additional advice such as whether a train is 1min 'up' or ½min 'down' or is running well, or 'shaping' badly will be given. All this type of information is continually circulating to each controlling point and to the overall traffic-control office in Manchester.

This theoretical traffic-control centre, encompassing Manchester, Salford and their surrounding networks, was not as efficient in these densely congested areas as perhaps it would have been when first introduced by the Midland Railway Company some 50 years earlier in the Sheffield, Derby and Nottingham districts. The local arrangements of box-to-box 'circuiting' was much faster and consequently more productive in relation to speed and efficiency.

Messages received and sent from 'circuit end' boxes could be amusingly ambiguous and invariably cryptic, in particular if you did not possess the ear of a 'local'. In this locality, a message forwarded 'Main Line Monkey' told Bury West Juction box that a Rochdale-Bolton train was passing Heywood. Equally, 'Brewery Bacup 36 and Tups, flyer Bury' would be deciphered as a Brewery sidings (Manchester) to Bacup mixed freight was now passing Castleton Junction with a load of 36 wagons, his next traffic stop would be Ramsbottom, locally known as 'Tupsarse', and he would skip his usual stop at Bury EL yard, providing there was no traffic to be attached. 'Edge Hill Healey Mills 60 and Todd, banker Bury', denoted the Edge Hill (Liverpool) to Healey Mills (Yorkshire) with a load of 60 wagons, and that he needed a banker on Broadfield incline from Bury Loop Junction, his next traffic stop being at Todmorden marshalling yard. A train 'circuited' from 'Moon Rakers' would denote Middleton, or from 'Boiler Shakers' would mean Radcliffe. From 'Trotters' to 'Puddings' would signify Bolton-Bury.

Traffic working here was so utterly contrasting to the strict passenger timetable operating I had been accustomed to at Bury South Junction, only 4 miles away from here on the East Lancs section and, again, to that of the terminal station workings at Bacup. I was beginning to relish the rapidly successive changes of environment that I was experiencing, and to become eager for the next move. It evidently would never be in my nature to become domiciled permanently in one box. As a pub-crawler may well state there are no two pubs alike in this county, equally it can be said there are no two signalboxes alike.

Normanton, Wakefield, Mirfield, Brighouse, Healey Mills, Crofton, Halifax, Bradford, Leeds, Pontefract and Dewsbury in Yorkshire, along with Fazackerly, Aintree, Edghill, Westhaughton, Moston, Ordsall Lane, Oldfield Road, Newton Heath, Agecroft and Patricroft in Lancashire, were names constantly on the tongue. Despite my unfamiliarity with the traffic over this stretch of line, only a short time was needed to train the box. The frame was extremely straightforward but, nevertheless, after taking over seven days later, I became a little apprehensive when informed that owing to staff shortages, and the failure to fill a second vacancy which had arisen here in the past few weeks, I would be required to work continuous 12hr shifts for an unspecified period. Coupled with an hour's bike ride at the beginning and end of each shift, a total of 14hrs per day did not appear particularly attractive; especially when something in my bones warned me of a nasty winter ahead.

Head down over the handlebars on the descent into Bury's smog at 5am the following week, and then out of the saddle to climb Heap Bridge brow, dodging tramlines and picking the smoothest path through boneshaking cobblestones, I began to pray for the next promotion. That should be a Class 1 box near to the city and I could then move my home and enjoy a more sedate and easier journey to work. As keen a cyclist as I was, and eager to achieve a maximum fitness in preparation for a full season of cycle racing, it needed all my known psychological powers to convince myself that I was revelling in leaving home at 4.30am in cold, foggy and rain-lashed conditions to cycle these 13 undulating miles to work. After a strenuous 2-mile start, the road took a 1 in 10 climb out of Rawtenstall to assist in speeding up a healthy blood circulation, and with no time to dismount and walk up any of the remaining hills, the route was in no way an easy one. Following a 12hr night shift, no signalman appreciates his relief arriving late, and the man I took over from was well renowned among drivers and fellow signalmen to be a stringently unco-operative chap. I was consequently unable to come to any unofficial arrangement or compromise and be able to travel by an early train. Despite all drawbacks, however, I persevered for the next three punishing months.

During my brief sojourn, I found to my surprise that the night shift suited me best. Cycling to work for a 6pm start was far more pleasurable than the early morning ride, and the work itself was certainly of more general interest and reward than that provided by the monotonous passage of scheduled trains in the daytime hours.

Throughout the night it was necessary to return bank engines to Bury Loop Junction as quickly as possible following their assistance of a freight on the 2-mile incline. Should the density of traffic on the down line cause it to be impossible to return a banker immediately, it would be a matter of only ½hr before the 'block' would be put on at Bury Knowsley Street Station, despite the quadruple tracking throughout two vital sections at that point.

The normal procedure when a banker 'dropped off', was to hold him on the main line in front of the box if possible, to await clearance of a down train, and then quickly to route him over the crossover road down to the advanced starter and into the section ahead, when acceptance was obtained. If this was impossible to do, one bellowed out of the box to the driver, telling him to draw ahead, and he was then brought back on the loop line to await despatch a little ahead of the box at a ground disc signal.

This move was forthrightly impressed upon all newcomers and when taking the examination for this post, the trainee had the relevent facts of the

1915 accident at St Bede's Junction on the NER vividly recounted. Nineteen people had died in that tragedy.

Leaving an engine on the main line to await a 'road', even if no consequent delay would ensue, was never a sensible thing to do and was frowned upon, particularly if no track circuiting existed, as was often the case. Such was the situation that led me into making another serious blunder, so easily accomplished when extremely busy and working in black and foggy conditions.

I had received 'train out of section' for a fast-moving down freight from Heap Bridge a little sooner than expected, and a following 'down' freight due to be signalled at any second from Heywood box had not materialised, doubtless because he was losing time somewhere. At last! a 5min margin; yes I could get the banker back. I rattled off a 2-3 and took 'line clear' from Heap Bridge. A quick reversal then of the crossover road and the ground signal changed from up to down main line, then the inner home and starter signals positioned and I dashed to the window. 'Right away Jack', I confidently shouted to the driver. He was ready, and quickly away. Already he was gathering speed as I crashed the window back into place and the sudden and horrible realisation hit me that he had been stood on the loop, and not the main line. The driver had not looked down to the first ground signal which was required for the move, but had merely taken my word for it. He saw all the other three signals ahead showing green, and bolted like Reg Harris at the start of a ¼ mile handicap on Fallowfield track. At the speed he would have taken the crossover road, he hit the buffers head on. The fireman was almost flung head first into the firebox and the driver was extremely lucky to suffer only a few cuts and bruises after catapulting across the footplate.

Fortunately, the buffers were sadly in need of repair and disintegrated completely following the impact and the debris was flung 6ft ahead. The locomotive was unscathed and the two footplatemen were extremely co-operative about the whole matter, considering the unpleasant shock they had both received. It was one of those incongurous situations where, had an enquiry been held, the driver would have taken the brunt of the blame. Fifteen minutes later the engine was safely on its way, and further co-operative action from the Yardmaster on the following day ensured a subsequent report, stating that the buffer stops had been rendered useless during normal everyday shunting duties!

The current and rising concern of post-war staff shortages, motivated by the retirement of men who had carried on working over the age of 65, and aggravated by the rapid spiral of factory wages overtaking those of railway employees, was beginning to show stark evidence. It was a sad situation. Only once during my whole signalling career was I ever to be relieved by a signalman's Supervisor, which was due to this appalling shortage of staff. It was here, during a 6pm-6am shift, when I had no option but to request relief. At about midnight I was experiencing a particularly severe attack of conjunctivitis, a very painful eye affliction. Following two or three hours of actue soreness and severe watering, I was unable to carry on safely and knew well the likelihood and consequences of making a serious mistake if I tried to hold on until 6am. I telegraphed for urgent relief but none was available, and at 3am the Area Supervisor arrived and I was immediately put on the footplate of a down coal train, dropped off at Bury where I took a taxi home.

This heralded the beginning of serious travelling problems to Broadfield box. Following a day's rest and suitable treatment with eye drops and ointment, I was back cycling to work again. The first day of that terrible winter struck, and there was the biggest snowfall and freeze-up of the century which I knew was an end to my work. In no way could I continue to work a 12hr shift, or indeed a normal 8hr shift, for that matter, without residing or lodging much nearer to the town. Houses everywhere were almost impossible to rent at that time, and the thought of buying one was a vision almost undreamed of by the average working man of that time. Reluctantly, I was forced into taking demotion to a box at Fernhill sidings, a little north of Bury, where again, due to the ever-present staff shortages, this normally three-manned post had become recently a one-man box, with a 10hr working day shift.

It was a bitter blow to me at the time. However, I reluctantly took solace in the sure promise that when housing shortages were overcome, I could break out of the Rossendale Valley where, reluctantly, I now seemed to have become trapped. The quest for the elusive big boxes of my ever insatiable desires would evidently resume in the not too distant future.

CHAPTER 11

The Valley Again

It started as a gift from heaven! But bad luck was to dog me from the very start at this once busy block post. A regular 10hr shift starting at 7am and finishing at 5pm, with the added bonus of 2hrs overtime pay was a duty not many railwaymen would ever be presented with.

The reduction of traffic on this line was most noticeable to me, returning after absence of four years. Troop trains, munition trains and other essential wartime movements had ceased and, due to the continual deterioration of the permanent way, rolling stock, locomotives and the general economic chaos of war-ravaged Britain at that time, there was no evidence of a return to pre-war pride and prosperity. Rusty levers, tarnished brass block instruments, filthy windows and floor linoleum would at least give me plenty to occupy my mind between the passage of trains.

With a bike-ride of only 9 miles and no need to leave home until 6am I soon came to realise what a tremendous difference these extra few hours made. More often than not by this time at least one car had passed along the road and made tracks through overnight snow. This made for an easier ride, following in the ruts made by a heavy car tyre.

For two days only I was to be fortunate. Then without warning, what we knew as the big 'Dollop', the worst snowfall I ever recall fell over 24hrs, and with it came Arctic conditions which were to last for many weeks. It covered the entire length and breadth of Britain and resulted in the greatest paralysis of communications the country had ever witnessed. Hundreds of miles of main-line track, despite herculian efforts by thousands of railmen and prisoners-of-war, were repeatedly blocked. These men were working entirely at the mercy of the elements for weeks on end.

Beyond Stubbins Junction, the Rossendale Valley was isolated for a whole week, to name only one of hundreds of areas in the same predicament. Huge snowdrifts blocked all road traffic movement at the 'Quarrymans' north of Edenfield, and again on the south side near Shuttleworth. Along the wide open stretch of road beneath Grants Tower, where the M66 motorway now sprawls, a massive barrier of snow obliterated any sign of the highway and defied anyone to attempt an entry into the more temperate streets within the borough of Bury.

No sophisticated snow-clearing equipment, as seen today, existed for road clearance in those days. It was the railways that took first priority and that was where labour was diverted. For seven days or more, with youth and pigheadedness on my side, I defied it. Two, three and even four hours I took, riding, sliding, dragging the bike over defiant snowdrifts and plodding, bike on shoulder to defeat the elements and get to work somehow. On several occasions, it was as late as 10am when I at last put the box into circuit. The fact that it was predominantly a block post merely delayed trains and did not cause an entire stoppage to traffic.

Shunting out the wagons from Fernhill sidings and the corporation yard was now abandoned due to the atrocious circumstances and the pilot engine which came daily and brought with it the signalman's can of drinking water was cancelled. The whole rail system was in total chaos and, of course, in those years organised road transport, as we know it today, was virtually non-existent. Had it been operating, it would have become totally paralysed under these catastrophic conditions. At least, despite the overall adversities, the trains did keep moving.

Within a very short time industry all over the country was grinding to a standstill and the relentless elements achieved a situation which even Hitler had failed to accomplish during a six-year bombing campaign. Though oil and electricity had now become a large factor in the fuelling of factory machinery, 'King coal' was still the dominating agent, and continued to play a major role. Passage of coal trains was given priority over passenger trains and consequent scenes of irate passengers hurling abuse at a signalman, who shunted their train in order to let through a slow-moving coal train, were frequent. To add to the passenger's discomfort, and further fuel that indignation, the steam heating pipes were often disconnected in order to make savings on the locomotive's coal consumption.

On one or two occasions, before the road home was opened up, I 'hitched' a lift on the footplate of an Accrington-bound freight as far as Ramsbottom marshalling yard. The bike was precariously perched on top of the engine's coal stack, a position which disconcerted me more than a little, as it was no 'ordinary' bike. It had cost me some very hard-earned cash, and was primarily a road racing bike, sporting an almost irreplaceable French 'Simplex' 4-speed gear.

By mid-March things were back to normal and I revelled in the regularity of the hours, with the bonus of overtime pay and the overall 16-mile ride which I was pleased to consider an ideal daily training run. In my locker I kept a coarse towel and spare clothing and, on arrival 15mins before my allocated time, I enjoyed a vigorous rub down and a complete change of jersey and shorts into the rough and dry serge of railway issue.

Something previously unknown was now happening to the recruitment of railway men. Young men without any previous railway experience whatsoever, in either station or engine-shed duties, were being recruited to train for this work. Within six weeks it was possible for these men to be in charge of a signalbox! It was a situation unprecedented in pre-war years. Most of these recruits, demobbed after spending up to six years in the forces and having been unemployed prior to 1939 during the thirties' depression, were totally unsuited. They were extremely unfortunate men, having no trade, and with no guaranteed job to return to after the war and, they had now to take the first position that became available, and the one which paid the best wages. By now the tragedy was that the railway companies, having been stripped of their old pride and bankrupted by a savage six-year assault on their resources, were now having to pay inferior wages compared to manufacturing industries, and the directors and management were content to shrug their shoulders knowing that nationalisation was only a matter of time.

Some of the first of these recruits from the labour exchange in Bury were allotted to Fernhill box for training in rules, regulations, and given any other necessary guidance to induce, persuade and eventually transform them into signalmen. Between working the box and during any spare time at all, I was to teach them all the ramifications of the absolute block system and generally prepare them for examination a few weeks hence in Manchester where, if passed out, they would be allocated a suitable Class 4 vacancy. With the first two men, I put my heart into it; after all, it was a subject I enjoyed anyway, and I carefully interpreted as many of the 240 rules which applied to train signalling in the company's standard rule book, and made a little sense to them of the 36 regulations and corresponding appendices existing in the book of absolute block regulations.

Whilst making this almost inextricable and tedious studying as interesting as possible to them, I attempted to illustrate as graphically as I could, the emergency regulations and, most importantly, the precautionary measures used. Sometimes I would refer to the many situations I had faced myself and, in addition, I related many accidents and their causes. Some of these stories, if somewhat 'gory', were considered most useful in securing the keen sense of responsibility required, in a man who soon would have the power to safeguard, or destroy, the lives of 100 human beings in one simple move. What of the 3-2-3 'Blocking back in section' signal, the use of lever collars, the most essential use of Rule 55, the ordering out of the box of any unauthorised staff, particularly during a busy period when a man's concentration can be fatally distracted?

Bearing in mind all these factors at the time, the most catastrophic rail tragedy in British history would have been averted had the most elementary of these rules been carried out. Of the 227 dead, and a larger amount suffering serious injuries, the bulk were troops of the 7th Bn Royal Scots. Five trains in all were involved in this massive pile up, three passenger and two goods, the wreckage taking 24hrs to clear. Nineteen coaches were completely gutted by fire. This all took place at Quintinshill near Gretna Green Junction, 10 miles north of Carlisle on the L&NW Railway, on 22 May 1915. Because of wartime censorship the public in general heard little of the holocaust until after 1918, and a very rare outcome of the subsequent enquiry was that the two signalmen responsible for the tragedy served prison sentences for manslaughter, after criminal negligence was shown to be the prime factor.

The first serious mistake in this short chain of errors was the failure to use the 'blocking back in section' signal. The second was in not placing lever collars on the protecting signals as a reminder that a train was standing on the up main line, and third was the incorrect carrying out of Rule 55. The train register book was correctly signed by the footplateman, but his failure to ascertain if collars had been placed on the signal levers protecting his train had, to a certain extent, my overall sympathy. Whatever fireman, walking into a signalbox with perhaps 30-90 levers could be expected to know at a glance which levers apply to his train? It could well take a trainee signalman three days before he himself had the slightest idea. The final contributing factor had been the continued presence of the relieved signalman and two goods guards, all chatting together, and who had no right whatsoever to be in the box at that time.

To emphasise all these contributory factors to the trainee signalman, I vividly described the scene at Quintinshill that morning when, at 6.50am in broad daylight, the up troop special, carrying a full load of 15 coaches and travelling at high speed off Beattock bank, smashed into the local stopping train to Beattock. In addition to the 'local', two goods trains awaiting a 'road' were occupying the up and down relief lines and into these three trains smashed the locomotive and wreckage of the Scots troop train. On the down line, travelling at high speed and too late to be stopped, was the northbound 'Night Scotsman' from Euston; 600 tons in weight, hauled by two locomotives and 13 coaches, three of which were sleeping cars, ploughed into the wreckage strewn across four tracks within one minute of the first smash.

This story, along with other relevant incidents helped me to interpret the otherwise tedious and perplexing rules and regulations. From the apparent disinterest shown, I was not a little surprised to hear that on the day appointed to take their examinations, they had handed in their notices, taken their pay and had presumably gone in search of more easy money. This situation was happening over and over again. With no stretch of the imagination could I say the work here was at all exciting; on the contrary, it was particularly dull and in every way demoralising to me, after previously achieving a Class 2 status. Nevertheless, I was enjoying the hours of work tremendously, and when I was informed I was to be transferred back into the Rossendale Valley in order to be nearer home, I was uncertain whether to take the news with joy or trepidation.

Until I arrived there I little realised that one of the system's 'cushiest numbers' awaited me. The box was at Union Mills, Cloughfold; the time, early summer 1947. By now, changing areas and boxes, or learning a new frame and surroundings was becoming part of my everyday life. Together with Union Mills box, Cloughfold Station level crossing box had also to be worked on this roster, and this came as an added relief to the otherwise dull and undemanding work at this particular post. The duty roster of 8am to 4pm were hours that only in my wildest dreams could I have anticipated.

Union Mills sidings had, by that time, been relegated to a small yard needing shunting but once a day, and the box had become merely a block post between Waterfoot and Cloughfold boxes. My hours were 8am-1.15pm in the Union Mills box, and 1.30pm-4pm in Cloughfold crossing box.

Sunday work compensated for the loss of overtime or night-duty extras and, indeed, a more sedate and suitable existence I could not imagine. The job here was extremely boring, but there was always a little something to break the monotony. There was the intrepid Maggie, a brazen, well-famed and discreetly-to-be-avoided 'local' who regularly crossed the line to Glendale cotton mill, voicing her obscene views on all and sundry; in particular on all the local males who, according to her, were the most sexually well-endowed in the valley. Her raucous comments, imparted with a voice that could reputedly sink a battleship, were deliberately unheard by the fair sex, but augmented, and often affirmed, by the male population. Her vociferous suggestions on many occasions all but deposited her into Rawtenstall courtroom, along with Fred, another character of the day who was forever 'flashing'. He surely had a lucky escape when using a local widow's letterbox for his suggestive displays. She was a little closer to the spring flap than he had imagined!

The Stationmaster was forever tantalised by a young clerk from Bacup. This clerk, by the name of Arthur Heyworth, was a very bright lad and invariably had completed the daily accounts well within the prescribed time and, apart from issuing tickets, he had little left to occupy his time. On occasions, the Stationmaster would tear about in a rage seeking out his missing clerk, who would be found later nonchalantly sunbathing on the station roof or perhaps laying a stone on top of the same official's office chimney and creating almost panic when the room was enveloped in choking smoke. There was always, of course, the eternal permeation of gas, well-known to every Rossendalian. If you should be dozing on a train late at night in a smoke-filled compartment, even with the window tightly closed and blinds drawn, the perpetual stink would penetrate the carriage with ease and you would be well aware that you were in the vicinity of Cloughfold Station.

It might have been my least impressive posting yet, had it not been for a close encounter with adversity after a Bacup-Manchester train overshot my home signal at danger and was within inches of taking the crossing gates and a persistently awkward motorist with it. This happened at the station crossing, and aptly demonstrated the incongruity of the regulation stating that crossing gates with normal everyday road traffic passing between them, did not consititute an obstruction within the normal ¼ mile clearance needed in advance of the outermost stop signal for the acceptance under Regulation 4 of a train from the box in rear. The driver of this particular train rushed back to the box swearing profusely and assuring me he would report the matter. He evidently did, for I received a request for a report which I duly made out and returned to head office. He had placed his own head in the noose!

At even the quietest and most tedious of boxes there can be an occasion, albeit very infrequently as in the latter case, that shakes one out of complacency and demonstrates the ease with which a catastrophic situation can develop. A common habit, often used to assist the signal linesman or to 'shake' a frozen signal arm back to danger, was to 'trip' the electrical locks on a track circuit. The danger of so doing was dramatically demonstrated at South Croydon on the Southern Railway in October of this particular year. As so often is the case, the tragedy happened during the rush hour and in thick fog between the hours of 8am and 9am. The signalman concerned had overlooked the presence of a train waiting at his starting signal, tripped the electric locking protective mechanism, believing it to have developed a fault, and accepted a second and fast moving train. The resulting smash cost the lives of 32 passengers and maimed many more.

Away from the hurly-burly of busy rail centres, I now found the regular nights in bed, replacing unnatural night-duty shifts, and the bonus of 'office hours' during the day, to be extremely beneficial to my pursuit of cycle racing and, without doubt, I reached a pinnacle of fitness never before attainable when working irregular hours. Significantly, however, boredom shortly replaced this new-found manifestation. A call to return to signalling work which was accompanied by a strong basis of interest was awarded a major boost following a holiday in Dublin. Passenger guard Ted O'Shea of Bacup had relatives residing on the outskirts of the Irish capital, a little to the south and in very pleasant surroundings. They owned a guest house and Ted had arranged attractive discounts for local railwaymen. A visit to the Republic with its added attraction of 'coupon-free' clothing and food, coupled with an allowance of a free pass for the crossing, was too good an opportunity to miss. It would be 7 years since we had tasted boiled ham and farm butter, unrationed sweets and chocolate. Most of these luxuries were still unobtainable and stark austerities were still in evidence across the whole of post-war Britain, although two years had passed since the VE and VJ celebrations.

A bus strike was currently in force in the Irish capital, apparently nothing unusual to the Irish, but to us in the UK it was something of amusement. A major strike had been unheard of since 1926. Over the past 8 years it would have been illegal, at any event, though highly unlikely to have ever been considered by the then co-operative trade unions and management of wartime Britain.

Together with our cycles and a pair of ruck-sacks replacing suitcases, my wife and I boarded a late train to Manchester Victoria and, after crossing to Central Station, we caught a further train to connect with the night boat-train at Chester. Night travel and other restrictions are part and parcel of the concessionary ticket allocation, and although frustrating at the time, can have interesting compensations. To be compelled to make a change at

Chester, instead of taking the through Holyhead boat-train from Manchester, gave us time to have a pleasant stroll round the station, take a cup of tea and generally reminisce about bygone days when this famous line to Holyhead on the island of Anglesey was first conceived.

Rumbling through that most unusual of bridges, the tubular Britannia, I contemplated on how many passengers were aware of the unique stone lions which guard the portals. In the distant past my father had held me back by the legs whilst I dangled precariously out of the carriage window to stare at this sight as the train rounded the curve towards the bridge. The aftermath of that episode was, of course, an eyeful of hot sparks and smut from the engine, and an inability to see anything else but tears for the next five minutes. Nineteen lives had been lost during the construction of this bridge and on more than one occasion I was almost to add to the toll.

It was well worth the discomforts of a 4hr battering on what is reputed to be the roughest sea-crossing around our coastal waters, to enjoy an entire fortnight of complete freedom which the Republic of Ireland provided. We found the country free from the rigid austerity we in Britain had become accustomed to ever since that fatal day in September 1939. To be able to walk into a shop, request almost anything you required without being asked for your ration book or coupons was almost a forgotten memory. To see hundreds of cyclists intermingling with the almost incessant flow of traffic on O'Connell bridge, and carrying no cycle-lamps after dark; to watch women balancing on crossbars; these were offences that would have brought an immediate and rapid first step into any British courtroom to receive a fine of 7s 6d (37½p).

Altogether it was a superb and most welcome break, but I almost marred it by my unfortunate first and, I assure any customs officer reading this narrative, my last attempt at smuggling. A Swiss wristwatch was almost my undoing when passing through customs at Holyhead. Watches of any reasonable quality, at any price, had been virtually unobtainable for several years in the UK and the temptation to purchase one, even at the then exhorbitant price of £10 stirling proved too much, and I succumbed to the enticement in Dublin city. Following a 10min grilling by the officer, I almost cracked and I was a trembling wreck after clearing the docks and station. Never again, I assured myself; the experience was never worth it.

As so many people conclude, a holiday gives not only a complete rest from everyday work and its associated anxieties, but a time to relax and perhaps take stock of the future. The future seemed bleak and no signs of any immediate boom appeared to be hitting the Rossendale valley. On the contrary, the cotton industry was in continual decline, property prices were plummeting and no plans for the introduction of replacement industries were visible. Perhaps this was also happening in the Manchester area, though we were not sure. Happily stretched out on a comfortable seat in Dublin's Pheonix park, we resolved to purchase a house in the valley, look for quick promotion and higher pay to effect the mortgage repayments, and make further efforts in raising a family. The latter part of this project was, without doubt, the simplest and would prove the most pleasant. Arriving home in the early morning after the night journey from Ireland, we slept until early afternoon. Waking up later and rampant with earthly desires, I decided to put the plan into immediate operation. So in wild abandonment, we enjoyed the pleasures that nature had bestowed. Then, with my youthful lust appeased, I threw back the bedclothes, gave my partner's bare bottom a hearty slap, jumped out of bed and, naked as the day is long, flung back the curtains and in all my pristine glory stared straight into the face of an open-mouthed window cleaner. The effect was shattering, and it took a full three seconds before the curtains blotted out this captivating display of female beauty and vibrant male wedding equipment. I gather the window-cleaner took this exhibition as due reward for his work as he never did include that day's task on his monthly bill!

Finding a property within our price bracket in the immediate vicinity of Manchester proved impossible, so with a little reluctance we were forced into buying locally. With nagging doubts regarding a promotion that was further afield, I awaited something more financially rewarding to show up on the Bacup branch. Within a short time a vacancy arose at Waterfoot Goods box, and although it was the same Class 4 grading as the box I already worked, it at least produced a larger pay packet due to shift work and Sunday duty at Stacksteads box. Furthermore, I knew the work was far more interesting, and it was not with any undue sorrow that I said my farewell to Cloughfold and its long roadside barrier of garish upturned railway sleepers, in the autumn 1947.

CHAPTER 12

A Step Out

It would have been some 20 years since I walked the rough cobblestoned slope to Waterfoot Goods yard. This was also the access road to the signalbox and what a change had come about! Passing the weighbridge, and its accompanying office on the left, brought many memories flooding back. The big warehouse and goods loading bays, on the right, lacked their teams of shire horses, stables, bays of fodder and nostalgic odours and had been replaced by articulated 'Karrier Kobs' and the paraphernalia of petrol driven lorries. Electrically driven cranes were replacing the large hand-operated winches, along with their heavy and cumbersome gear.

Crossing the line to the box now, it seemed little else had changed. L&Y, L&NW and LMS tender and tank engines were, as ever, shunting the yard. My old home, Railway Cottages, still stood on the lineside a little towards the station, and in Bluebell Woods beyond the river the majestic trees stood proudly like sentinels, guarding my many personal secrets. These stalwarts could tell so many a sensuous tale of my early exploration into the mysteries of life, and bring a nostalgic blush to the cheek of one of the young maidens of Waterfoot.

Walking into this signalbox, barely ½ mile from the very house I was born in, induced in me a most peculiar sensation of inescapable entrenchment; was I to be forever trapped on this fast declining branch line? When was I to be given my next opportunity to sever the invisible cords that circumstances had dictated, and return again to the main-line work that was my sole and ultimate goal?

This section of the old East Lancashire Railway was not without its historical and fascinating interest and, after learning the frame and studying the local supplementary regulations, I came to realise the unique layout of the three Glen tunnels. They needed a very careful study in order to answer correctly the questions which would be put forward during the examination on regulations appertaining to any emergency that should arise.

Soon after the through line from Manchester-Rawtenstall was established in 1846, work was commenced on the next phase to Waterfoot, or Newchurch as the station would then be known. It was completed and operated as a single line two years later. In 1852 the single-line track was extended to Bacup, passing through two short tunnels, Newchurch No. 1 and No. 2, in the Glen. When competition came later from the newly laid Rochdale-Bacup line in the 1870s, it accelerated the necessity for double tracking from Rawtenstall, through to the proposed new and enlarged station at Bacup. Problems caused by the geology of rock formations in the Glen and the original line's close proximity to the river, entailed a third and separate bore having to be driven through. This became known as Thrutch tunnel for the up traffic and was opened in 1880.

Tunnels and their construction I had always found to be a most fascinating subject. Although shuddering at the very thought of walking through, or having to work in one, I nevertheless had some strange compulsion to read of the trials and tribulations of the great surveyors and engineers, and of the heroic feats and utter misery under which the navvies of those early pioneering days had to work. Not only in the construction of the long Alpine tunnels of Europe, or through the Rockies of North America, or the Andes of the south, do we count the number of lives lost in thousands; here in the UK there are many famous tunnels, used daily at the present time with little thought spared for those great engineers and workmen of the last century, many who laid down their lives in order to give this country the most densely knit railway network in the world.

Our longest, the Severn, though by no means the earliest, was built by Sir John Hawkshaw and opened in 1886. Our oldest, at Talyllyn Junction near Brecon in Wales, was built in 1812 as Napoleon and his army were retreating from Moscow; first used for a horse-drawn tramway, it was eventually widened in 1863 to take the trains of the Brecon to Merthyr and Hereford Railways. Not far from here, a mere 20 miles to the south, Richard Trevithick had taken the world's first steam engine for about 10 miles from Pen-y-Darren to Abercynon in the high Glamorgan valley of the Taff. Of the four trans-Pennine tunnels, all have their captivating stories.

Totley, the longest and most southerly, is not so familiar to the intercity traveller. The route on which it serves is less traversed, but is an extremely picturesque and captivating artery of the Peak District, transporting a great proportion of ramblers into the National Park. It was built in 1893 and the length is 6,230yds.

Woodhead, a little to the north, was built with an extreme urgency in order to twin the two rapidly expanding cities of Manchester and Sheffield. So, too, was Standedge, a further leap northwards, and connecting Manchester to the big wool towns of West Yorkshire. Northernmost of these illustrious bores was Summit tunnel, so named on account of the portal at the eastern end; standing at the highest point of this Leeds-Manchester route. This tunnel was opened in 1841 after a very long delay expressly resulting from fierce opposition by the Rochdale Canal Co, then a very powerful force. Striking north to the junction with west and north Lancashire routes at Toddmorden, the line then follows through the Calder Gap, one of the few natural fissures that splits the whole Pennine chain from the north Midlands to their links with the Cheviots in Scotland.

A shorter route than that followed by other engineers in their quest for speedier travel between the booming areas of Lancashire and West Yorkshire, was that blasted through the high bleak moors at Standedge.

This, a three-mile, 60yd tunnel was unique. Having water troughs lain within, it proved to be the only one like it in the world. There were two reasons for this phenomenon, firstly it was the only level stretch of line between Huddersfield and Manchester and, secondly, a ready water supply was available from the canal running alongside it. The trans-Pennine canal tunnel itself was built 30 or so years previously and at 666ft above sea level and 5,698yds long, became the highest and longest in the UK. It was the third of the trans-Pennine canals in existence but unfortunately, owing to its extreme narrowness, was the least used. Eventually, at this point, four tunnels existed, one canal, two single-line rail, and one doubled-tracked rail. Woodhead tunnel, perhaps publicised a little more and made visibly obvious due to its western portals standing in full view of the main road alongside, was first opened in 1840, though several changes were made to it in the early years. In more recent years, it became the first intercity line to use the overhead electrification first pioneered on the suburban Manchester City-Altrincham line.

Box tunnel on the Great Western Railway, Brunel's controversial but self-confident bore through the chalk of the Bath district, was still swallowing some of the world's fastest trains one hundred years after sceptical directors of the GWR Board had confidently warned it would collapse within a very short time!

Probably of little note to railway enthusiasts, the ½ mile Cucksey tunnel between Redhill and Ashford on the South Eastern has it own intriguing little story for posterity. Edward Pierce, the enigmatic Victorian villain was almost plastered to its walls in the year 1853 during his successful Great Train Robbery.

Longest of the Alpine tunnels, the Simplon, 12¼ miles, took the world's record for achievement during the great pioneering years and along with Lotschberg, 9 miles; the Appenine 11½ miles; Mont Cenis, the oldest, 8½ miles; and the Gothard 9¼ miles and containing 13 block sections within; all became legends in their time.

Mulling over these feats of engineering and tales of untold hardship was forever a joy, but the thought of working perpetually in a signalbox situated five miles inside the illustrious but claustrophobic 'Simplon' sent a cold shudder down my spine. Optimistically and, as ever, perusing the vacancy sheets, I would have closed my eyes to that position. Not that it was likely to appear on a British list.

Subsequent to a week's training here at Waterfoot and a further few days at Stacksteads station crossing box, where duties were shared with the regular men, I settled into the routine of this comfortable two-shift box, though for how long that would be, I was never sure. Things were to change in another way as on 1 January 1948, nationalisation of the entire British Rail system was put into operation. It was no surprise to anyone as it had been forecast for years, having been considered as long ago as just afer the First World War. The pity was that, whereas nationalisation of the electricity, gas, coal and road transport enterprises presented the country with most profitable assets, the railways, pitifully neglected and ruthlessly exploited by necessity over the war years, were an immediate and total gross liability. Young socialists like myself now eagerly and confidently awaited announcements of wage increases and conditions equivalent to postal workers and other civil servants, the promise of enterprising plans for modernisation and expansion, and electrification of all main lines. Also the reduction of bottlenecks by an immediate move to quadrupling many more miles of track. All these wonders would soon happen, we were sure. The more mature of our compatriots were far more sceptical and forecast the end of rail travel in Rossendale within the next decade. Had not the passenger services between Bacup and Rochdale been withdrawn only last year? That in itself was a foreruuner of sinister things to come.

In June, my wife presented us with a son once again. It was a happy occasion but, allied to my recent discontent on the Bacup branch line, it led subsequently to a decision that in future years I was to deeply regret.

For some considerable time a local cycle dealer had been offering me a tempting position and salary, and when a Bolton firm, again in the cycle retailing business, did likewise and offered me a position at their Rochdale branch, I was not in the mood to let the chance go by. After all, the pay was 25 percent higher than I was receiving at that time. The hours of 9am-6pm were regular and I would be alleviated of the constant worries associated with winter road conditions. A late arrival following the 13-mile ride to Rochdale would be met with noticeably more sympathy than that meted out by a railway company. Together with these inducements it was suggested that in a very short time I may be transferred to manage the Manchester branch, a proposition I viewed with relish. This shop was on the south side of the city, a 20-mile bike ride, but I still considered the job worthwhile. I was apprehensive to a small degree, but took the plunge and broke my railway service in the autumn of 1948.

My life over the next 18 months was in a marked contrast to that I had experienced as a railwayman. For all that, I cannot say it was uninteresting and I certainly did not live to regret my managerial experiences, as they were to pay handsomely in later years. The break with shift-work and, in particular, with night and Sunday duties was difficult for me to grow accustomed to for some weeks. Notwithstanding, within a few weeks and with the realisation of its compensations, there came a surge of activity that was to benefit me tremendously. Accepting honorary work as secretary and treasurer of the Rossendale Wheelers and Rossendale Road Club, too, coupled with business management training, produced a new interest which would prove extremely advantageous within a decade.

Cycling 40 miles a day to and from work, and having Sundays free for racing, along with numerous trade perks, helped enormously in attaining a few reasonable achievements in the sport. Given the added advantage of increased leisure time, my interests expanded in both writing and reading.

My narrations in general were confined to work as cycling correspondent to two local newspapers and to editing a club magazine. Leisure reading, I confess, continually drew me to topics of railway interest above all else and within 12 months of breaking ties, the obsession of my life was causing me to have niggling doubts as to whether I had chosen the right course.

For all that, cycling itself had taken a deep hold on me, and whether touring from Scotland to Cornwall, or racing in Northumberland or Surrey, I was blissfully happy. But to be employed permanently surrounded by cycles, selling, purchasing, repairing or whatever, presents one with a totally different aspect, and whether it is easy to adapt one's hobby into an interesting and successful livelihood is extremely debatable. To some, the fusion is quite successful but for myself, in 1950, the novelty was wearing transparently thin.

September of that year found us with a further addition to the family, a daughter, who my wife had conveniently arranged to deliver on the morning of my own birthday. I believe it was this happy event that provoked me into sitting down quietly one evening and taking stock of my present situation. Over the past few days a magazine feature dealing with the illustrious and pioneering times of the *Orient Express* had rekindled my latent ruminations of a return to railway signalling. Two or three days later, my ponderings received added fuel. Along with other branch managers, I was informed of a takeover by a larger city firm who appeared to be wrestling with the competition of the big Curry and Halford concerns. Both these latter companies had, up to recent years, been predominantly retailers of cycles and their components. Indeed at my firms Rochdale branch we habitually handled the more technical repairs that Curry's were unable to carry out. Now we were informed that without any necessary professional skills we would be retailing radios, radiograms, other electrical items and prams. Business in this field was booming, we were told. Prams would be stocked in large quantities as the population explosion accelerated into full swing. As a final blow we were instructed to work until 9pm on Saturday evenings. This was the last straw. Often a 50-mile ride was necessary after finishing work on Saturday evenings. This was to obtain lodgings in preparation for an early morning Sunday Time Trial. Thus, following a private meeting later in the day, I and two other branch managers gave notice to quit.

Without hesitation, I telephoned through to Inspector Grey, the Area Supervisor at Bury, and with an optimistic but conciliatory note, requested an interview. 'I'm not surprised at all, my boy,' was Mr Grey's greeting. 'I did expect you back within the first six months!'

Obtaining employment of any nature and almost anywhere in the country presented no great problem in 1950.

Little was changing on Britain's railways during the early years of nationalisation. Pay and conditions were still rapidly falling behind those of other industries, be they nationalised or privately owned, and vacancies were consequently in abundance. Promotion was, therefore quite rapid and despite no priority being given on account of my previous years of service, I could expect to climb from porter/signalman to at least a Class 2 post within two years. A signalman's vacancy was shortly expected to materialise in Bury itself but, in the meantime, I would be temporarily allocated a porter/signalman's post at Bacup. My sudden relegation from a position of shop manager to a humble porter/signalman, and the accompanying drop in pay, would be compensated by overtime and Sunday working.

One week later, I stood once again in those stuffy and antiquated head offices at Victoria station awaiting the routine medical tests and preparing to face inevitable admonishments of some bowler-hatted, starch-collared individual who would further lecture me on the follies of having terminated my services to the railway. Indeed, to a railway company where employees start their careers at the age of 14 and continue unimpeded and without hindrance until they reach the grand old age of 65, my actions were totally inexcusable. Two hours later I was free, and for the umpteenth time shook the dust of these dingy dens of authority from my shoes. Afterwards I took the opportunity to visit a few of my old haunts in the city. In retrospect, I could not have more suitably spent the remaining few hours. I returned home thoroughly rejuvenated and prepared for the third, and hopefully final, climb of the elusive ladder to the top.

Bacup station, 1950: My God, what a shock! Only five years ago I had worked this bustling junction. Look at it now!

The death knell I had heard jingling on this branch line two years ago was now ringing loud and clear. The station buildings and platforms were decaying fast, both goods and passenger services had been drastically cut; and the Rochdale branch, to all intents and purposes, was as good as closed. The engine shed was a shadow of its former self; locomotives were completely void of the pride and polish of the defunct LMS. I had no doubt at all that the days of this depot, and the entire two branches themselves were numbered. A deliberately conceived and spuriously engineered campaign to 'wind down' was in force and, doubtless when a few foresighted people spoke out against what was happening, a sly attempt would be made to prove to the Valley people that they did not really need a railway at all. The almighty motor-car was on its way!

An overwhelming rape of these great Pennine branch lines was taking place. They were once the big profit making source of the 'East Lancashire' and 'Lancashire and Yorkshire' railway companies. This subjugation had commenced at the outbreak of war and since the cessation of hostilities little remuneration for damages, or cash for modernisation, was being made available. Twelve years of almost total neglect, coupled with current government policy, was relentlessly grinding in the rust and spreading decay which would be unstoppable, and further assuring the Transport Commission of the success of its ultimate closure policy.

During my period of training on the shed box frame, I took a stroll around the drastically diminished locomotive complement and, whilst chatting to an old friend, learned that Jack Nathan, Bacup's 'Champion' driver had recently severed both his legs whilst operating the turntable. After receiving that somewhat depressing news, I chose to walk further up the incline and spent time reminiscing at Britannia Station, now closed to passenger traffic. At a little under 1,000ft above sea level, this was the highest point of the L&Y system and at a location where, in the winter of 1939-40, a passenger train was completely snowed under. It was not at all an inviting hill town, particularly in the depths of winter. I had refused a lease on a house here five years previously when first stationed at Bacup. A particularly biting wind and snow squalls were blowing off the moors on that occasion and when viewing the property my wife gave a resounding and very sensible NO!

Looking ahead, I was confident that the next few weeks would soon pass by and I would say goodbye forever to this line. Seen in its full maturity in the mid-twenties and thirties, I had now no desire to see it dying. The incessant thuds as Billie Wibden banged his dented head on the porter's room wall, I saw as a prelude to the station's ultimate dismantling. He was as mad as a hatter, and so should I be if I stayed here much longer. Within four weeks I thankfully received a mesage to report to Bury Gas Sidings, and was subsequently well clear of the area when the valley's railway system finally disintegrated.

CHAPTER 13

Quick Steps up the Third Ladder

Bury Gas Sidings box was a totally misleading title. It was a neat and very typical block post, positioned midway between Bradley Fold East Junction to one side, and West Bury Junction to the other. Bury West controlled the western approach into Knowsley Street Station; and Bradley Fold East the traffic from Bolton, to either the Radcliffe Loop or to the main Bury line. Gas Sidings box itself, in addition to acting as a block post, positioned coal trains into the gas works sidings and brought out the empty wagon and coke trains.

As is often the case, when a box is lying between two junctions three or four miles apart, it is vital to split the sections, thus avoiding consequential delays when either of the junction signalmen is crossing a train and unable to accept another approaching train due to the clearance regulations. Although the volume of traffic was now far lower than that of the golden age of rail transport, or during wartime, it nevertheless warranted a 24hr manned box at this point. For me, after the customary couple of weeks needed to settle in, it was the psychological momentum I had been awaiting ever since leaving Broadfield box four years ago.

The unending succession of coal trains on their eternal cross-country hauls from the vast coalfields, of Yorkshire, to the ever-hungry factories and ports of Lancashire; the heavy freights, the local and cross-country passenger trains and night return specials from the west coast resorts all made it worthwhile. It was great to be working again amongst those all-round locos, the Stanier 'Black Fives', heading the expresses. Now there were 842 of these versatile locomotives in service on the system, their taper boilers and neat lines closely resembling the GWR 'Castles', and perhaps giving the clue as to where Stanier spent his early years, in Swindon's evocative GWR works.

I was so pleased to have realised the futility of continuing to work on a fast fading branch line, that I was soon revelling in my work again. No longer did I have qualms over the early morning 10-mile ride. Staff shortages, housing problems and a new breed of supervisors had contributed to a change in the over-strict outlook of the past. So long as signalmen changing over shifts did not falsify the train register book entries, and they agreed mutual arrangements regarding their time sheets, no unnecessary questions would be asked.

Observation and anticipation are essential factors, in even the most simply laid out signalbox, and a signalman must forever be 'on his toes'. The

'Train divided signal' 5-5, along with the 'Train running away on wrong lines signal' 2-5-5, and the 'Obstruction danger' signal, 6, are probably the least welcome bell signals of the eight or more emergency rings. The operation of Regulation 20 appertaining to every situation, and the consequential action to be taken when a train divides in section, is the constant fear of any signalman or driver. In the days of the loose linking of coal trains and almost all freights, except the most important, Bury 'hollow' was a notorious black spot, and a goods guard needed special skill in keeping his hand brake in suitable check. He must avoid wheel skidding at all costs but keep 60 or more wagons' links on the stretch and then fully release the brake on the Irwell Viaduct at the same time as the driver moves from his vacuum brake and takes up the regulator for the climb. A well syncronised operation would avoid the fatal 'snatch'.

On a, fortunately, dry and clear morning some weeks later, I was to experience my first and, not regrettably, last experience of putting Regulation 20 into practice after fourteen years of simulating such an occasion. On the up line I had accepted an express from Bolton, and having taken 'line clear' from Bury West, all signals were in the off position on the falling gradient from Bradley Fold Junction. On the down line a 40-wagon coal train had been in section for ½min when I took 'train on line' for the express from Bolton, and crossed the desk to enter the usual details in the train register book. With my back to the window, there was something ominous in the sound of that approaching 0-8-0 L&NW stalwart that made me swing quickly around. The frightening sight of half a coal train approaching fast confirmed the split-second thoughts that raced through my mind. As many moves in as many seconds were now needed. All signals were quickly thrown back to danger against the up express which had now passed the distant at clear; 2-5-5 'train running away on wrong line' signal to Bury West; 4-5-5 'training running away on right line' signal to Bradley Fold box in addition to the 'obstruction danger' signal; and, lastly, I threw back the advanced starter against the front portion of the divided train. Due to the incline there was no danger of the loose rear portion catching and colliding with the front, and the driver was well aware of what had happened.

The rear portion of the divided train had been brought to a stand by the guard and, after protection of this by placing detonators at the prescribed distances, he hurriedly came forward. A 'wrong line' order was issued for the front portion to set back in section and recouple, using the unbroken links of the leading wagon. Cautioning the driver of the up express which had overrun the outer home signal but eventually stopped without mishap in front of the inner home, things were soon back to normal.

Emergency signals such as 'stop and examine train' and 'train passed without tail lamp' were comparatively commonplace. The former was usually caused by a porter's failure to notice a carriage door handle at 'half cock', or a door handle having closed onto the first catch only. The latter signal, a little more serious, was often due to a tail lamp being invisible during thick fog, or because the light had become extinguished.

An emergency situation experienced here some months later followed a most unusual mishap. The day was a Saturday and it followed a Cup Tie between Bury and Blackburn Rovers. The away supporters were returning to a football special awaiting them at Knowsley Street Station when, unknown to them, only a miracle saved them from untold carnage. Spanning the four tracks, a timber bridge of glass and steel-lined construction connected the two main platforms, and on this day it tragically failed to support the pounding of an enthusiastic and hurrying crowd. With an enormous crack the 60ft bridge split and, along with its helpless and shocked cargo of humans, plunged down across four main lines.

Bury West sent a hurried 'obstruction' danger signal from this box, but it was too late. The Bolton-Rochdale service train, which was already in section, had passed both West Junction's distant and outer home signals. Only extremely prompt action by the driver, who was passing under the EL railway bridge when he first sighted this heaving mass of humanity and wreckage, saved an enormous tragedy. With only feet to spare, he halted his train and quite amazingly not one person was killed. Two hundred people were injured, 15 seriously, and one died later in hospital.

Having now experienced and dealt satisfactorily with every emergency situation at some time or other, it gave one a certain pride, also a little something to chat about when signalmen met 'over a pint'.

Track laying on a big scale, now surrendered to outside contractors, was in progress. On a 12hr Sunday shift, with single line working put into operation, I saw manual track-laying the like of which would never be seen again. Mechanical aids, apart from the standard 'hopper' ballast wagons, were not much in evidence. Characteristically, there would be a burly 6ft 6in Irish foreman overseeing a few hundred Polish, Ukranian and Irish navvies. The promises of Sundays with double pay, accompanying bonuses, and visions of a wild night out in the town, were the only incentives necessary to ensure several miles of track relaying in one day. Specially adapted railway carriages were provided for these tough international navvies as they traversed the country. These were their homes as they pursued their gypsy-like existence, sleeping in numerous railway sidings over the entire system. Rough handling of these men was needed, according to the big foreman. Next week they could well be attracted to higher pay on the Snowy Mountain project in Australia, or even to the local Thirlmere aqueduct tunnels now under construction to augment Manchester's water supply. The foreman informed me that to keep rigid control and dominance, a good supply of whisky and a heavy fist was required. Sticking out my puny 38inch chest and stretching my 9-stone frame to its full height, I was compelled to agree, then thanked the good Lord for a regular home and a comfortable family life.

Within a few months, the forecasted promotion came and I was saying farewell to yet another post. By pure coincidence, I was returning again to

Summerseat box which, in recent times, had been raised to Class 3 status. I felt confident it was goodbye temporarily to this line. Within a year one of the five Class 2 boxes in Bury would surely be mine. By now the transfers from box to box were becoming almost a ritual, anyway, and it was the only conceivable way to achieve the ultimate goal: Special Class.

Returning to Summerseat box for the second time, I took as a matter of course. Seven years had elapsed and the drop in traffic flow came as a shock. Freight had been reduced by one-half and passenger services had been cut back considerably. Ironically the post, previously a Class 4 position, had been re-rated under new arrangments to Class 3 status, the assessment having been based on prewar traffic. It was not for me to complain, although it did seem a little unjust to some Class 4 signalmen I knew on other lines, whose work load had increased.

The local people were continuing their faithful patronage of the railway because, as yet, there was no bus service into the village. Access by road was difficult, and the narrow and very steep drop from either of the two main roads was not suitable for public transport. Only a day was needed to refresh my memory of the frame and local supplementary regulations. These had not changed. Regular passenger traffic, though thinned out considerably, was held rigidly to the old pattern and could not be easily forgotten. Manchester-Skipton expresses speeded up as before, gathering steam for the slow climb from Stubbins Junction to Haslingden, before facing the hostile 1-in-40 drop from Baxenden summit into the vicious curve of Accrington Station.

The volume of night traffic could not be compared at all to the density I had previously known. The consequent drowsiness that overtakes one between 3am and 4am, familiar to all night workers, now became a nightly ritual. Following a heavy day of domestic work, and after having had little sleep, I found this consistent danger overcoming me one summer's night. It was hard to believe, for at 'Nickleson's' lodgings for racing men, alongside the A6 trunk road and parallel to the west-coast main-line, I had spent many sleepless nights due to the unending roar of express freights and night sleeper trains.

How it could be possible for me to fall asleep here whilst on duty, I shall never know. It happened, however, on this one and only occasion. It was within barely a minute of receiving 'train entering section' from Ramsbottom for an up freight that I virtually 'passed out'. Eight minutes later, alongside the hot stove, oblivious to everything, I was brought round by a frantic ringing of telephone and block bells from the signalman on either side. A complete train of 70 wagons had rumbled by unheard and was now three miles ahead and my signals were still off! No injury was done, and only a minimal amount of delay was caused, but the incident certainly brought self-recrimination and made me think carefully of the situation at Thirsk on the North Eastern Railway many years earlier. The results of a signalman falling asleep on that occasion had ended up with an Edinburgh-

King's Cross Express ploughing into the rear of a goods train at 60mph and killing eight. A verdict of 'guilty of manslaughter' had been given against the signalman concerned.

Vacancies for stationmasters, up to recent times a much esteemed position and a very difficult grade to break into by operating staff of the old LMS, were now becoming frequent. When James Ingham, Stationmaster here offered to put my name forward and give me the necessary training, I was all but tempted to take the plunge. However, a close friend of mind, Bill Suffle, Stationmaster at Helmshore, gave me a rather different picture, stating that my weekly wage, which takes into consideration overtime and night duties was far in excess of what he himself received. Progression and the long-term benefit of a pension were attractive, but money in the hand now seemed a far more practical necessity whilst raising a family. Indeed, Bill himself left shortly afterwards to work on the Rhodesian Railways, whilst I settled down and patiently waited for promotion to Bury or the Manchester area.

Patience can be rewarded in many ways, so goes the saying. Mine was rewarded, or otherwise, as the reader may determine, by a few hair-raising experiences with two local young ladies of easy virtue. Without a cinema, and the present-day luxury of television which diverts mature girls from a natural pursuit, it was my good fortune to receive their persistent and not easily shunned attentions when leaving work at 10pm. Perhaps I was endowed with a weak will to resist the fruits of temptation, or gifted with a strong desire to flirt with danger, I know not. The resulting advances, I admit with a bow of shame, were unresisted and if stone walls had eyes and ears, they would tell many a tale of promiscuous passion and sensual cavortings in the depths of Summerseat woods. All good things come to an end, however, and in the autumn of 1951, the promotion I had yearned for, and eagerly awaited, was just around the corner.

This year had seen the Festival of Britain. It was the country's turning point after 12 years of austerity. The entire population was rising from a decade of enforced stagnation. There was a general desire to break with the old system, for better or for worse, and this year heralded the post-war boom that waited the nation. By contrast my own years had been wonderful, with a return to the work I idolised, success in the sport I had grown to love, a young family and a dear wife. Now to cap it all, here on the vacancy sheet, staring at me in face, was promotion to Bury Loop Junction Box, Class 2! In my heart, as I dropped the application into the office letter-box, I knew it was mine. Two weeks later, confirmation came.

An artist's impression of the signalman's aspect. (*Courtesy of Steve Bradshaw*)

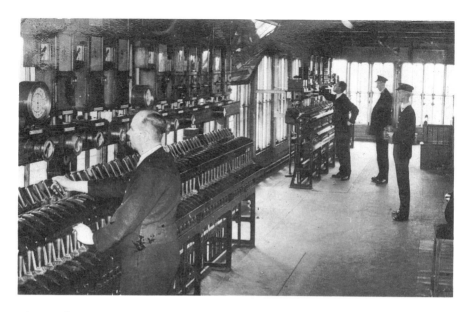

A typical LMS semi-electrically operated signal box c.1935.

Waterfoot c.1900. The old East Lancashire Railway Co's yard is seen to the left close to the author's birthplace. *(Courtesy of Lancashire Libraries)*

Helmshore station and signal box c.1900. *(Courtesy of Lancashire Libraries)*

Haslingden Station and a Manchester to Colne stopping train. A typical pre-Beeching scene. *(Courtesy of Lancashire Libraries)*

Haslingden Station c.1962.   (*Courtesy of Lancashire Libraries*)

The Night Scotsman. The 10.25pm King's Cross to Edinburgh c.1935.

Preparing locomotives at the LNER Stratford depot for the holiday rush, c.1936.

LNER express freight the London to Scotland overnight service c.1936.

The interior of Bury South Junction 1939. Signalman Llewelyn Griffiths. Note the newspaper over the gas light to comply with the war time blackout regulations.

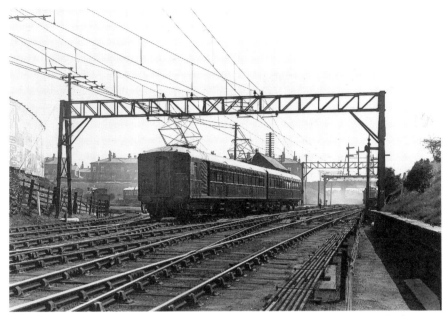

Bury South Junction 1939. The electric train on the left is passing into platform 1, and an up Manchester train is standing in the Bay platform. The absence of advertising on the bill-boarding is due to war time restrictions.

Skipton to London express approaching Bury South Junction Box in 1938. This view is from the box window.

Ilex Hall Carr signal box.

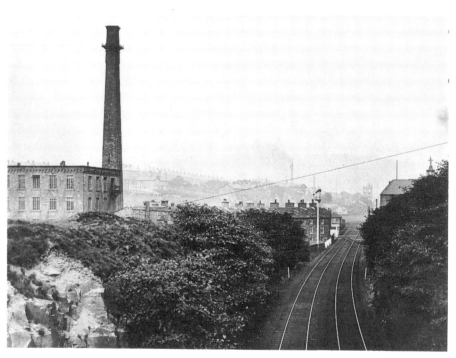

Approaching Rawtenstall with the West Box half visible. St Mary's church is seen in the background. *(Courtesy of Lancashire Libraries)*

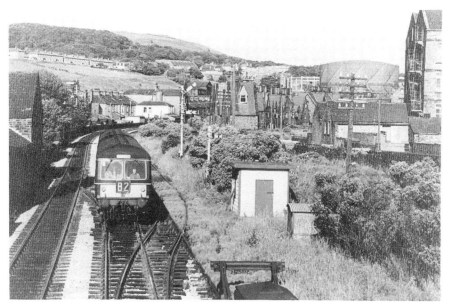

View taken from the footbridge at Ilex Hall Carr just before the closure of the old East Lancashire line from Rawtenstall to Bacup. (*Courtesy of Lancashire Libraries*)

Cloughfold station and signal box 1947. Junior booking clerk, Arthur Heyworth stands guard whilst the author sprints to the top of a signal post to snap this picture.

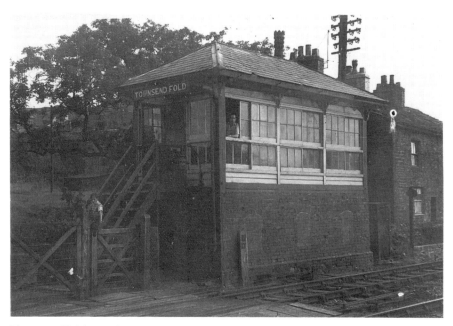

Townsendfold signal box 1957. *(Courtesy of Tom Wray)*

Rawtenstall West Box in 1957 and the foundations of a new box before Beeching's axe fell a year or two later. *(Courtesy of Tom Wray)*

Bacup locomotive shed c.1870.   (*Courtesy of Bacup Natural History Society*)

Bacup locomotive shed c.1900.   (*Courtesy of Bacup Natural History Society*)

Bacup Junction and goods yard, c.1920.   *(Courtesy of Bacup Natural History Society)*

Bacup goods yard and signal box c.1920.   *(Courtesy of Bacup Natural History Society)*

Bacup terminal c.1920. *(Courtesy of Bacup Natural History Society)*

The author working Summerseat signal box in 1942.

Talyllyn Junction and West Signal Box on the Brecon – Merthyr line.
(*Courtesy of Gavin Morrison*)

A typical country station scene, Talyllyn Junction in the late 1950s.
(*Courtesy of H. Allen*)

"Block Telegraph Train Register" Book, for Double & Single Lines

UP TRAINS

Description of Train as Signalled. (See instructions inside of Front Cover.)	TIMES OF SIGNALS FROM AND TO STATION IN REAR.						TIMES OF SIGNALS TO AND FROM STATION IN ADVANCE.						DELAYS.
		REPLY SENT.						REPLY RECEIVED.					
	"Is Line Clear" received.	"Line Clear" through.	"Line Clear to Clearing Point only."	"Section Clear, but Station or Junction Blocked."	"Train entering Section" received.	"Train out of Section" sent.	"Is Line Clear" sent.	"Line Clear" through.	"Line Clear to Clearing Point only."	"Section Clear, but Station or Junction Blocked."	"Train entering Section" sent.	"Train out of Section" received.	
1	2	3	4	5	6	7	8	9	10	11	12	13	
4	6.39	6.42			6.51	6.58	6.39	6.39			6.57	7.3	5.30 L past
2.2.3.		7.1		6.58	7.2	7.12	7.3	7.6			7.11	7.20	4.18 N tar

Fireman. J. Bloggs Rule 55 8.29 am.

R.& Bradshaws on duty 6.0 am.

Fogmen called out 7.30 am.

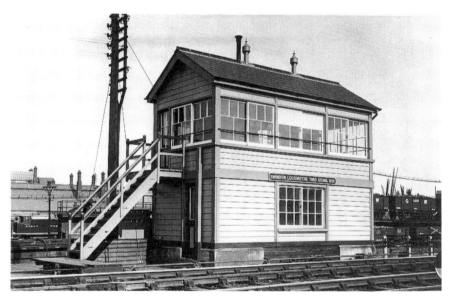

Swindon Loco signal box. The very last one worked by the author.
(*Courtesy of Swindon Railway Museum*)

CHAPTER 14

Obstruction Danger

Loop Junction, lying to the east of Knowsley Street Station, was to Class 2 working what Bacup Junction had been to Class 3, namely the worst. Or, if you were a glutton for punishment, as I forever would be, it was magnificent.

This box marginally escaped Class 1 status, (my ultimate goal) the very light Sunday traffic being the cause. With the exception of the comparatively quiet periods of 10am-12noon and 2pm-4pm, the remaining hours were constantly demanding, due to a rather heavy frame and the high level of mental stress needed in traffic control. At all times there was the overriding necessity to be at least three moves ahead in this elaborate game of railway chess. A belated decision to 'put the block on', whilst freights were approaching from three directions, could 'stitch up' both Knowsley Street and Bolton Street Stations for at least an hour.

Splaying out from the double track at the foot of the bank, the facing junction split traffic in to up and down main line to Loco Junction on the Bury Connecting line to Radcliffe, Bolton and Manchester, and to down slow and fast lines through Knowsley Street Station. On the up side, the convergence of the slow and fast lines into one main line ran over the notorious hand and mechanically operated catch points, lever No 34. From my days as a signal lad in South box, I well recalled the casual remark, 'Oh yes, No 34 again!' should there have been trouble at Loop Junction. Those reflections, echoed many times along with other moderately exaggerated talks of the workings of this infamous 'Hell Hole' had subconsciously implanted in me a strong fascination and a secret desire to be stationed here. This wild acceptance of largely shunned posts was, no doubt, instrumental in the rapid promotion I was now experiencing.

As had been the case at Bacup Junction, I was aware within a few hours of taking charge here that this was truly my vocation. Then with only a week behind me came the challenge of a 12hr night shift. My two-week training period had taken place between the hours of 6am-10pm and the impact of meeting an almost incredible and unbroken continuity of traffic from 10pm-4am came as a mild shock.

The unending succession of heavy night-freights rumbling down the bank to be dispersed over one of the three diverging routes; traffic signalled over three up approaches to be systematically routed in preferential order onto one main line only; one of the two bank engines, each permanently in full steam to be slipped out of their siding and onto a passing heavy freight. All this to the accompaniment of night-long marshalling in the L&Y goods yard by pilot engines, and accompanied by the shrill whistling of L&NW 0-8-0s

115

or the mournful cries of a Stanier 2-8-0 'blowing' for a banker. Between East box and Loop Junction, any newly arrived resident to Heywood Street or its accompanying streets would initially have experienced many a sleepless night.

Should any being have wished himself to be steeped forever in railway history and lore, he need only have stood for one night between the hours of midnight and dawn between these six main lines. This paramount L&Y stronghold in the first half of the twentieth century would have kindled an inextinguishable flame and imprinted an indelible picture which would never be erased. I know, because that is what it did to me. If ever a signalbox was hand-cut and tailor-made for me, this was significantly the one and, as the year 1952 progressed, it revealed the happiest railway signalman employed on British Railways.

In marked contrast to any monotonous nightly drudgery, one can often find a lighter side to compensate for such a situation. It came here in the form of a gratuitous and very mysterious nightly striptease act. Towards the end of Heywood Street, overlooking the railway bridge and by good fortune in clear view of the signalbox, was an eye-riveting bedroom window which at 10.30pm, with sublime regularity, revealed its none-too-well-guarded secrets. Unashamedly and totally premeditated, the curtains were left wide open, the bedroom light switched on, and the Heywood Street 'Salome' commenced her late evening ritual, silhouetted and framed to perfection against the clear glass. Lasting some 20mins or more, this captivating performance regularly caused 'loss of steam', 'slipping wheels', wagon hand brakes 'hard on', or one of many suitable excuses for slow shunting in the vicinity of the box during that specific half-hour. Foggy nights were not popular!

Frequently, pleasant attractions of this nature would be interspersed with matters of a more serious nature. A potential runaway down the incline was not uncommon. Drivers of non-vacuum braked heavy coal trains were expected to bring their trains to a stand at Broadfield, and request the guard to pin down brakes on several wagons before descending the bank. This act was rarely performed and, when subsequently encountering Loop Junction's gantry of three home signals at danger ½ mile ahead, drivers would be heard blowing rapid short whistles as a warning. More often than not, the section ahead was cleared with time to spare, but on more than one occasion, the pressure of 800 tons against an 80-ton locomotive would prove too much on a wet rail and a cursing Wakefield or Edge Hill driver would bring his sliding train to a standstill 100yds ahead of the offending home signal. Block signalling allows for these eventualities and no harm, apart from a possible delay, will transpire. The normal friendly liaison between locoman and signalman usually 'square up' the episode.

Spanning the River Roche, at the foot of this incline was the viaduct on which I had stood many a night shivering whilst on guard duty in wartime.

Had it been able to speak, it would have told many stories of near runaways and apprehensive footplatemen, but also, and in marked contrast, the thrills of single and sometimes double banking of heavy freights, overloaded excursion trains and 20-carriage empty stock trains on their return to Lightbourn Sidings. No better thrill could be enjoyed than that of standing here observing or, better still, be holding tightly to a brake-van verandah-rail when a bank engine, its chimney stack belching black smoke and its lethal 70tons catching your moving train, makes a shuddering contact and quickly compresses up to 80 wagon buffers behind the leading engine. Almost instantaneously, the regulator is wide open and the driver is whistling his presence to the leading driver who, in turn, acknowledges with a long-drawn-out code. The overwhelming and truly magnificent sight of power that only steam traction can aptly demonstrate is set in motion.

The continous traffic flow through the night normally ran quite smoothly, when we were given advance details of train loadings and information as to whether bank engines assistance was needed or not. This advice was given from as far away as 10-15 miles and thus the control of traffic was made comparatively easy and, coupled with experience, it eventually became second nature. Quick thinking and replanning are vital, however, especially when at very short notice a driver whistles for water or banker assistance when passing Gas Sidings box, and your signals are all Off for a through run on a very tight margin. These situations are the test. Either you are made to be a true signalman or you are not.

In October of this year came one of Britain's worst rail accidents, claiming the lives of 122 people. This, the year in which Britain's first ultra modern 'panel-operated' signalbox at York was put into operation, we witnessed a most devastating tragedy. Not of the magnitude of the Quintinshill holocaust, it was nevertheless to prove beyond argument that whatever amount of sophisticated electrical and mechnical safety devices are installed, human error remains the overriding factor and must never be overlooked.

It was on 8 October at 9am when scattered and jumbled reports were buzzing along the grapevine of box telephones. Apparently, the overnight Perth-Euston sleeper car express had ploughed into the rear of a crowded local stopper somewhere near London. When the facts were eventually clarified, it transpired that the up express, travelling at 60mph and hauled by a class 8P 'Pacific', had overshot both distant and home signals at danger and violently smashed into the rear of the stationary commuter train. The signalman in Harrow Station box did all he possibly could, but was unable to stop a down combined Liverpool and Manchester double-headed express, which itself then ploughed headlong into the two wrecked trains. It was a catastrophe of the first magnitude. The result was a holocaust not witnessed on Britain's railways for some 35 years.

The subsequent and intensive enquiry, showed that signalling and locomotive maintenance was all in order, and though his negligence was never proven, the deceased Perth express driver, a top link man, was to take full responsibility for the tragedy.

Most signalmen, and in particular those who have experienced operating in an area of dense traffic working, come to possess a sixth sense, accompanied by a nagging and inner premonition that one day, sooner or later, they themselves will be witness to, or become involved in, a catastrophe, however small. As with a road-vehicle driver, an engine-driver, an air-line pilot or a ship's captain, the higher the mileage covered, and the busier the lines of traffic, then the sooner this is going to happen.

My own personal experiences had produced a small crop of scares during my years behind the levers, but the most overwhelming spectacle was that of a Stanier 8F 2-8-0 relentlessly thrusting tons of derailed metal and timber against Heywood Street bridge. As is so often the case prior to any serious accident on land, sea or air, the unpredictable elements have played a major part in setting the scene. On this particular black and rain-lashed night, I had brought the Bolton-Healey Mills heavy freight to a stand on the up fast line, from where it would detach its quota of Bury traffic and be shunted into the goods yard. Often the up fast line was used for this purpose at night, leaving the slow line for fast-moving through traffic. This may seem rather contradictory, but the reason was that, due to a heavy roll when switching from fast to up main, through trains were given a much smoother ride when passing at speed along the slow line. After the head shunter had uncoupled behind 24 of the 70 mixed freight wagons and vans, the driver whistled to draw ahead beyond the box and clear the trailing points from fast to main in readiness for the set back into the yard. This required No 34 lever to be operated, thus locking the spring catch points, and with signals lowered, the move commenced. Due no doubt to the atrocious weather, the shunter whose responsibility it is to stand alongside the main-line points and hand signal when the train cleared them, was many yards away under the bridge and taking shelter from the high wind and rain. Eventually, he flashed the red light to stop the driver, followed by the white signal to authorise me to reverse the trailing points and set up the road for the reversal into the yard. Fate, however, decreed that the last wagon over the trailing points, which was the leading one for the reversal, was a double bogie bolster wagon carrying several tons of used rails. Because of the excessively long wheelbase of these wagons, I felt nothing whatsoever on the point lever when pushing it back across the frame. Owing to the distance involved and the excessively black night, the shunter had grossly misjudged the position, and the leading bogie wheels for the set back still remained on the up fast, and the trailing set of wheels on the up main. All was now set for this monstrous tonnage to attempt a reverse over two separate tracks. Ground signals were lowered and a tremendously expensive night's work was put into motion.

Within 30 seconds the bogie bolster slewed at 90 degrees across the two tracks and was pushed forward and thrust deep into the ballast, as sleepers cracked and splintered like matchsticks. Rails now yawned apart and steel chairs split as if made of cardboard. This tearing, screeching and cracking of timber and metal had swung me into instant action, but fate was now playing the ace card; that Class 8 monster was blowing steam everywhere as it bore down towards the box. Despite all my efforts with a red handlamp and reverberating calls, the unstoppable loco thrust relentlessly forward. It pounded on until it could pound no further. Every wagon of the entire 25 was savagely derailed and when, ½hr later, steam cranes and breakdown equipment arrived, arc lights were set up to reveal a scene that was absolutely devastating.

If any potential steam-locomotive purchaser needed a worthy demonstration of the incredible power of a Class 8 2-8-0, the stark proof was here to be seen. The up fast, slow and main lines were dangerously and totally blocked. Within, and stacked on both sides of the bridge, were the precariously perched tangled and twisted remains of 400 tons of rail wagons and their contents. Three 15-ton wagons stood perpendicular on their buffers!

I had known by the earsplitting sound of point rods being mangled near the box that my own safety was far from secure, and the sinister illumination from the firebox and the engine tender with its adjacent wagon coming within inches of the box confirmed that. Well over 100tons of firebreathing and steam bellowing metal leaned towards the timber signalbox which was not conducive to relaxation for the next few hours! Fortunately none of the other four main lines was fouled and standby emergency workings were put into operation until 9am, when the tracks were eventually cleared and reopened.

Resounding talk of a big modernisation programme for the ensuing year gave rise to some speculation. Renewal and expansion of the Bury-Manchester electric system would speed up the area's increasing potential commuter traffic, and an overall increase in vacuum-fitted wagons would prove a vital factor in clearing freight-trains more quickly through the bottlenecks of these industrial regions. Over the grossly overloaded stretches, for example, between Rochdale and Bolton, quadruple tracking was a priority in order to combat the increasing infiltration of road transport and bring back much of the heavy goods traffic lost to unfair competition. What idyllic and utopian dreams we harboured of a railway transport system of the future!

Popular Blackpool with its sea and sands, illuminations and other attractions, necessitated the running of endless excursion trains, on weekends, full days, half-days and evenings, all converging on Preston to make the final 'block to block' run into this most famous of west coast resorts. The bulk of these heavily loaded trains came from the region's densely populated Lancashire and Yorkshire towns, and often an overloaded return excursion, running in an extremely tight margin, would be checked through our three short sections as Knowsley Street to await clearance of a decelerated predecessor on Broadfield incline.

This 'concertina' action gave an interesting and colourful insight to the many 'carryings-on' of some groups of revellers, no doubt moderately lubricated before departure at Blackpool. Coaching stock used on these well patronised excursion trains was very carefully selected, and not in any way in the interest of passenger comfort. Carefully avoiding the new or well maintained carriages, old and more often than not non-corridor coaches, void of toilet facilities, were selected and deemed suitable. In particular, to menfolk, urinary problems were common, and on the slowing down of these very early morning specials a carriage window often flew open and an offending item of male anatomy would be thrust out to dispense its acrid fluid onto the trackside, or onto all and sundry alongside. Shunters on night duty knew well, or very quickly learned, the danger and degradation of standing within 6ft of these late night specials!

By now, my fast-broadening mind was well accustomed to the sights of mild, and even passionate lovemaking in non-corridor stock, but the display I was unwittingly given by a small group of Kama Sutra disciples positively made my eyes boggle. It had been necessary to draw forward and hold one of these specials at my inner home signal, and their specific compartment was directly in my vision. Had the five or six frisky young travellers been acting out a scene in a pornographic film, I could well have comprehended their complete abandonment. However, their obvious enjoyment was immense, and more than apparent by the giggles and laughter accompanying the actions. Suffice it to say, the information was passed along the line, and at least the next two signalmen were allocated a fleeting glimpse as the train regathered its speed.

Whilst this form of light relief was to bring many a smile in later years, it was the near tragic collision of a night return Blackpool excursion which haunted me for many years to come. For some mysterious reason, which I never fully understood, and considered an almost criminal omission, was the lack of catch points, or run off points at the merging of the fast and slow lines beyond the up signal gantry. This was the crucial factor in the near tragedy on that dark autumn night in September.

At around midnight 'line clear' was requested by Tom Brown, signalman at Bury East box, for a 15-coach empty stock train returning to Lightbourne carriage sidings. I refused and contacted Bradley Fold West for information on the running of a Blackpool-Bradford return special, due to pass through at 12.10am. Other information showed the empty stock train to be running badly. It was now rumbling by Bury Gas sidings, whilst the express was to this side of Bolton Rose Hill Junction, crossing the Darcy Lever Viaduct and three minutes 'up' on his booked timings. That settled the matter. I would hold the empty stock train and give the express an unhindered clear road.

Within three minutes of accepting the heavy slow runner on the up fast, 'train entering section' was received, and two minutes later the train hissed to a stand at the gantry home signal. At the same time that I had been given 'train entering section', I had refused 'Is line clear' on the up slow for the express which was evidently running very fast. 'Line clear' was obtained first from Heap Bridge box and now, with the empty stock train at a stand, 'line clear' was given to East box for the Blackpool-Bradford and I made a few very fast moves across the frame to clear all signals. No sooner had I dropped the yellow distant lever catch into its notch, when the shrill whistle for East boxes distant, interlocked with that of Loop Junction owing to the short sections, was clearly audible. The acknowledging short blast clearly echoed again and the driver now faced a total of eight clear green lights in succession as he raced up the hump out of Bury Hollow and through Knowsley Street Station at full steam. This train was really moving!

It could have been only 10 seconds after making my rapid moves and pulling 'all off' that, walking to the desk to make the train registry book entries, I instinctively heard an ominous binding of wheel flanges over the fast to slow line points some 100yds away. Looking up quickly and into the black night, two parallel engine lights were moving forward under the bridge. Instantaneously, I realised the driver of the empty stock train had mistakenly taken the wrong signal and was about to split my trailing points and already was directly in the path of the oncoming express by an engine length. Never in my life have I moved so fast. All up signals were thrown back to danger, the 'obstruction danger' signal was sent to East box, the trailer points rammed back over, and I was at the window with a red hand-signal, screaming my head off to the approaching driver.

As Tom Brown took the hastily clattered 6-bell 'obstruction danger', the express was within yards of his clear home signal and travelling at maximum speed. A sudden reversal to danger of two brilliant green lights met these unfortunate footplatemen. Only an extremely alert and experienced driver could ever have stopped this heavy and loaded-to-capacity train in a manner in which this man succeeded in accomplishing. A dry rail did help tremendously, no doubt, and with a blinding shower of sparks, the like of which I had never seen before, this hurtling mass of steel was almost raised in the middle as it came to a shuddering stop within feet of the hastily reversing empty stock train.

The guilty driver had realised his almost disastrous mistake. No more than two minutes elapsed before his train was back clear and, with no point damages apparent, my signals were cleared a second time for the ill fated Yorkshire-bound express. Amidst the clouds of steam and sand still blowing from the overworked ejectors, the regulator was lifted and the train was quickly on its way again. Startled passengers were staring out of windows into the blackness, having no doubt experienced a rough shaking during the past few minutes, but in a typical Blackpool excursion mood they would soon forget it. As for myself, the delayed shock brought with it a nauseating and sickly sensation. For a couple of minutes it overcame me, and I sank into a chair. The cold perspiration was trickling from my forehead and I was shaking violently. The comforting fact that I had done everything correctly and averted a certain smash gave me no effective solace at all at that moment.

When the drawn-faced and evidently shocked driver of the empty stock train, accompanied by a pilotman burst into the box, it was some minutes before my voice returned. 'Stopping for steam', was as good as any other excuse for the visually shaken driver and his very careless pilotman and subsequently, after all other delayed traffic was cleared a 'road' was given ½hr later.

The reporting of this extremely close encounter with disaster did not really enter anyone's mind. Should no enquiries as to train delays be made, no statements would be forthcoming. All the necessary details were entered in the train register books of the boxes concerned and were there to be examined if the need arose. Whatever impressions or visions passed through the mind of the unfortunate engine driver, I shall never know. Suddenly, and without the slightest advance warning and at very high speed, he was confronted by two signal gantries, every signal thereon showing a frightening red aspect and, in the dim lighting from the street lights, the grim outline of another train crossing his path a mere 500yds ahead. Did he really surmise the truth of what had happened? Did he believe he himself had, per chance, mistaken the distant signals? The questions never arose and judging by the way he was driving that night, he would doubtless arrive in Bradford 'on time'.

Suffice it to say that this incident was the most traumatic I experienced during my signalling days and was to give me many a minor nightmare in the ensuing weeks. It brought to mind Norton Fitzwarren in Somerset where, 13 years previously, similar circumstances had caused an almost coincidental smash. The Great Western Railway, even after allowing for a substantially lower overall route mileage than its brother, the LMS, had, in comparison, an extremely good accident-free record.

At Norton Fitzwarren, however, fate played a cruel and doubly bad hand. Here, in 1890, a signalman's error had wrecked a Plymouth-Paddington *Cape Liner* special and now, again, 50 years later, a driver's fatal mistake brought a total death toll of 27 lives. As in similar circumstances to those at Bury Loop Junction, the driver had mistakenly read the wrong signal for the line on which he was travelling. At Norton Fitzwarren two factors alone averted an accident of far higher and horrendous magnitude. Firstly, that of the open catch points protecting the merging of two main lines, the lack of which I deplored at Bury Loop Junction; and secondly, without any doubt, pure and unmitigated luck.

When the driver of the Paddington-Penzance sleeper car express, travelling on the down relief mistakenly took the through line signal showing green from Taunton, he headed straight for the open catch points protecting the down main and an extremely fast moving newspaper train running several minutes early. With a 'King' class engine, regulator wide open and a heavy train behind, the driver's sudden realisation of his inextricable situation came too late. Seconds later, as the overtaking newspaper train's rear coach passed, the sleeper train ploughed through the open trap points at speed, resulting in the 110ton locomotive and six coaches spread-eagled across all four main lines. Had the speeding newspaper train been a mere half-a-train-length behind, and consquently not observed by the driver of the night sleeper, the results would have been appalling.

The reader may well consider my writings to be morbid and perhaps imbued with a deep fascination of rail catastrophe. Far from it, the relating of these factors, their circumstances and precautionary measures, are all part and parcel of a signalman's training. His occupation exists primarily to prevent trains bumping into each other, to put it simply, and that is the overriding element and significance of block signalling. The controlling and regulation of traffic to its various destinations, though of prime importance, must take second place to the paramount teaching: 'one train, in one section, at one time'. It must be said that the safety records for railways are very good. Statistics taken for 1975 showed 6,366 people having died on Britain's roads, whilst the railway claimed the lives of a mere 84! Then, as now, it was a well-known fact that it was far safer to enter a railway carriage than it was to cross the public highway. That old adage had held ever since the invention of the motor vehicle.

Extremely content as I was in a box where monotony was virtually unknown, I admit nevertheless to regularly scanning and eagerly awaiting the advertising of a higher class post on the fortnightly vacancy lists. Frequently and unfailingly, situations of a higher classification were to be found in the more affluent southern regions, particularly in areas of car production. Luton was an almost certainty on the 'all areas' list, but in the summer of 1954, in a district far in contrast to the rolling plains of Bedfordshire, a post was advertised which sent an ecstatic tingle of anticipation rushing through my veins. The position advertised as 'Special Class, Rest Day Relief Signalman, CARNFORTH'! It took my breath away. Where better indeed, throughout the whole of England, could anyone be fortunate enough to be employed? It was adjacent northwards to the ever-magnetic Lake District. The limestone Yorkshire dales were to the east; the purple-heathered hills of Bowland Forest to the south-east; and historic Lancaster, gateway to the somewhat brash but equally tranquil resorts of Lancashire's coast, to the west and south.

I knew Carnforth, its environment and its surrounding regions very well. As a racing man and cycle tourist, there were few roads in the neighbourhood on which my wheels had not turned. Relatives in Lancaster had endeared me to the city as a child, and camping alongside the river Lune with several scout troops in the early thirties had thrust upon me an almost secret personal claim to these hills and adjacent valleys.

With the ink barely dry, my application was resting in the Inspector's office and I prayed dearly for days to come that I would be awarded this heaven sent gift from above.

Away to inspect the job, and thrashing hard on the pedals three days later in the Trough of Bowland, I tried hard to reason why this seemingly most attractive position had been advertised outside its normal promotional area. In recent years it had become quite common to see high classification boxes announced in the fast-growing industrial regions of south-eastern England and the London area itself, where wages were now chasing employees. Rarely would this occur in a rural setting such as Carnforth, where the railway itself was the major employer of labour. The obviously disturbing possibility was that no one locally wanted the job, implying that it was of a particularly hard nature and had none of the additional perks that accompany a desirable post, such as Sunday work or night duty pay.

Arriving on the station after an exhilarating 50 miles ride, I contacted the signalman in 'No 1 box' and received his permission to go along to the box for a look around and intended to ask him a few searching questions regarding this, and the other several boxes in the vicinity I would have to work. I dumped my racing bike behind a pile of new sleepers at the platform end and, feeling rather conspicuous and out of place in racing shorts and club jersey, strode off, keeping a wary eye open, as all up signals were cleared for a through train. A couple of minutes later, I needed no further confirmation to dispel any misgivings of a misjudged job application. As I gingerly picked my way over rails and masses of point rodding and signal wires, a piercing long-drawn-out whistling vibrated through the station buildings and the *Royal Scot* thundered through. Then, as I gripped the handrail of this imposing box, came the realisation that my arrival could never have been better calculated.

Through the slipstream of dust, flying cigarette packets and miscellaneous debris, I strode eagerly up the signalbox steps to be greeted by a most friendly local signalman who, during the next half-hour, gave me a helpful run down on the five boxes that I would work as a special class reliefman. My premonitions were positively confirmed. Since the recent reduction in the working week from 48hrs to 44hrs, a fortnightly rest-day had been adopted for signalmen working eight-hour shifts and this type of relief position had therefore come about. No night or Sunday duties were involved. Normal eight hour shifts between 6am and 10pm would be worked in these few, but extremely busy, boxes, accompanied by no extras, save for a very small remuneration for Saturday working after 2pm. In terms of classification, however, it was the top of the ladder. I would leap two grades altogether and automatically take the next 'regular' special class vacancy.

Nothing could dim a burning desire for this post. For almost a further two weeks I paced about with baited breath, but bitter disappointment transpired in the end. A senior man had been appointed and, as I had anticipated, the vacancy had attracted a substantially large number of applicants. Perhaps it was the bitter pill I found hard to swallow, or maybe the eternal gipsy in my blood, that now turned my thoughts to the fact that I had worked Loop Junction for almost three years. That was indeed a record for me. I was more than happy here, but my wandering star had shifted in the sky and was beckoning me yet again.

The thrill and anticipation of a busier intercity main-line box had no doubt been fired by my visit to Carnforth and, later, after spending a week in the close proximity of the GWR Paddington-Bristol and South Wales line, the seed was well and truly planted. I became pregnant with a burning motivation for new ventures. If I failed to find a Class 1 box in more cheerful surroundings than Manchester now that top vacancies were cropping up all over the country, then it was apparent that I was going about things the wrong way.

This little mental foray into the highly improbable chance of obtaining a vacancy in some distant national beauty spot was abruptly dashed when, some weeks later, 'Rose Grove East, Class 1' appeared at the head of the vacancy sheet. In went another application form without a great deal of forethought. After all, Rose Grove, a little to the south-west of Burnley, was but a mere seven miles distant from my home.

Recently, on a mad impulse I had been talked into buying a 500cc-speed twin motor-bike by my enthusiastic friend, Jack Eastwood at Broadfield box, a truly garrulous individual. Despite a nasty pile-up on the cobblestones and tram lines of Spring Street in Bury, directly in front of the illustriously named 'La Scala', which was followed by a further front wheel skid and crash on ice-bound roads at the 'Quarrymans', Edenfield, I was still confident that the early morning start would present no hazard. The main A56 trunk road, crossing the 'Waggoners' at 1,000ft, was a notorious black-spot in winter snow and ice, but there was nevertheless the alternative 13-mile route through Accrington and Huncoat.

Parting company with a two-wheeled vehicle at speed was a nasty habit I had become accustomed to during my 20 years' cycling and, although never having suffered a broken bone, I had been knocked unconscious and dragged from the road on at least 10 occasions. Motor cycling was yet another challenge and, indeed, I was enjoying the new experience. At that time, I possessed no nerve whatsoever and potential accidents were mere suppositions and purely hypothetical.

I sat back, patiently awaiting the outcome of this latest application, with the premonition that my venture would take me to a fearful post, not universally desired.

Consistent with the anticipation and mental stress experienced whilst awaiting the outcome of any promotional undertaking, I'm sure no person works to their true potential. Lack of normal composure and patience, coupled with the presence of a sense of instability was, I am sure, responsible for a most simple and stupid mistake that all but cost me any promotion during this tedious period of expectation. It was so ridiculously simple, it became a huge joke amongst fellow signalmen within days.

All freight trains at this time ran with a brake-van coupled to the rear of the train, and a guard was always in attendance, predominantly as a brakesman in addition to his more mundane duties of bookkeeping, and so on. Attached to the rear of the van, as with all trains, is the ever-important tail lamp, there predominantly to confirm to signalmen that the passing train is complete. At the sides of the van, high above track level, are the two side-lights which, after dark, exhibit a red light to the rear and a white light forward towards the head of the train. Their purpose, apart from rear protection, is for the driver to observe when he intermittently looks back along his train to ensure it is still complete, particularly when taking an incline where many a snatch is common and causes great stress on the coupling links.

At 1.10pm and in broad daylight, with regularity every weekday, the empty coal wagon train, Bury Loco Junction-Crofton, departed on time and had a clear and uninterrupted passage on the 'Connecting Line' and then made short work of the steep Broadfield bank. As neat as one can imagine, a Fowler 7F 0-8-0, with 59 symmetrically layered coal empties, and a brake-van at the rear, trundled gently along. So it was that Thursday afternoon, with a friendly short whistle from the engine crew as they clattered by, the train gained speed for the incline. Now the brake-van passed and a raucous shout embellished with suggestive signs I well knew the meaning of, came from the old guard I remembered well from shunting days. Following a suitable reply the train passed on, and the 'train out of section' was given to East box. What myself, the east box, and the Loco Junction signalman had not observed, whilst distracted by the guard's friendly waving and comical gyrations on the verandah, was that he had fixed his sidelights correctly, but failed to attach the most important item of all, the tail lamp!

Passing Heap Bridge, the guard had settled down inside the van to commence his bookings and the observant signalman at that box, attentive and undistracted, observed the omission. Very correctly, he carried out all the emergency regulations which involved, among many other actions, throwing back his signals against a passenger train moving at high speed down the bank, and generally causing havoc with the train timings over the next few hours. The consequences of a signalman failing to observe a missing tail lamp are synonymous with suspension, and 'form ones', and rightly so. It is a very serious crime indeed and, in particular, when three men in a row have committed precisely that. Consumed by remorse, we all three pleaded for leniency due to extenuating circumstances, but the result was a foregone conclusion, and we each received a 'form one', plus an ignominious one day's suspension. I was confident that this would positively assure my current Class 1 application finishing in the waste bin.

Within a week of this frustration, I had cause to 'blow my top' and blasphemously order painters and carpenters out of the box, one of which was an old school friend with whom I have never since come into contact. The occasion arose during an extremely busy period at about 9am when these men, who had in all probability completed just one hour's work painting the outside of the box, decided it was time for a 'brew up', and confidently sat themselves in a corner with their 'billie cans' and 'tommy boxes' to enjoy their, doubtfully, well-earned 'bait'. Not content to eat and chatter quietly amongst themselves, they took out a deck of cards. That was enough!

It is a signalman's moral and legal right to order any individual, including even authorised persons, out of the box if he considers their presence to be detrimental to the paramount safety of his work. I have never seen three men depart from a box so swiftly, including their canvas bags and belongings which I hurled after them through an open window.

Friday of the same week came and along with the customary weekly pay packet there was a letter attached confirming my appointment to Rose Grove East box with instructions to report to the local signalmen's inspector in Blackburn the following Monday. It would be a fallacy to say I was anxious to leave a box which for the past few years had given me total satisfaction but I simply had the over-riding desire to get to the top, and the attraction of higher pay was the driving force.

All good things come to an end. I cleared out my locker on the Saturday, phoned my workmates and bade them a sad farewell, and mused on what was in store for me in an area not very far away, but where I was acquainted with not a soul.

CHAPTER 15

Class 1 Achieved

Compared with Spring, September is not an ideal time of the year in which to train in a new box. Nevertheless, it can be said that although the evenings are drawing in, there is a brief respite before the fogs and other hazards of traffic control rear their ugly heads. Burnley town, lying deep in the folds of Pendle Hill, the Rossendale Forest, Entwistle Moor, Worsthorne Moor and Hameldon Hill, was particularly prone to fogs, aggravated in no small way by the belching chimneys of the surrounding cotton mills and augmented further by smoke from the big locomotive sheds, the large hump marshalling yard and the huge power generating plants at Hapton and Huncoat.

In the late nineteenth century, the region was a major crossroads from the four points of the compass. West to east provided a vital crossing from Liverpool and the west coast towns to the densely populated centres of West Yorkshire. It climbed through the Holmes Chapel and Lancashire's Calder Valley to reach its summit at Copy Pitt signalbox, then it took the long plunge into the Yorkshire Calder Valley at the county boundary and went on to Todmorden, where it linked with the busy Manchester-Leeds main line. From north to south, traffic was heavy from Skipton, Colne and Nelson, where cotton tycoons had for the past one hundred years, patronised the many daily expresses into Manchester and Salford. That is not to say that a substantial amount of farmers from the Craven country of the Dales did not also use these luxurious trains provided by the old L&Y in the heyday of rail travel. Skipton-Salford expresses were plentiful at that time and gave an additional boost to the L&Y's most lucrative movement of goods traffic. In marked contrast to modern times, in the early 1900s Salford cattle market was the hub of meat distribution, dead or alive, encompassing the entire north of England, and consequently it was a mecca for these hardy dalesmen.

In harmonious co-operation with the Midland Railway Company, this route had been made an important link in the 'alternative' route to Scotland from Manchester, a subtle move to break the L&NW monopoly. In 1875, when Midland trains had become press labelled and well known as the 'finest trains in Britain', many were the wealthy Mancunians who took the through express passing through Bury, Accrington and Burnley to arrive at the extremely smart station at Skipton, ready for their change to the Midland and on to Edinburgh or Glasgow in a stately Pullman coach.

After a tough primary interview, I was told to spread my learning time over all three shifts at my new post and pay particular attention to night working as this was heavy, and of a far different nature to that of the daytime turns of duty. An hour later, I was walking proudly into my very first Class 1 box. First impressions were somewhat frightening, the frame displayed 86 levers, and was a total length of some 50ft. By the brute force that the signalman was exerting to wrench over the black point levers and yellow distants, it appeared to be not only a frame of considerable length but also a very heavy one, as I soon discovered.

It also transpired that up to recent years, a train-register boy had been employed here but he had now been withdrawn for economic reasons and no train-registry entries were made, with the exception of emergency records. This was unusual but the reason became more than apparent by the time I had finished my spell of training. Purely and simply, it was a box demanding little other than brute physical force and lacked the overriding interest of traffic control. At that time I wished that I had not been so hasty in my actions, and was less impulsive in applying for anything and everything that came along. Major control of the Rose Grove zone was exercised in effect by the two junction boxes on either side, and apart from the passage of through trains, the bulk of the work consisted of dealing with the unending stream of trains into and out of the 'hump' mashalling yard. Coal trains and cross-country expresses from east to west consistently carried the same titles, but different timings to those familiar to me on other trans-Pennine lines and, although the heavy frame rightly designated it a 'hard box', the workings themselves were comparatively straightforward to comprehend. In the fullness of time, I mastered that long frame and was duly examined on both the box itself and, having encroached from 'foreign' territory, the block regulations and rule book in addition. Satisfaction given, I was then told to take over on the night shift the following Monday, an order which I mutely cursed. Night duty here, as my learning period had already demonstrated, was particularly hard and, subsequently, after three nights my back and arms were causing agony. My stomach was not in good shape for some time either, due to the strain it was taking whilst getting the 'feel' of this strange frame, but within a very short time, this aggravation had disappeared and I had settled into these new surroundings.

To the Blackburn side of Rose Grove Station was West Junction box, a special class post, controlling entry into the station from the main Accrington line and from the nine-mile Blackburn-Padiham Loop with, additionally, the entry and exit of the locomotive shed under its control. Unless I moved elsewhere, this box would now be my ultimate goal and I was giving serious thoughts to moving home and coming to live in the Padiham or Whalley district, a more attractive venture than continuing to live in my native Rossendale, where industry was declining fast and property prices plummetting.

When my wife suggested we abandon house-searching in this area and make a complete break with the north, perhaps moving to the south Gloucestershire region, my ears pricked up. She was tentatively alluding to an area where we had spent several short holidays in recent years, and this was indeed very close to Swindon, the Great Western stronghold and railway mecca of the west country. Indeed, what a marvellous idea, but was a transfer at all possible? Surely there were signalmen's vacancies to be found in that region, and were we not all now one united railway system, with interchanges of staff a strong possibility?

The eternal and uninterrupted clatter of wagons in the marshalling yard, and the shunters calls and curses sounded less harsh and progressively mellow over the next few days, as I carefully pondered over the ramifications of such a decision. Yes, I concluded, I would apply for a transfer, then the irony of it all struck me, would my ceaseless moves ever come to an end? Instinctively, I gazed above for my wandering star; doubtless it was now in the southerly heavens, but for how long I knew not; it had one more move to make to the west, perhaps one day it would do just that. At first, my application received a cold reception, apparently due to staff shortages in our own vicinity, but a second request brought back a vaguely evasive reply stating that no signalmen's vacancies existed in the Swindon district and, furthermore, a transfer to another region would result in the loss of seniority and a return to Class 4 status all over again. I took up the challenge, however, replying that it was of no consequence and, if necessary, I was prepared to demote myself again to a goods shunter's grade. I had done it before, so why not again? That was probably the most foolish thing I did on the spur of the moment. An immediate reply was forthcoming from Paddington stating that the post of head shunter was available at Hinksey yard in Oxford and I could be transferred there within the next two weeks.

Never have I had to move so fast! I replied in the affirmative and the die was cast. My house was advertised and sold the same day. Four days later, I was moving out the furniture to place in storage and my wife and children were taking temporary residence with her father. Within a further four days, I was saying goodbye to Burnley, my friends and relations, and to my native county which I would not have cause to work in again for the next eight years. On a bleak December Sunday, suitcase in hand and a borrowed one-pound note in my wallet, I was leaving Manchester by lunchtime on board a south-bound express.

CHAPTER 16

God's Wonderful Railway

It must have been whilst relaxing in the strange confines of a Great Western carriage from Wolverhampton to Oxford, lazily contemplating the ever-enchanting pictures of Cornwall's coastline and Brunel's bridges that adorn all compartments beneath the luggage rack, that the full reality of what I had done really struck home. Only three months ago I was working a Class 2 box which had become the pinnacle of my early ambitions. Work that I so dearly loved, yet enjoyed for so short a time, was cast aside. Now here I was, heading for a shunter's post in a completely unknown quarter where I wouldn't be acquainted with one mortal soul and, yet again, would have to commence on the long, slow grind to the top of the tree.

Feeling utterly dejected on arrival at Oxford Station, I found myself dragging a grossly overloaded suitcase around endless streets to seek out some reasonably priced lodgings. This was not at all easy in a university city, overpopulated by thousands of students in temporary accommodation. After a weary three hours, with the evening light fast fading, I had to settle for bed and breakfast at 13s (65p) for the night, an extortionate price at that time to a man accustomed to a 'pie, pint and night's doss' for 5s (25p). After being shown the room, I informed the landlady I would have to be up at 5am for the 6am start and she all but suffered a heart attack. Never did any of her students or commercial travellers rise so early, she indignantly retorted, and finally condescended only to make me a cup of tea at that unearthly hour and see me off the premises. I thought it was far from an endearing welcome to a northerner although I knew most southerners were rude, thoughtless, aristocratic anyway and, in addition, were unable to speak the King's English correctly!

With a large hole bored into my one and only pound note, I strode out into the chill frosty air that Monday morning, oppressed by apprehensions, yet somehow emotionally elated by reminiscences of bygone shunting days during the war. I made a very strange sight. To see a goods shunter arrive on duty carrying a large holiday suitcase, standing hesitantly in the shunter's cabin doorway, presented an amusing spectacle to both the night-shift gang signing off, and my future mates arriving for the early shift. The Yardmaster kindly relieved me of the case and stored it in his office. Then, after giving me instructions for learning the yard workings, he advised me of a suitable area in which to seek lodgings later in the day.

Shunting duties here in Oxford's Hinksey marshalling yard were far different to what I had been accustomed to in Lancashire 12 years ago. In the first place, the floodlighting was something we had been denied but had grown accustomed to in wartime, and here also I found there was an abundance of pipe-fitted vacuum vans and wagons. I was more familiar with the perpetual hooking up of loose-linked wagons with the traditional 6ft ash pole, and it seemed strange to be crawling between these more sophisticated vans, hooking up by hand, screwing up the link tension bar and coupling steam vacuum pipes. It was a continuously hazardous task, fraught with danger, as the shunting engine squeezes up the buffers and you either make a good connection, or fall flat on your face on the frost-covered sleepers and ballast, feet spreadeagled within inches of the rails and feel the shuddering 15 tons of an engine, spewing hot steam above your head.

When daylight came two hours later, it revealed a much larger marshalling yard than I had anticipated and quadrupled main line. In the turmoil of selling my home, moving my furniture into storage, settling my family into temporary accommodation and generally gathering my wits for this all-too-sudden transfer, I had found no time at all to make a detailed study of the geography of this Great Western main line from Paddington to Birmingham and the north-west. Trains were passing frequently, with hardly an interruption, along this Didcot-Wolvercot Junction line and were going to I knew not where. This was the case with traffic in the yard, which was marshalled for trains to destinations with which I was only vaguely familiar, over a large part of the south-east of England. If wagons were labelled to towns in the west country, Wales or the north, then I had a reasonable idea of which train service they would be set aside for. Otherwise, it was obviously going to take far more than one week to learn the traffic workings, let alone the yard's layout, if I was to pass out as a head shunter within the next few weeks and achieve the wage standard that was needed to pay lodgings and send money home.

When break time came at 10am there was the usual rush for the shunter's cabin and its warm interior, where water boiled invitingly on the hot stove. The adopted system among the men here was to buy packets of tea in rotation, and the brew was made in a gigantic enamel teapot. Gingerly placing my 'traditional' Lancashire mill striped pint pot on the scrubbed table-top in the midst of six or seven small GWR refreshment cups, I awaited the reaction. It soon came with several good-natured utterances and humorous quips such as: 'We thought it was only Yorkshiremen who took extra rations,' or 'Is that what the LMS use for fire buckets?' Clogs were not worn in this area as they were in north-country yards and ex-army boots were common. Looking down at my tattered shoes eight hours later, I knew where the bulk of this week's wages would be spent.

Two o'clock found me again with suitcase in hand and making a start to my quest for lodgings. Taking the Yardmaster's advice, I made for the bar of a small pub in Mill Street, not far from the station and, pleased to find only a couple of regulars occupying the place, I ordered a 'gill'. Apparently, this demand meant nothing in these parts. When I changed my request to a 'half' it did the trick and I partook of my first glass of southern ale for 6d (2½p), almost 25 percent higher cost than in a northern town, something that made me comprehend the far higher cost of living in the south.

The landlord was a very pleasant individual, allowing me to eat the remnants of my own stale sandwiches along with the beer, and when I later asked him for information regarding lodgings in the vicinity, he gave me an address to visit closeby which was within five minutes' walk of the station.

Holding on tenaciously to my remaining 6s (30p), I crossed my fingers and approached the house a little timidly, over-conscious of my financial embarrassment. There proved no need for apprehension. The lady who answered my tentative enquiries was extremely pleasant. Her last lodger had departed only two days previously and she was only too pleased to take me, despite my eloquent excuses for requiring meals at extremely awkward times. When I stutteringly apologised for being unable to provide a deposit, having no wage due for four days, she unhesitatingly offered to loan me cash if I was in need. My impression of the citizens of the south was immediately lifted to a higher pinnacle.

On my third day I was carefully considering what my next move should be in the light of the rather inextricable position in which I had voluntarily placed myself. It really had been a rash move. Before long, though, a Class 4 signalman's post would undoubtedly become available, if indeed there was not one already existing. Tantalisingly, it was the wrong division. Swindon was the district I wanted, and it would now be necessary to apply for a further transfer from out of the London division, which was reluctant to part with any valuable staff.

Showing lamentable self pity, I poured out my tale of woe to the Yardmaster who proved most sympathetic and arranged for me to be interviewed by the local signalmen's inspector the following day. Finding a ready-trained signalman in his midst was indeed a great delight to this man and, subject to the usual examinations, he informed me a Class 4 box was available on the outskirts of the city almost immediately. When I put forward my desire to be transferred to Swindon, however, he was most disappointed, but nevertheless arranged for me to be transferred temporarily to the passenger station, where I would take up parcel porter's duties pending his efforts to secure an interview at divisional headquarters in Bristol.

At least I had now planted my two feet on Great Western soil, or Western Region as we were now expected to refer to it, but the indignity of plummeting from signalman, Grade 1, to porter Grade 2, was a bitter pill to swallow. Adopting the rigidly self-imposed posture and stance of a new recruit, I reported, cap in hand, as I had done 17 years before, at the Stationmaster's office the following day – and it cut into my ego like a sabre.

What I viewed in the next half-hour as the Stationmaster himself walked me around, explaining the porter's duties here, gave me a rude awakening. Admittedly, I had only worked for short periods on railway stations, and only on two occasions had I stood on a GWR platform in pre-war days, but the change that had now come about was staggering. The indifferent attitude of the staff, the filthy platforms and neglected condition of the station buildings' paintwork, the dirty and untidy uniforms and, finally the strikingly apparent disinterest from station foreman downwards, was appalling. It was a far cry from personal memories of Pontypool Road Station in South Wales in the 1930s with its immaculate staff, bright shining brasswork, glistening paintwork on the station buildings, and an overriding air of unrehearsed efficiency. Dozens of four-wheeled trucks were piled high to a point of overbalancing, apparently abandoned, along the platforms. It left a lasting impression on me. It was as if I was witnessing the beginning of the end of railway pride. And so it proved to be. In this day and age, the only proud railmen left appear to be the unpaid enthusiasts, fighting to obtain a mere glimpse of a bygone age.

Labour was the overriding problem, I was informed, and with high wages available at the Morris motor-plant in the suburb of Cowley, only the dropouts were left available for porter duties on the station. If these men worked efficiently and carried out their allotted duties, consisting primarily of parcel-van loading, with attendance to the arrival and despatch of passenger trains a second consideration, then the task did prove quite demanding. A large proportion of the retail distribution of motor cycles was centred here at Oxford, and manhandling 650cc heavy bikes was shunned by all. When pushed a little, reluctant staff would absent themselves under the pretence of sickness. Many were partially disabled and returned repeatedly to the 'dole'. Under these circumstances the situation became chaotic and almost intolerable, and I observed on one occasion the Stationmaster himself sweeping snow from the platform, leaving the foreman powerless to intervene, and some half-dozen down-at-heel porters furtively hiding about the station entrance ready to solicit the occupants of incoming taxis. This vocation was known as 'quilling', with the strongest of the pack usually to the fore and ready to grab the most gullible of travellers who displayed affluence and the demeanour of a good 'tipper'.

Train arrivals produced the same diabolical situation. Five minutes before arrival of any 'cream' trains, the entire eight-men gang, deftly herded together a matter of only 10mins earlier, would slyly disappear when only a total of three men were necessary to attend to both train and passengers. After only four or five days of this frustration, circumstances got the better of my usually calm temperament and the loss of my composure, albeit but temporary, could well have cost me my job. Work had been particularly hard that morning following a 4am start on a bitterly cold morning. Fish trains arrived very early from Grimsby and Hull and were shunted into the up bay. In these days, prior to the wide use of refrigerated vans, fish were boxed with layers of chipped ice and the well-worn and often damaged crates were bound with strips of thin and treacherous metal. None of us could afford to purchase the industrial gloves really necessary for this type of work. Blasphemy was the only release from the incessant boredom and pain of mauling hundreds of these boxes, bursting all round and scattering the protruding ice everywhere as they were loaded and stacked into the road vans for delivery to Mac-Fisheries and other retailers across the city. Only when the ice turned red could your fuddled brain take in the fact you had received a very nasty cut from the vicious steel bands.

At 7am with that job completed and barely time to straighten our backs, the foreman ordered four of us into a parcels van for off-loading. There was the usual mad rush for the inside job, leaving the last man to stack the outside platform trucks. A little after 8am, with my head down, sorting in a far corner, I suddenly became aware that I was working completely on my own. The crafty trio had disappeared. By that time, with four hours of hard graft, my numb and bleeding hands were causing me understandable irritability. These illiterates were not going to make a fool of me. With my blood really on the boil, I stormed down the platform, oblivious to passengers awaiting the London 'fast', to discover the first of the missing three culprits sitting nonchalantly drinking tea in the refreshment room. That was the final straw!

I confess my temper got the better of me. With one hand I knocked the cup from his grasp and, as he rose, my right fist caught him square on the chin, causing him to recoil and fall backwards, taking the table, an assortment of crockery and two empty chairs with him. As he scrambled to his feet, I ordered him back to the parcels van, even though I did not hold one scrap of authority to do so, and he ran like a hare back up the platform. Fortunately, as the commotion ensued, the London train was drawing into the station and the few alarmed passengers had dispersed quickly from the buffet and were boarding the train before they had time to think about what had happened or, worse still, to lodge a complaint.

Somehow, however, and within minutes, the Station Inspector had the story and I was summoned to his office post haste. A mere five minutes had elapsed when I stormed into his seat of authority and, with my temper unchecked, expounded my eloquent views on what I thought about the station's operations, the total lack of authority by himself and other supervisory staff, the fact that I myself did the job I was paid for, unlike the majority of the rabble employed here who spent half their time 'quilling' and dodging. Furthermore, not one of the entire gang of men I was supposed to work with on parcel and mail sorting were at all sure if Edinburgh was in Cornwall, or Cardiff in Kent. Their contemptuous and unconcerned slinging of parcels destined to any or every part of the country, without the remotest idea of where the next tranship point was situated, was beyond my belief. Unburdening myself of all these pent-up emotions took probably a couple of minutes and then, as I returned to a more rational state of mind, I shuddered at the thought of what could be the potential outcome this outburst.

In pre-war days fighting on duty would court instant dismissal, synonymous with the penalties for theft or drunkenness. The net result of all this however, stunned me. Ten minutes later, I was upgraded to Parcels Porter, Grade 1. I thanked my lucky stars I managed to express all my views first, and the Inspector had given me a sympathetic hearing. When I calmed down we had a sensible discussion and the outcome was that he arranged for me to be put in full charge of parcel and mail despatch. Ironically, my knowledge of the immediate surroundings was negligible and the locality of many of the smaller outlying stations in the neighbourhood were, as yet, unknown to me. Realising that it could well be several weeks before my transfer came through, I was content to make my work as interesting as possible.

One finds many inconsistencies and thoroughly inconceivable anomalies in the field of countrywide distribution of parcel traffic by both road and rail. I would encounter road transport irregularities later in life, but here at Oxford I saw many of the glaring examples of inefficiency that lead to the warranted public complaints of incompetence. At Oxford, if you posted a parcel at the general post office at, say, 4pm addressed to someone in Newcastle-on-Tyne, 200 miles away, the chances are that the package would be delivered by noon the following day. If you had taken the same parcel to Oxford Station to be forwarded by rail, it would arrive in all probability three or more days later! Paradoxically, a parcel left at the post office would travel by GPO van to Oxford Station, be despatched on the Swindon to Sheffield and Newcastle night train, its loading being under the supervision of a GPO official, then it would be offloaded again on Newcastle Station the following morning, conveyed by the GPO to their sorting office and, subsequently, to the consignee within hours. On the other hand, this very same parcel, consigned from Oxford Station parcels office, was likely to be stacked on a platform truck along with hundreds of others, unheeded for up to two days before it was eventually and hopefully despatched on the correct service to Newcastle. Should the same intolerable perplexities prevail at this Tyneside metropolis as existed here in the reputedly highest seat of learning, then heaven help the general public. For a great number of years the liaison between the GPO and the railway companies had been more than excellent and, here again, I found splendid co-operation to be evident. Following the arrival of the nightly loads of mail bags, letter mail was scrutinised most carefully by the watchful eye of a GPO official during its transit into the passenger train guards van, and parcels mail received further keen observance, checking that all bags were being loaded into their correct vans.

The battle to clear an unchecked backlog of parcels was unending. When success appeared to be on the horizon, some demon would raise its ugly head and thwart all our efforts. The scheduled passage of the Royal Train one evening caused the attaching of one coach from the down bay to the GC train to Sheffield to be suspended for over 20mins and in order to keep the train to a respectable late running time, many truck loads of parcels were of necessity left behind. When I came on duty the following day they were still there! If the Royal Train caused this to happen at one station alone, what were the repercussions throughout the entire journey!

An occasional word with the Duchess of Marlborough who, along with the Duke, travelled regularly on a morning 'fast' to Paddington, broke the monotony of the job. I am sure it gave her quite a surprise when I first refused the tip she proffered, adding that I was already paid by my employers to assist passengers if they requested any help. The giving and receiving of tips had perpetually caused me abhorrence. The Duke himself was a very tall man of exceptionally few words, but who could expect a conversation with so illustrious a person as the resident of Blenheim Palace.

Some weeks later, on an appropriately sunny morning, I reported for duty and was greeted on arrival with an urgent message to catch the next service to Bristol where I was required for examination at Temple Meads Station, in preparation for a transfer and signalbox posting at Swindon. Success at last! It had taken several letters and a whole succession of verbal pleas, but at long last it had all come to fruition. Armed with a much-treasured and glowing reference I had received from my old supervisor, Chief Inspector MacNiel of Manchester, no time was lost in preparing for the journey. Although sorry to leave the excellent lodgings I had enjoyed here in Oxford. I could not have been more anxious to pack my bags.

CHAPTER 17

Into the Hub of the 'Western'

Running into Temple Meads Station, I cast an optimistic eye on the impressive East Junction box with its staggering total of 23 block instruments and over 300 levers. Secretly, I wondered if ever I would be privileged to work alongside the other few men required to work a box of this size, or would I eventually be fortunate enough to work one of the two special class boxes we had passed in Swindon.

Chief Inspector Old was the man chosen to interview me, and I wandered through the impressive offices in an equally impressive station until I was directed to the correct door. The way in which I was both greeted and subsequently questioned by this most genial person was in marked contrast to the way things were done in Manchester, a bastion of the 'we' and 'you' attitude. His approach was impeccable and, within seconds, I was put at complete ease.

Although I had by now experienced many encounters with high-ranking head office personalities, and always deemed myself to have adequate confidence, there was, nevertheless, a nagging tension present which was always a constant irritation when attending examinations and interviews in this type of surroundings.

I need not have held any such apprehensions however. Following an initial questioning of my general block-signalling capabilities and a further interesting discussion on the minor but quite important variations of the Western train signalling regulations, Mr Old read the reference I had procured from his counterpart in Manchester. He appeared suitably impressed and then passed me on for a medical examination.

Finally, a return to the office of Chief Inspector Old, and confirmation that I was suitable for taking a post in Swindon. I was to report at the office of Inspector Cotterill the following morning at 9am.

Close to four months had passed since my wife and I had made the decision to uproot ourselves and set Swindon Town as our target. Now, after applied patience and a little cajoling here and there, it was finalised. Tomorrow would see me happily installed in the town we had chosen, the town which owed its very existence to those illustrious personages Isambard Kingdom Brunel and Daniel Gooch.

Over 30mins waiting time for a return train gave me the opportunity to steal a walk down to Temple Gate and gaze back at Mathew Digby Wyatt's flamboyant and most outstanding castellated station facade. My wife and I had previously noted its captivating appeal when cycling along Temple

Meads nine years previously, but my second and more detailed study of the building proved to be extremely stimulating.

Ambling back up the station approach, an interesting thought crossed my mind. The 4.30pm ex-Bristol-Paddington was none other than the *Bristolian*, now back to its pre-war timings of 1hr 45mins for the 118-mile run to London. There was no need whatsoever for me to rush back to Oxford, so I thought I would take this train to Paddington and then return via Reading and Didcot. After treating myself to a beer in the refreshment room I quietly awaited the 4.30pm drawing into the platform with its seven chocolate-and-cream coaches and a sleek green diligently polished 'Castle' class locomotive, completely absent of any frills to portray its latent power.

Instead of having to stand in the corridor, which would have been necessary when using a warrant had the train been fully loaded, I was fortunate to find a vacant seat, and watching the 4.15pm Paddington express leave from an adjacent platform, I settled back to enjoy this surprise treat. Next to me sat another lone passenger, a gentleman who was quietly observing my obvious interest in the 'goings on'. Within a short time we were chatting together and exchanging reminiscences of this particular train and its compatriot, the pre-war *Cheltenham Flyer*.

The *Cheltenham Flyer*, unlike the *Bristolian* never officially held its illustrious title. In railway timetables, it was merely shown as the 2.30pm Cheltenham-Paddington Express. After its inaugural run in July 1923, with nine coaches and headed by the 4-6-0 locomotive *Saint Bartholomew*, it set up a new record from Swindon-Paddington of 72mins for the 77¼ miles and the train soon caught the imagination of the press. Hence it became the 'Flyer' and by 1929, the start-stop run from Swindon, scheduled at 75mins was easily shortened to 70mins with a clear run and the train at that time was officially named 'fastest in the world'.

Today, promptly as ever, our train pulled out of Temple Meads at 4.30pm dead, and unimpeded by the slightest shudder or hint of a slip the *Bristolian* was quickly into the climb to Stoke Gifford and travelling at a deceptively high speed into Chipping Sodbury tunnel. On the Somerford straight I made a rough calculation and found we were moving in the region of 85mph before a check came for the severe curve at Wootton Bassett West box. Through Swindon town now, the blurred outline of the massive rail works rushed by as we sped over the very spot where, in December 1933 whilst crossing the lines, the great Churchward aged 77 was ironically killed by an express headed by a locomotive of his own design. Again a high speed was reached through the vale of The White Horse and sustained on the approaches to Reading, with a final burst through the lower Thames Valley. At 6.14pm this fastest train in Britain pulled into Paddington Station one minute early, having covered the 118 miles at an average speed of just under 70mph.

Perhaps another day, and on a much slower train, I might see more clearly the outlines of the big boxes at Swindon, Didcot and Reading. This day they were merely a blur with their presence only signified by a slight roll over the points and my own pre-studied composition of the track layout. The hasty decision to travel on the *Bristolian* had produced a memorable experience and to me was comparable only to a journey on the *Mancunian* over the Rugby-Euston 'race track'.

Returning to Oxford, packing cases and preparing for the necessary tramp around Swindon in search of accommodation now held no qualms. I was a man about to return to his rightful and true vocation, and about to work happily among trains, the like of which I had never experienced before today. Oozing with confidence following the satisfactory reception in Bristol, I was a little surprised to see what appeared to be disapproving glances as I alighted from an early morning train onto Swindon Station. Several porters and, in particular, the Station Inspector of whom I requested directions to the Signalling and Traffic Inspector's office, scowled with obvious distaste towards my head. Only when removing my cap a little later, did I realise the true gravity of my insulting behaviour. On the front of my cap, as had been the case for the last 20 years, there rested the miserably unimpressive 'L.M.S' chrome-plated badge. Here amidst the heavy gold braid and imposing cap badges of the GWR still worn with reverence by all supervisory staff, I had the effrontery to stroll nonchalantly along the station and cross these sacred Great Western rails to the office of Inspector Cotterill, in the very core of Western territory. That matter was prudently and promptly rectified by Assistant-Inspector Lockett, who despairingly handed me an even less impressive British Railways' badge and the offending rival company's insignia disappeared quickly into my pocket and subsequently into oblivion. The link was now broken forever.

Entering the smoke begrimed Bath stone offices, which had ostensibly seen little change since they were built with the stone hewn from Box tunnel over 100 years ago, the overwhelming spiritual presence of a bygone age dominated one's every thought. It was a feeling of a binding of tradition, the compulsive moulding of a family of deeply dedicated railwaymen, a feeling of belonging to, rather than being simply a paid employee of a world-renowned, yet comparatively small company which was large only within its own concepts. I had previously been unaccustomed to such formality and it was strange to me when Mr Cotterill rose from his desk, walked around it to shake hands and then talked across, and not down, to his subordinate. I was even to be addressed as mister, and not by my surname alone, or by the official title, 'Signalman Bradshaw'.

What I had witnessed in my very short association with the Western region brought home to me the truly tactless decisions that were taken in 1923, when the big amalgamation caused unnecessary fusings of powerful and bitterly opposed companies. The incorporation of the long-standing enemies, the Midland and LNW Railways was a glittering example. This, above all, had generated mutual and deep resentment between the ruling camps in Crewe and Derby, and any traditions and loyalties among the workforce which had existed was brutally sabotaged forever.

Temporarily my mind had wandered on to other things but I was soon drawn back to the gilt-framed photographs of GWR locomotives, imposing portraits of their builders and everywhere, in respectful evidence, the characteristic picture of the cigar-smoking Isambard Brunel greeted you in these cream-walled GWR offices here in Swindon. It is said that in the houses of railway workers at that time you were much more likely to find a Gooch or Churchward locomotive painting adorning the living-room wall, than the ever-traditional wedding photograph. That fact, I could well believe, following the introductory interview with Mr Cotterill and my subsequent wanderings around this railway town.

Kingsdown Road signalbox on the short Swindon-Highworth single-line branch was to be my first posting, pending a main-line vacancy which could be expected within the ensuing two months. Now I had just three or four days in which to learn single-line 'token' workings of which I had had no previous experience, and to learn the Kingsdown box, the smallest I was ever to see. This itself proved no great problem, but tramping the streets of Swindon over the next few days searching for lodgings or rooms, was by no means an easy task. Hopes of a quick house purchase were severely dashed after enquiries in the three or four property agents' offices. Ninety pounds was the residue from my sale in the north and would have proved ample for the 10 percent necessary for a mortgage deposit in most northern industrial towns. This was far from a reality in the south of England however. A comparable property in this area would command double the price and I had come to terms with this fact. Until promotion loomed, with the accompanying necessities of overtime, night-work and Sunday duties, no further cash would be forthcoming to increase the mortgage deposit required.

Scouring intrepidly through this town of a 50,000 population during the next few days enabled me to learn most of its geography, and to study a great deal of its short but world-renowned history. Any item of high technical engineering manufacture bearing the inscription 'made in Swindon' would, the town proudly boasted, be accepted as the very best the world over.

Illustrious street names abounded: Gooch Street, Dean Street, Collett and Churchward Avenues; even Stanier Street, in respect to the GWR assistant chief who deserted to the LMS; all were so named in honour of these great men.

The massive railway factory covering all aspects of GWR operation from locomotives to laundries, carriage and wagon shops to signal and telegraph operations, all were here, and at one time, the whole complex employed a total 14,000 work force. Close by was the railway housing-estate, its streets of Bath stone neatly laid out and named after towns served by the GWR network. And beyond stood the noteworthy buildings that lay testimony to the work of a lesser known, but philanthropic Swindon chief, Joseph Armstrong. The hospital, health centre, school, church, swimming and washing baths were all the work of this man, who believed fervently in the great achievements of Robert Owen, a Welshman who incorporated theories of scientific management with workers' amenities and care, to motivate his highly successful venture in New Lanark, Scotland.

Brunel had chosen this particular site, a short distance from the village of Swindon, in 1840. The population was a little over 1,000 in 1800 and he gave Daniel Gooch, a 23-year-old Northumbrian and protégé of George Stephenson, the task of building a factory and new town. This he did in no uncertain means. In 1850 the population had exploded to 7,000, with cesspools flowing into the unpaved streets and alleyways. Health warnings were issued and rigorous methods were applied by Armstrong to combat the fast developing filth and squalor. So was conceived a unique liaison between management and workers that was to remain a paramount factor for 100 years. Daniel Gooch himself donated £1,000 towards the building of the hospital, and a small deduction from wages assured all Swindon's railway employees medical treatment substantially in advance of anything known at that time.

By the turn of the century the new town of Swindon had doubled, and doubled again its population, and 95 percent of the employable labour was engaged by the GWR.

The Midland and South Western Railway, a line built later to give a service from Cheltenham-Southampton, was the second company to thrust into Swindon, its route crossing over the GWR and passing through the old town. It provided a most useful service for the Manchester, Liverpool or Leeds traveller, having connection with the *Pines Express* and the *Devonian* at Lansdowne Station in Cheltenham. Single line it may have been over most of its length, but it provided a quick and efficient service for liner connections at the Southampton terminus. It was known to local railmen as the 'Tidley Dyke', a mysterious *nom de plume* the origin of which I never did discover.

Finding accommodation in Swindon proved difficult. The town council had embarked on an expansion scheme, and preferential treatment was being given to housing an influx of London expatriates who were being encouraged to take up employment in the many new manufacturing industries now springing up in the town. There was scant help, therefore, from that quarter and, after several days of fruitless enquiries, I hit upon the idea of paying a visit to the Citizen's Advice Bureau, an organisation relatively unfamiliar to me at that time. Within two hours I was jubilantly rewarded and sending the good news to my wife I suggested she left the children in the care of relatives and come post haste to Swindon where I had obtained furnished accommodation. Then she could help me in further attempts to find a family house. At least we now had a roof over our heads and I felt a great relief as the next few weeks sped by.

Now installed in what must have been the cushiest signalbox posting I have ever enjoyed, the opportunity arose to seek part-time work in order to augment a very low income. Jobs were abundant in the fifties and success soon came with the offer of work in a local cycle shop at hours to suit myself, wheel-building and carrying out general cycle repairs of which I had had previous experience. In a very short time my wife secured some furnished accommodation for us which was far more suitable, and our children were thankfully able to rejoin us. Our family was now reunited after an eventful six months and luck still played a kind hand. An offer of hospital work for my wife gave us a total of three jobs between the two of us, and a mortgage deposit and permanent home were again in sight. Six weeks was all that was needed, and we were ready to install ourselves into a town house and become citizens of our adopted borough. Our next offspring would rightly be able to claim being born a true 'Swindonian'.

CHAPTER 18

Onto the Main Line

The normally exhausting task of mounting a full-scale house removal over a 200-mile migration proved to be not a traumatic and exasperating operation, but a task of pure joy. It signified the climax of a vision we had set out to accomplish six months previously in the confines of such a dramatically contrasting environment. The stark hills and smoke-shrouded valleys of the industrial west Pennine towns were in distinct contrast to the vividly lush pastures of agricultural Wiltshire. Furthermore, the dense complexity of the overlapping tentacles of rail communications surrounding Manchester was so different to this long, lone high-speed track skirting the feet of the Berkshire and North Wiltshire Downs.

At first light, local hostelries could not favourably compare with a north-country pub, where the strains of a honky-tonk piano, and the sight of the player's accompanying pint on the polished top would be a foregone conclusion. However, on this monumental weekend when I chose to sample the local brew, the friendly west country accents surrounding me carried an intonation of welcome that would forever endear me to these West countrymen. There was no need to heed the warnings of my workmates in the north, who always held a foreboding in respect of all forms of humanity south of Birmingham. People in general were little different from their counterparts in Crewe, Derby or Doncaster. They were all doing the same job anyway. If their accents were softer and more mellow it was understandable, and wasn't that to be expected in this rolling countryside? And when it came to heaving and mauling heavy furniture into our new home, the friendly cup of tea and welcome were equally sincere as that which we could have expected in our native Lancashire.

Kingsdown Road signalbox was a far cry from the large box I had last worked. Whereas that had been surrounded by power stations, cotton mills, a huge engine shed and marshalling yard, this totally insignificant post was situated almost four miles out of town, encompassed in lush green pastures and primarily a block post only on this little-used line from the town of Highworth to Swindon. A short branch line into the Vickers Armstrong factory was used once or twice a day, and two or three passenger trains rumbled through the pretty countryside from Upper Stratton Station to Stanton Fitzwarren and Hannington Halts, finally running alongside Bydemill Brook, a tributary of the Thames, and up the short incline into the old town of Highworth. I was very pleased because I had not only achieved my ambition to work on the Western, but also in the specific area chosen, and I was even more delighted when the first main-line Class 3 vacancy came along.

Two weeks later, my ultimate dream came into fruition and I was appointed, subject to passing the usual examinations, to Shrivenham box, six miles east of Swindon on the main Paddington to Bristol and South Wales line.

How often in what now seemed a distant Lancashire hometown had I studied keenly the intricate railway maps and noted all boxes both east and west of Swindon town, where one day I may be privileged to work. Now it had all come true and one week later saw me cycling out on the comparatively easy seven-mile journey from home with a head swimming in hypothetical wanderings, and visions of subsequent postings to Reading, Didcot, Bristol or Swindon which, in the course of time, might be within my grasp.

As a Class 3 position can be rated, Shrivenham provided an average workload, and the layout and workings were reasonably straightforward. There was double track on the west side to Marston East box, and quadrupled on the east side to Ashbury crossing box by up and down main, and up and down relief lines. These latter lines served the station, in addition to providing a refuge for slow-moving goods trains. Small goods sidings were situated on both up and down sides, although the up side special sidings, laid in 1943 for American ambulance trains to offload casualties for the local US hospital, were now closed.

Whilst learning the box, a little bit of history was related to me and, surprisingly, imparted without constraint, as references to accidents on 'God's Wonderful Railway' were seldom forthcoming. Apparently, it was here in the year 1848, that six passengers of the midday Exeter-Paddington were killed when Daniel Gooch's *Sultan* 8ft single driver ploughed through a horse-box, and wreckage of the smashed van tore through the following train. This had happened within a stone's throw of where the box now stood, and long before block signalling existed on the system. More recently however, a matter of only some three years past, a near tragedy occurred with the up Weston 'slip' train between here and Uffington, the next station ahead. By accident, on this particular morning the guard had somehow slipped the Didcot portion after passing Knighton box and the signalman at both Uffington and Challow had almost fatally misread the multiple tail lamps on the main train, and sent 'train out of section'. The following up slow passenger train had been accepted and all signals cleared. Only quick and concerted action on the part of permanent way men, who had observed the situation, had averted what could have been a major accident and a severe blow to GWR's long-established record of safe travel. I made a mental note to pay particular attention to the regulations regarding slip train signalling in preparation for the forthcoming examinations at Bristol. Slip train workings were something completely new to me as they had been withdrawn in the LMS field of operation many years previously following a few narrow mishaps.

Together with additional track circuiting and more 'lock and block' workings, the GWR had added the celebrated ATC (automatic train control), a revolutionary invention which gave great credence to GWR's boast to being Britain's safest railway. This ATC was, again, something new to me. Placed within a few yards of the distant signal, a crucial signal displaying either clear or caution to a driver in order to dictate his speed, a ramp is positioned between the running rails. Under the locomotive frame a contact with the ramp activates a bell in the cab if the signal is showing clear, or a siren if the signal stands at caution. Not merely a safety precaution, in foggy conditions this innovation had been instrumental in achieving a much higher degree of good timekeeping.

Of paramount importance at Shrivenham was the need to become familiar quickly with necessary 'margins' required by the manifold classification of freight trains on the down road. Responsibility for the acceptance of trains onto either the up main or up relief was taken by the Ashbury box signalman.

The passage of a slow freight taking 10 or 12mins to reach the next relief line at Marston East box, meant that pathing of the *Bristolian*, or a similar fast closing up to Didcot, required a diligent and almost instant decision to be taken as to what you were going to do with this freight. Although the control system, put into operation first by the Midland and used extensively on the LMS, was not considered to be perfect by any means, here on the Western it was virtually non-existent. To ascertain the position of a down fast was laborious work. First one had to contact Challow, and then perhaps Foxhall Junction, Didcot East, or even speak to the signalman as far back as Goring. A vital 60 seconds could be frustratingly lost in this tedious process and the freight could easily miss a clear 'distant' and, consequently, would come into the 'relief'.

Quadrupling of the lines here, and at Challow and Wantage Road, in the early thirties had caused speculation but now there was to be a return to this policy. Obliteration of this continual source of freight delays could be imminent following a veiled suggestion of a government modernisation plan in the pipeline. Simultaneously a scheme would surely be promoted for the quadrupling of the track throughout, from Didcot to Swindon, and both freight and fast moving passenger traffic would run unimpeded and independently. Thus the transport of goods and coal, at one time the prime source of profit of railway operation, could again take its rightful place in the nation's integrated transport network. Existing roads and the proposed new motorways, too, would benefit with an equal distribution of what was surely becoming the biggest mass movement of vital commodities the country had ever witnessed.

In recent years, I had often been pressed to learn a box quickly, no doubt due to staff shortages, but I found little of that attitude here; precisely the opposite in fact. Told to make my own arrangements with regard to what shift I worked, whilst learning the frame and traffic workings, the time was equally spread on both night and day turns of duty. After a fortnight, and feeling fully conversant with the traffic, Inspector Cotterill was contacted and informed I was ready for examination.

He arrived the following day and examined me on all aspects, later stating he was fully satisfied and would arrange for my visit to Head Office in Bristol the next day. Returning again to Bristol's divisional headquarters did not raise the awesome spectre it had yielded six months previously and, when confronted by Chief Inspector Old's deputy in place of his good self, I deemed that as confirmation of having passed muster on his original scrutiny and furthermore that I had been accepted into the auspicious GWR fold.

The examination was quick and to the point. Noticeably questions were framed around the emergency Regulation 20, train divided, in the wake of the recent 'slip train' scare at Uffington. Never can one anticipate the forthcoming form of interrogation, and a quick retort of 'rising, at 1 in 834', to a query on the gradient from Shrivenham to Marston east, raised a complimentary flicker of the eyebrow. He was satisfied within an hour and I was discharged, free to take an hour's relaxation before returning to Inspector Cotterill's Swindon office.

Time to celebrate, I thought. Yes, I would treat myself to a hair cut, singe and shampoo in the smart subway hairdressers. It proved very expensive at 1s (5p). The places I usually frequented were called barbers and were only conversant with a 'short back and sides', at the modest charge of a 'tanner' (2½p)! This was something different, however.

I took a stroll into the city centre and around the cobblestoned streets to the old docks. They were marvellously fascinating. Was this where young 'Jim' set out on his remarkable adventures to Treasure Island? Unequivocally, Bristol was an impressive city in which I would like to spend a little more time on some future day, together with a return visit to the city of Bath. This superb trail to the West Country, its magic and traditions already well established, was taking a profound hold on my emotions.

Although 20 years had passed since untold hours were spent on Manchester Victoria Station enshrouded in teenage visions and aspirations; my mind was captivated as a child on Blackpool's Central Station's departure platforms, watching endless trains pulling out and heading for some distant city I never expected to ever see, the fascination had never died. Wandering from platform to platform on Temple Meads this brilliantly sunny midday, these old reminiscences not only returned vividly, they multiplied and brought a new impetus to my faith in the future of Britain's railways.

Now that the Western Region had obtained a little autonomy and authority to make a return to its traditional colour of chocolate and cream on selected coaching stock, a most welcome return of individuality and a hint of decentralisation was creeping back into the system. Being distinct from the mass uniformity that state monopolisation was forcing upon us, it was pleasant to observe the 'crack' trains displaying a hint of their former glory. The spick and span green and black 'Castles' and 'Kings' with their polished brass domes belied the latent power that could be generated by these ever-so-silent locomotives as they glided to a stand. I do confess, though, to clinging forever to my most cherished sight, that of a Stanier 4-6-2 'Duchess Pacific' pulling out of Euston with a night 'Scotsman'. However, here I was, deep in the land of Gooch, Churchward, Collett and Dean, and I must proclaim their names with reverence, and that of Stanier with tongue in cheek. Only scathing oratory pertaining to the LMS could one expect to be tolerated in these confines.

Passing through Temple Meads Station at this time of year, locomotives from both camps were commonplace, hauling their long holiday trains and regular services from the West Country to the northern cities, to South Wales, and to London and the east. Those Crewe-built locos heading trains to the Midlands and North outlined Stanier's GWR influence, their taper boilers a by-product of Churchward's 'Stars', as indeed were the 'Castles' and 'Kings' of C.B. Collett.

Hurrying down to platform 1 to view the 'King' that was pulling into the station with an up Weston-Paddington, my thoughts turned to ghosts of the past, and what sheer amazement would be stamped across the faces of those pioneers of a mere century ago, if they could but stand alongside me and see now the fruits of their endeavours: the irrepressible Brunel, who had engineered the line from London to Bristol, and the young engineer he brilliantly chose to bring from Stephenson's works in Newcastle to become his chosen locomotive engineer. At the age of 20, Gooch had begun work on the locomotive that would eventually head the first train into this city on 30 June 1841, and achieve a then remarkable time of four hours. What a compelling sight they would now witness. Churchward, without doubt, possessed the brain that lay behind Britain's world supremacy in steam traction that was predominantly witnessed in those record-breaking days between the two world wars.

I gazed up admiringly, at the King of all 'Kings' facing me now which was none other than *George V*, No 6000, with its 135 tons of lethal power. Some 30 years ago it had made its famous record-breaking run in the USA and it looked not a day older. Its alien transatlantic bell, placed midway between the express headlamps, was a compulsory attachment on that occasion in the USA, but by good fortune it was donated to the GWR and it served as a glittering reminder of the visit by this renowned engine to the Ohio and Baltimore Railroads Centenary in 1927. The staggering performance of this locomotive had impressed both USA footplatemen and public alike, and forever more the 'Kings' would epitomise the ultimate symbol of Great Western Locomotion. Watching the 'Kings' effortless start towards East box, the sudden thrill of anticipation sharpened. Tomorrow would see me back in charge of a main-line box afer an absence of over six months, and in all probability signalling this very train, and many other equally illustrious trains.

It was time to return to Swindon and I boarded the next train which had stops at Bath and Chippenham. Brunel's superbly engineered route reveals many notable points of interest along its way. The long low stone viaduct when entering the lovely city of Bath blends admirably with the surroundings, and is of particular charm. Immediately after Bath comes the 1 in 100 climb through the famous Box tunnel, to herald an impressive panorama of Chippenham town from the high viaduct and, on leaving the station here, the prestigious names of Westinghouse, synonymous with rail travel for over a century, peers down from a nearby factory. Just a few level miles along the upper Avon Valley, and the regulator is wide open for the 1 in 100 climb up Dauntsey Bank to Wootton Bassett Junction, and after the link with the South Wales Line, a final burst is made for the gently falling gradient into Swindon.

On returning, a brief visit to Inspector Cotterill's office confirmed I would take charge the following day at 2pm, so grabbing my bike from one of the thousands in the cycle stands that surround the Swindon works, I rushed home to celebrate. Now my feet were planted firmly once more on the second rung of the ladder towards my new goal!

CHAPTER 19

Auspicious Trains

The *Flying Dutchman, Red Dragon, Torbay Pullman, Royal Duchy, Capitals United, South Wales Pullman, Bristolian, Zulu, Pembroke Coast Express, Cheltenham Flyer, Merchant Venturer* and *Bristol Pullman* are all names synonymous with auspicious 'Western' trains and have been romanticised and written about over many a decade by the GWR publicity departments. Some have passed into the annals of railway history, and a few of the others still in service were using the 'Berks and Hants' route from Reading. Many of these I would be signalling through today, I mused.

No amount of mountain sheep passing through imaginary gates on a high Cumbrian fell had induced sleep the previous night. However many signal boxes a man learns in his lifetime, he will forever hold a deep sense of apprehension, and even some fear as the hour approaches to take charge and work completely alone. When the man he relieves waves a cheery goodbye and walks away down the steps, the butterflies stir ominously in the pit of his stomach.

The express roars by, the train out of the section is given, and is immediately followed by a request for 'line clear' for a partially 'fitted' freight. Perhaps your relief line already holds two waiting trains and the last thing you want to do is to block a 'fitted' behind two coal trains. Are you going to run him or not? Is there a margin? Where is the next express, due in 15mins at that very moment? There is no time to dither. A 'distant' check to a heavy express travelling at 80-90mph will mean a 4min delay which the driver will be unlikely to recover before Bristol or Newport. A locomotive travelling at these speeds consumes a staggering 1cwt of coal every three miles and the fireman, after such a severe check, will shovel an extra 1cwt into the firebox. The icy and stony stare you will recieve from the passing driver will leave you in no doubt as to his feelings for you, or your parentage. Those, and many other consequential forebodings, were scurrying across my mind as I set out that late summer day in 1955.

For seven miles the journey was in sharp contrast to the one I had been accustomed to in the foothills of the Pennines. From the east side of Swindon, from the multitude of streets that adjoin the railway works, the monotonously flat road took me through Gorse Hill and Lower Stratton, along the route of both the railway and the Wilts and Berks Canal to the old Bourton Wharf, then into the 'Royal' county of Berkshire and, finally, round the back lanes to reach the box by cutting through the down goods yard.

After the customary greetings had been exchanged and the necessary information given with regard to what trains were in section, the point attaching most importance appeared to be that the '12.55 Paddington' was two minutes 'down' at Goring. This was another way of passing into your hands responsibility for what subsequent decisions were taken. Charlie Thomas then waved a phlegmatic cheerio, accompanied by the laconic paraphrase 'it's all yours now', and he was gone. I was on my own.

The tip that the 12.55 Paddington was two minutes 'down' at Goring was now evident, and I turned out an empty coal train immediately on receipt of the 'train out of section' from Marston East for the down 'Old Oak Common-Whitland Milk'. I should have had second thoughts. Hardly had the empty coal train cleared the down starter when the potential 'clanger' registered. Perhaps I could blame the 'butterflies' for overlooking the obvious fact that although the express had left Paddington late, the driver was probably doing his utmost to make up time. This proved to be so. At Wantage, he had successfully regained almost a minute, and when my 'distant' eventually dropped for him, he was all but over the ATC ramp. This fact was substantiated as the train roared by and the fireman smilingly 'cocked' his thumb.

Traffic at this box was virtually continuous both during the day and at night, and there would not often be a 'clear block'.

By 10pm I had signalled the *Cheltenham Spa Express*, the *Bristolian*, the *Red Dragon*, the *Capitals United* the *Pembroke Coast Express* and a host of other main-line trains. Up to that time, these names had been but visions crossing the impressionable mind of a young train register boy. Shortly the Paddington-Penzance Travelling Post Office, would roar by to pick up the Swindon mail at speed on the catching mechanism at Stratton Green. Almost 80 percent of Britain's mail at that time was handled by the railways and, in this, one of many travelling GPO trains, mail would be sorted inside these red windowless coaches by hand, at the astonishing rate of 60 letters per minute. Along with the Grimsby and Hull fish trains, the milk trains, the Avonmouth banana trains, the Fishguard 'Sleeper', the Penzance TPO, a succession of parcels trains and the flying 2.15am Paddington-Bristol newspapers, that was the work of the night man. At 9.55pm precisely, the latter arrived for duty. His name was Fred Goodenough and he possessed a car. That was something of a talking point in the fifties; perhaps he had a 'day job'!

It had proved an extremely satisfying day to me, and that night I enjoyed the sleep of an utterly relaxed and totally contented man. Over the next few weeks, there would be time to relax and take stock of my surroundings. Soon I made the acquaintance of several of my workmates. In this occupation, they are often heard but rarely seen in person. I decided to rectify that anomaly and proceeded to visit several of the boxes between Swindon and Wantage on my rest days. In the immediate area, my co-signalmen were Ken Griffiths at Marston West; Bill Reeves at Marston East; Cyril Thomas at Ashbury Crossing; Bill Curtis at Knighton box; and Gordon Groves at Challow.

By now, despite a very short time spent in the region, the long 'Ahhs' and 'Ehhs' were creeping into my everyday speech, but the heavy Lancastrian overtones remained overwhelmingly dominant and were a constant source of amusement to the West Country inhabitants. To Bob Tanner, signal and telegraph linesman, to Jimmy Tichener, signal lampman, to relief signalmen Harold Blewett and Charles Early, it never ceased to cause merriment. On occasions, when Sid Tyler, 'Brush' as he was commonly known, had need to telephone for information he would invariably adopt an excellent north-country accent and for a few seconds have me totally perplexed. Yes, these good people were splendid to work with.

Swindon town, despite an ever-increasing influx of new industries, was, at heart, still a railway town. Its warm-hearted citizens and basic desire to welcome all newcomers, as its very existence for over a century had proved, played a notable part in aiding my family to settle in quickly.

A term used by locals, and taking a little while to become adjusted to, was the statement 'My husband's inside'. This could well be the response when you innocently stated to some neighbour that you worked on the railway. The first reaction was that the person concerned was expressing profound joy at the fact that her husband was serving a jail sentence. When the ambiguity was clarified, it appeared her husband, his father and possibly his grandfather, all worked 'inside' the factory of all factories, the railway works.

All too evident, when admiring the efforts of a Swindonian's attempts at house painting on both the interior and exterior, was the abundance and interminable application of chocolate and cream paint, needless to say the traditional colours of the GWR's coaching stock. It was lavished here, there and everywhere. Indeed when I came to burn off this extravagance from my doors and window frames, the oozing residue wailed out its dying shame to the over-zealous workman who had unofficially removed it from the company's carriage and wagon shops.

Within a few months, my LMS (or 'Load 'em, Move 'em and Smash 'em', as the GWR man would eloquently refer to the Midland) image was fast fading. I was well and truly becoming an accepted Western man. To make friends quickly and enjoy a mutual comradeship, and having regard to my previous experiences when moving to a new town, I have found it prudent to disagree most fervently with the locals who condemn out of hand their own town and all its assets. A response in glowing terms of how wonderful their town really is, and how much more interesting it has proved to you than the town you have come from, can pay a huge dividend. In effect, it was a cowardly way to attain rapid acceptance, but I admit to adopting this practice and over the years it has often been advantageous. In any event, when migrating to a completely different environment it is essential to convince oneself that it is the best place on earth, and soon you will believe it. As stated so often: 'Home is where you make it,' and loss of identity, homesickness and loss of old friends are then made so much easier to bear.

Back in the box at Shrivenham, I was noting that 'Castles' hauling the

Cheltenham, the *Bristolian* and the Pullmans to Bristol and Swansea were a regular feature, whilst the new 'Britannia' Class 7s, or a 'King' were heading the heavier *Red Dragon, Capitals United,* and *Pembroke Coast Express.* In September came news of the locomotive *King Richard III*, No 6015, setting up an 'official' high-speed record of 108.5mph whilst hauling the *Cornish Riviera* at Patney, near Savernake in Wiltshire. It was by no means a national or world record but at least the first time the 'Western' made an official recognition of what their locomotives were capable of achieving in the field of high speed.

Together with that and many other great feats acclaimed by this renowned GWR legendary locomotive, it was fitting that this latest accolade should be coupled with the name of the prestigious *Cornish Riviera.* Of all the illustriously titled trains in Britain, among them the *Royal Scot*, the *Flying Scotsman*, the *Irish Mail*, and the *Brighton Belle*, the *Riviera* can claim everlasting fame. Initially named the *Cornishman* in 1890, it later became known as the *10.30 Limited.* Then it took a more sophisticated image as the *Cornish Riviera Limited* but, finally, in 1935, its status secure and the Great Western flying high in national press circles, it was renamed once more as *THE Cornish Riviera Express.* Three hundred and five miles away from its bustling departure on Paddington's No 1 platform, it ran through the counties of Middlesex, Buckinghamshire, Berkshire, Wiltshire, Somerset and Devon, to the palm-lined shore of Penzance in Cornwall, year in and year out over many a decade. For 23 years it held a world record for the longest start-to-stop run, London-Plymouth, a total of 225 miles. Not until the combined power of the LNER and the LMS took up this enticing challenge in the late 1920s was it lost and rendered irretrievable. First 236 miles, and in succession 268, 299, 393 and finally 401¼ start-to-stop runs. The GWR could hardly shift the town of Penzance any further westwards; it was already virtually at Land's End and on the extreme tip of Cornwall. Thus it was deemed that future advertising was to concentrate on the superior comfort of the prestigious train and the unrivalled scenery that its journey provided along the exquisite coastline of both the Devon and Cornish Rivieras.

The need for powerful and reliable traction on these heavier trains was ever paramount and, of necessity, 'Kings' or the new even more powerful 'Britannias' were now in common use. In particular, the passage through the Severn tunnel called for utmost reliability and speed. Breakdowns in any long tunnel were a constant source of anxiety to any footplateman, especially to those with a train-load of potentially panic-stricken passengers. Locomotives of great dependability were imperative when negotiating this, the longest of Britain's tunnels.

By the mid-fifties, the sight of the huge 'Britannias' and 'Stars' was becoming commonplace. Striving hard to perform and, indeed, achieving a great degree of success, they were on a par with the high standard of their thoroughbred fathers, the Staniers, the Gresleys, the Colletts and the

Bulleids. On Sunday, 20 November of that year, however, a casual glance at *Polar Star* a 'Britannia' class, heading a Treherbert to Paddington special, brought no hint to me of the impending tragedy that was to be witnessed within the next 20mins. Approaching Milton, three miles west of Didcot, and due to engineering works that were in progress, the 12-coach special was signalled from up main to up relief. The distant signal stood at caution in order to check the train and bring its speed down to 30mph at the facing points crossover road.

The scene was set, but the subsequent chain of events were never fully established. It was believed that the driver for some unknown reason, after taking the ATC warning siren, knocked off the vacuum and in so doing failed to brake and, unchecked, took the crossover road at 60mph. The consequences were catastrophic. The 135-ton locomotive keeled over and together with the four leading coaches rent from the main train, plunged down the embankment. Only by a miracle were there not more than eleven people killed and ninety-nine injured.

The resultant wreckage proved a strong challenge to the engineering department and several days were to elapse before lifting gear, powerful enough to lift and re-rail the *Polar Star*, was brought alongside. When the departure of despondent press reporters and photographers had been noted, the time arrived to attach the locomotive to a depot engine and return it to Swindon works for renovation and re-naming. No 70026 would never again carry the name *Polar Star*.

In front of my box where I had need to shunt the two engines for the passage of an express, I saw the terrible scars inflicted on this huge locomotive. It had been the victim of one of those only too easy lapses in the concentration of a driver or signalman. Needless to say, I felt pity for the tragic death and sufferings of those Welsh families from the Rhondda, a little square of Britain that forever is destined to produce great actors, superb singers, astute politicians but, poignantly, a liberal sprinkling of pathos.

Taking a mental survey and reflection on the happenings of the past 12 months, it was hard to comprehend that over that short time I had been employed as a Class 1 signalman, a goods shunter, a station porter, a parcels porter, a Class 4 signalman, and now I had seen a return to the position of Class 3 signalman, a posting I had held on two previous occasions, the first more than ten years past. I hoped that only three consecutive moves would now be necessary to lift me to the ever-elusive Special Class status. Taking into consideration the promotional chances, it appeared that a period of between five and eight years would elapse before I could take a step beyond the Class 1 status I had proudly attained on the LMS. As the year 1956 approached it saw me overflowing with confidence and my sights were now aimed at the 172-lever Swindon West box.

A man in his mid-thirties finds himself lacking in a desire to seek new pasture, even one with such a prolific appetite for changes as myself. Now I felt a new-found security and an urge to settle in my adopted town. Nothing,

I thought, would dislodge me, and the image of Swindon's new power box of the future, a foregone conclusion to any foresighted signalman, would witness my retirement from signalling work in some 25-30 years' time. What crazy visions! Anyone holding such optimistic beliefs certainly had a shock to come!

One of the most irritating things as a signalman was the 'double back' or period where the changeover of shifts took place. An eight-hour break between turns of duty satisfied the company's legal requirements, but it nevertheless produced an unsatisfactory and potentially dangerous situation. After completing a 12hr night-duty shift from 6pm until 6am there came the seven miles journey home, breakfast and a bleary-eyed clamber into bed at a time when all the local children, and your own, were noisily preparing themselves for school. If you were successful in enjoying a full four hours' sleep before rising again, taking a meal and cycling the seven miles once more for a 2pm start, then you considered yourself extremely lucky. It was punishing, and if any mistakes were to be made, then they would surely come to light in the ensuing few hours. In both mind and body the readjustment was slow and a high degree of concentration was called for.

Omitting to forward the 'train entering section' under these circumstances for the 12.55 Paddington, due by at 2.15pm, and narrowly escaping a train delay was commonplace and would be guaranteed to bring me to my senses, and help me to shake off the overwhelming tiredness. Strong coffee appeared to be the antidote on these particular days which arose at three-weekly intervals.

Perhaps it was due to these circumstances that I unwittingly conversed with a fellow signalman on the local telephone ciruit. The 'fellow signalman' turned out to be a woman! On the signalbox cabin-to-cabin lines, not only was there an unofficial line to the signal and telegraph linesman's house, where his wife Stella would often be heard taking messages, but there was, in addition, a connection to the telephone exchange at Swindon Station and this had crossover lines to all railway departments and even to the GPO public system. Female operators were obviously in evidence there and twice on those particular changeover periods I was caught out by the very same young lady, in the process of employing descriptive adjectives of a blatantly colourful nature, and furthermore, the odd 'blue' joke. My moment of true shame came, however, when I was overheard by a young lady to whom I was later introduced. She listened silently whilst I lapsed into vivid oratory, portraying the abandoned scenes I had witnessed in a 'blue' movie shown in a London club. Only her discreet cough at the end of the recital revealed her to be a young lady who chose to listen a lot, and speak a little.

In 1956 I justified my move to the south, and the summer of that year convinced me I was to enjoy a much-improved climate and the statistics taken show that spring as the sunniest since 1922, and the driest since 1896. Apart from the personal satisfaction that I was experiencing, was the added bonus of my family being ensconced happily in their new environment, and feeling a security in the future. In August 1956 an urgent journey was demanded in order to visit relatives in Lancashire, but due to the short notice and inconvenient time of the day, the route via Gloucester or Cheltenham was impractical. A quick scan of the timetable produced an admirable solution. Provided the 4.05pm from Swindon was 'on time' reaching Paddington, and I positioned myself up front, a taxi could be taken post haste to Euston and the 6.00pm *Mancunian* boarded, to see me in Manchester a little after 9pm. This is what I did and the service proved excellent in all respects.

At 5.30pm, as we pulled into Paddington, I made a rapid leap from the leading coach and grabbed the first taxi in the rank and asked for Euston at all speed. No doubt inspired by my obvious haste, and despite the rush-hour traffic, the taxi driver used all his wide knowledge of the short cuts around Marylebone and Euston Road and deposited me at the station with ten minutes to spare. Rushing under the great Doric arch that dominates the forecourt of this London terminus, it struck me as an ironical fact that in 1835 the directors of the London-Birmingham Railway Company had refused the newly incorporated GWR access into this admirably situated station. What a great pity in the long term. Many millions of travellers with need to cross this metropolis over the past one hundred years would not have been faced, as indeed we were in Manchester also, with the enduring frustration of inter-station hassle. Possibly one of the few advantages of state control over that of private monopoly is that a more positive approach can be made to the all-round interests of the travelling public, a feature sadly lacking in the schemes of those early rail entrepreneurs, who were cash orientated and enterprising, but utterly ruthless.

After running virtually the entire length of the *Mancunian* in order to find a third-class carriage among the predominant first-class stock, I found myself close to the engine. Ignoring the frantic whistles for a few seconds, I sneaked a quick glance at the Royal Scot class locomotive, easily recognisable with its customary smoke deflectors which did little to detract the eye from the imposing lines of this now famed engine. These deflectors were a feature of most LMS 'Royal Scot' and 'Princess' class locomotives and I remembered that they had been fitted in 1931, subsequent to an accident enquiry deeming that smoke obscurity had been the prime cause of a driver mistaking the position of a distant signal near to Leighton Buzzard and running into a crossover road at high speed.

We pulled out exactly on time and I settled back. For some unknown reason I was feeling extremely snug and secure in a false sense of affluence. Possibly it stemmed from the abundance of first-class passengers on board this prestigious train. Certainly the gross amount of cash I carried with me at that time warranted no such composure. However, I had rushed away from home under duress and omitted to pack sandwiches, so tonight I would allow myself that little treat that only once before I had enjoyed. That was a meal in the restaurant car. Every day now I signalled through these glamorous trains without a thought of the luxuries provided for the privileged few. Tonight I would do it in style, and I booked second sitting with the attendant.

A good start had been made on the Camden Bank and the 'Scot' had the *Mancunian* rolling at full speed by Watford, and approaching Rugby I was settled in the dining car and speculating as to which of the passing expresses was our sister train, the *Comet*, on its return run to Euston.

This stretch of line, London-Crewe, was the busiest main line in the world and trains were passing each other at a combined speed of 180mph every two or three minutes. The old statement that to obtain the maximum comfort on a rail journey, you must be seated in a Midland coach on a Great Western track, I found now was irrefutable. Immediately following the smooth ride from Swindon to Paddington, the sway now evident on the LMS track was distinctly noticeable, but nevertheless was soon overlooked when taking into account the additional comfort provided by that company, and its predecessor's insistence on superior seating. All too distinct came the extra loud shock wave and consequential sway when being passed in the opposite direction. This, again, was in deep contrast to the effect produced on the Western, and could only be attributed to the closer proximity of the adjoining tracks which had never seen the like of Brunel's wide gauge.

In consequence of the cessation of broad-gauge workings in 1892, the GWR had laid the standardised track throughout its entire system, and the distance between tracks was increased considerably. What is known to railwaymen as the '6ft' became on the Western, almost an '8ft'. A fact I can vouch for in no uncertain terms. To be trapped between two passing trains on the GWR system was a great deal less hair-raising than to be caught in the similar situation on the LMS!

As the second meal-sitting ended, passengers were dispersing to their compartments to collect luggage and we were pulling into Wilmslow, along with Alderley Edge, a smart and affluent Cheshire town and the mecca of Manchester's business 'elite'. It seemed the train all but completely disembarked its cargo of bowler-hatted and brief-case laden passengers at this point, and it was an almost empty *Mancunian* that rolled into London Road Station 20mins later. I sped on foot across the city, knowing full well that the taxi fare saved would buy me a drink on Victoria Station, and from the Rochdale Canal Company's warehouse and at the foot of the station approach and down Cannon Street to Balloon Street, only ten minutes were needed.

It was in the station buffet, whilst waiting the last 'electric' to Bury that I bumped into an old acquaintance and, within seconds, we were into a spate of nostalgic rhetoric. When I last saw him, he was firing Ivatts and Aspinalls at Bacup shed, which was all of five or six years ago. 'Where have you been posted to now?' I asked, and he detailed a graphic story of the closure of Bacup shed, also the L&Y line from Rochdale to Bacup. He had seen the end coming a year before the axe fell and he had resourcefully applied for a transfer to Crewe. Why become redundant, he suggested, with nothing more than seven days' pay to keep a family whilst searching for alternative work in a town whose predominant cotton industry was dying only too quickly. Why not transfer into Cheshire, a county where mellow fields and plump dairy cattle stood in sharp contrast to the ravaged valleys of the industrial Pennine foothills? As a confirmed admirer of the wild and mountainous uplands I could have argued over that subject indefinitely, but the point of issue of course was the necessity of employment and the financial support of a family taking precedence over where and in what type of countryside one searches for solace and recreation. Discarding romantic notions, I was forced to agree with him wholeheartedly.

He had taken his family to Crewe, a town with strong similarities to Swindon, somewhat isolated on a vast agricultural plain, and settled down quickly, after readjusting himself to the markedly contrasting footplate work that he had been accustomed to previously. He held me enthralled whilst relating his experiences of firing on a 'Duchess Pacific' or a Stanier 8F on a Crewe-Euston or a Crewe-Camden Town run. Over the tough Carlisle run it was a far different proposition than firing, say, a Fowler 7F 0-8-0 or an Aspinall 2F 0-6-0 in the north Manchester environs.

Picking up his shovel in Crewe, he was unlikely to release it before Euston loomed on the horizon. But the personal satisfaction he derived from working on the footplate of so many illustrious named 'Pacifics' was more than compensation for a heavy day's work. A typical day's work, he added, could well consist of a changeover with a Glasgow crew on a 'Scotsman', taking that train on to Euston, bringing back the *Comet* or *Mancunian* to Manchester, or the *Red Rose*, the *Shamrock* or *Merseyside* into Liverpool, culminating in a return to Crewe on a southbound express. 'At the end of an eight or ten hour shift like that my wife discreetly refrains from asking me to bring in a bucket of coal', he laughed.

'By the way, did you know they have closed down the Liverpool overhead railway this year?' he asked. I was stunned by this news, as I used to sit up at those windows as a child, gazing wide-eyed from the comfort of those early electric trains across the whole expanse of Merseyside's major port. Visualising those huge berths and transatlantic liners, and the city pulsating with a dynamic enterprise, it was hard to believe that all was now on the wane. The closure of this pioneer of electric overhead railways must surely herald a foretaste of the winds of change. It would be no consolation to the citizens of Liverpool to admit that all ports have their day. Hadn't the cities of Bristol and Plymouth been the major ports of Britain for hundreds of years? Wasn't Cardiff, another of the nation's thriving ports on the verge of becoming a shadow of its former self? With the new age of thought and the overriding necessity of Britain forming a closer unity with Europe, the proximity of the South-Eastern ports would supersede those of the West coast and become the dominant gateway to the continent.

John was visiting relatives in Bacup and, after an all too brief chat, we parted company at Bury. Had we have met earlier in the evening, I have no doubt there would have been numerous and graphic accounts of battling through snow drifts with an Aspinall 0-6-0, or racing non-stop from Rossendale to Manchester with the *Purple Passion* pre-war express parcels train, or struggling with a Midland 'Compound' on Britannia bank. These and a hundred more prolific tales would have been shared over a pint in the 'Lord Nelson'. I left him to thumb a lift to Bacup whilst I did likewise to my destination in Tottington.

Having completed the task that brought me north I returned to Manchester two days later and decided to take the *Pines Express*, 10.20am from London Road Station. The *Pines* was a Bournemouth train and one on which staff travelling on a free pass were not eligible to use. The travelling ticket inspector would have every right to throw me off at Crewe or alternatively charge me full fare for the journey. With that in mind, and should the train be full, I would obviously use my discretion and stand in the corridor and hope for pity.

I had been quite surprised before departing from Manchester to see such a short train for a long distance express of this status. The reason became only too obvious when we pulled into Crewe. An equal number of coaches, comprising the Liverpool portion, were attached to the rear and within ten minutes a far more imposing train was heading south across Staffordshire. At Birmingham, a further two coaches were added and a second locomotive then coupled to the leading engine. All this meant scant notice of the long climb through Bournville to the summit of Lickey bank which precedes the two mile, 1 in 38 drop and provides a 'big dipper' effect to take the train rapidly into the 'eighties' and maintain this momentum across the rolling Worcester plain twixt the Malvern and Cotswold hills.

Cheltenham 'Lansdown' was the *Pines'* third stop and where I alighted to take the Southampton connection, this M&SW line provided an admirable service to Swindon Old Town. There came a 20min wait here and it gave me ample opportunity to take a refreshing cup of tea in the station's small and relaxing buffet. The entire atmosphere here was extremely tranquil after the bustle of big stations and it came as a surprise to note the deceptive efficiency of the M&SW service following departure into the South Cotswolds.

Perhaps the winding climb through the peaceful towns of Andoversford and Cirencester, skirting the Roman village of Chedworth, and viewing endless flocks of sheep grazing the rich fields on this scenic route, contributed to an illusion of slow travel. On the contrary, the timings were excellent and after three stops we crossed the GWR Gloucester line on the approaches to Swindon and a minute later the Bristol line, to roll into Old Town Station at 3.13pm. A little under five hours, including a 25min break at Cheltenham, was all the time the whole journey from Manchester had taken, and it was a time that I doubt could have been bettered by car in pre-motorway days.

This M&SW line from Swindon Old Town was to witness a sudden burst of activity in mid-November when refugees from the 4 November 1956 Hungarian uprising were coming into Britain in substantial numbers. At Chisledon, a village almost midway between Swindon and Marlborough, the disused army camp was hurriedly reopened to accommodate these refugees and special trains became numerous along the Paddington-Swindon main line, where they were later switched to the Old Town route at Rushy Platt M&SW junction to continue along the single line to Chisledon Camp Halt.

CHAPTER 20

The Spectre of the Diesel and Doctor Beeching

Often during my signalling career I was asked, 'Are you not lonely, all alone up there for eight to twelve hours at a time with no one to speak to?' On the contrary, nothing could be further from the truth. Unless I was working a box of very low classification, there was constantly telephone work, a 'boxer' or 'circuit' message to be relayed. There were block code messages to be tapped out between yourself and the signalmen on either side of you which linked you with your workmates, who might be anything from one-quarter to a few miles distant, so you were never conscious of a sense of isolation.

Monotony rarely crept into the daily workings at Shrivenham box. Each year brought its changes and almost every day there would be some form of variation to the set timetable routine, these being sometimes tinged with a degree of excitement. One such occasion came early in the morning of a dark night in January 1957. At 2am an ammunition train passed Knighton box with smoke and flames pouring from a hot axle box and Ashbury box, after receiving the seven bells 'stop and examine', rightly passed the signal on to me, so I was able to put back my signals, reverse the road from down main to down relief and bring the train to a halt at the home signal a few yards from the box.

Ammunition trains had recently become far more frequent in consequence of the Anglo-French attack on Egypt two months previously and they were a none too pleasant reminder of wartime days. No black out tonight, however, hampered the guard and footplatemen, who hurriedly detached the wagon and shunted it on to an empty siding to be dealt with quickly after the train had been recoupled and despatched. Slowly that particular night was unfolding into 'one of those nights' when nothing would go right. I had cycled halfway to work at 9.30pm before realising that I had left my sandwiches behind and I faced a 9hr stretch without food. That fact prompted me to take a hasty burst into Shrivenham village and visit Gages Fish and Chip Shop, and then later suffered the resultant soggy mass of warmed-up chips from the top of the signal box stove, taken in two helpings, one at midnight and the next at 3am.

When traffic was moving smoothly and reasonably to time a signalman could plan his visits to the toilet to appease the calls of nature, with a reasonable degree of success, but should traffic be out of course and erratic, as on this particular night, the results could play havoc with both one's patience and anatomy. I was thrown into a state of total mental confusion, something which all signalmen have experienced, running up the steps from an outside toilet, one hand grasping a pair of drooping trousers and rushing into the box to answer an impatiently ringing block instrument, or endeavouring to pull over a particularly heavy lever and eventually collapsing in an undignified manner, sprawled across the floor with his trousers dropped to the ankles. It was so often a case of try, try, try again. Endeavouring to roll a cigarette, it could be guaranteed that as the tobacco was halfway spread across the paper, a quick move would be necessary to answer a block instrument and the tobacco would disappear through the openings in the frame.

By 5am, it had begun to snow heavily and, to finish off a thoroughly miserable night, on my way home I found myself having to turn back on a snow-blocked road from the station and having to catch the first down 'stopper' to Swindon, a smoky train crowded as usual with railway-works employees, which was an experience I loathed compared with the open road and my own two-wheeled transport. After such a night session, every night worker will be familiar with the pleasurable ending of clambering into the warm position vacated by your partner as you roll her out of bed at breakfast-time.

Late turn usually followed the night shift and, though inconvenient to staff who were avid cinema-goers or keen socialisers, the hours did not present any undue worry to me. Indeed, a whole morning's freedom gave me time to devote more attention to odd jobs around the house, and the signalbox workings in the busy early evening period held far more interest than the corresponding early morning peak when both mind and body were in a disorientated state due to the early rise at 4.30am.

About this time, in the late 1950s, unusually long test trains were taking to the rails. The main line from Swindon to Reading offered an admirable testing area and trains of 20-25 coaches, including a Dynamometer car, were a common sight, headed by the British Railways 9F 2-10-0s, which on occasions passed at 80-90mph, creating an impressive sight. As these gigantic locomotives with their mammoth loads roared by, the crew on 'The Fly', our local goods train and daily shunter, would look up from their menial tasks with more than a little jealousy at their 'top link' colleagues.

'Where's Chapel-en-le-Frith?' I was greeted with when answering a telephone call from Didcot one February evening that year. 'Oh, I know it well,' I replied. 'I've cycled every inch of those roads and youth-hostelled all over Derbyshire. It's between Buxton and Manchester. Why?' 'Is it on the Midland?' 'Yes, well it was the London & North Western, then London Midland Scottish, but the way they're messing about it could well be Midland or even Eastern region; their trains run into Manchester,' I replied warily. 'Well, there's been a smash there today and a Midland driver at Oxford says several have been killed.'

In the course of time, I discovered this particular accident had come about in most unusual circumstances and had been caused by an extremely rare occurrence. The resultant facts probably procured a wide amount of interest amongst the railway fraternity, but little reached the national press as no passenger trains had been involved in the smash.

Derbyshire, or in particular, the predominating mass of the Peak District provided an abundance of extremely undulating railways. More than any other county at that time, the routes within its boundaries proffered delights of exquisite charm and rugged beauty, as any traveller on the Manchester-St Pancras journey would readily confirm. Cleaving through Millers Dale and Monsal Dale, what better tribute to the railway builders of the gallant 'Midland'. Northwards from Buxton, a spa town 1,000ft above sea level the old L&NW line climbs a further 100ft before commencing its long descent, crossing the Midland line at one point many feet below in the Doveholes tunnel, then down rapidly through Chapel-en-le-Frith, south to the Combs Reservoir.

Things went drastically wrong for driver John Axon on this occasion. His monstrous 2-8-0 class 8F suffered a fractured steampipe which rendered the steam brake totally inoperative and, at the same time, completely enveloped the cab in scalding steam. Behind him was a full train of loose-linked, non-vacuum-braked wagons and this load was impossible to hold. His firemen jumped from the rapidly accelerating locomotive and speedily attempted to pin down wagon brakes but it was a thoroughly hopeless and impossible situation. The train was doomed. With the gallant driver mercilessly thrown about on the heaving footplate and still making every possible attempt to control his runaway train, it ploughed violently into the rear of another freight train awaiting signals in Chapel-en-le-Frith Station. In the resulting devastation the signalbox was completely wrecked and buried amongst debris piled to a height of almost 30ft.

I never did ascertain what injuries the signalman suffered, but read in a subsequent publication that the guard of the stationary train had been killed, and that the driver of the runaway train had been posthumously awarded the George Cross, following his making an extremely brave but unfortunately futile attempt to avert disaster.

This was the year, too, in which we were to lose our well respected, and thoroughly likeable supervisor, Inspector Cotterill. He was promoted to Chief Inspector at Bristol and his replacement to the Swindon district was Inspector Millsom. Along with Mr Lockett, the assistant, he soon became popular and was respected by all.

Rarely does a situation arise where friction between a signalman and a departmental Inspector erupts into harsh words coupled with a contemptuous order to vacate the box. However, even a placid person like myself could be roused when under provocation, and Inspector Conduit of the Permanent Way department was just the man to incite such an outburst. In reality, he was a likeable person, but volatile, and despite a 'steaming row' we were to remain the best of friends. The heated argument arose when he demanded in no uncertain terms that a 'ballast train', returning to Swindon with his workmen, should take priority over the traffic of higher classification to which I had chosen to give preference. Like most signalmen, I took an instant dislike to anyone from another department telling me how to operate my box.

Situations of this nature often arose. Sometimes single line workings were put into operation on a Sunday whilst engineering works took place and, following an exhausting 10-12hr period of re-laying, men returned to their coaches on the ballast train and were forced to wait frustratingly for a seemingly endless time awaiting a 'margin' between more important trains. The build-up of higher classification traffic could well have become a serious problem and the consequential clearing of this backlog took preference, whilst the patience of these very tired men was sorely tried. These were the occasions when the Permanent Way Inspector burst into the box and demanded his train must follow the next express. After a colourful and highly charged exchange I ordered him out of the box, and that was a demand he had no alternative but to reluctantly comply with at all speed. I doubt he would receive extra pay for the long delay, but at least his men had no need to worry unduly; they were receiving double-time or at least time-and-a-half for their spell of Sunday work.

Overlooking the obvious adversities and irritations that accompany almost any job there were the perks to consider, and to a railman, prior to the advent of the workingman's car, privilege tickets, and the annual one or two free passes, were a congenial bonus. In particular, to the likes of myself, an inveterate traveller, they were indispensable.

The company, or rather the 'Board', 'Commission' or 'Authority', as it had now become known, was, thankfully, sympathetic to an application I made requesting concessions to travel to Sutton on the Southern Region where my eldest son was confined in hospital. Throughout the period he remained there, a weekly free pass was issued to enable my wife, or the two of us, to visit him, and considering the tedious journey involved this additional concession was deeply appreciated.

The 'privilege' arrangements offering a half-price fare opened up a whole new world to me, especially on the realisation of how speedily and economically I could reach London and its many attractions. Irresistably enticing were the concert halls and two opera houses, so I placed myself on their mailing lists to obtain advance details of forthcoming performances and an opportunity to take advantage of any reduced price early booking rates. To fully appreciate these excellent opportunities, it was necessary after finishing duty at 2pm to catch an afternoon 'fast' to Paddington and then catch the Underground. Initially, I would browse around Soho, followed by a very pleasant two hours in the opera house or concert hall, then I'd go for a glass of beer and an inexpensive supper in Edgware Road, before finally taking the 11.55pm back to Swindon. Cycling home from the station attired in a dinner jacket and bow tie must have raised many a passing eyebrow, and I'd get little sleep before rising for the early shift, but all in all it was extremely worthwhile.

In addition holiday passes were a great financial boost, enabling the whole family to travel free, albeit sometimes with frustrating restrictions. In 1955 we had taken advantage of the Western Region's Channel Islands' service, and spent a wonderful fortnight in Jersey. This year (1957) we decided to hire a caravan in Folkestone and were rewarded with our first journey ever on a Southern main-line train.

I was by no means impressed. My personal opinion, perhaps a little biased, was that the Southern, along with the LNER, had possessed one or two 'crack' trains; in the case of the Southern, the *Brighton Belle* and the *Golden Arrow* but, in general, their trains were rickety and unclean. They were a detrimental and shocking advertisement to continental travellers who were now taking an interest in touring Britain and would be forced to endure this antiquated and Dickensian journey from Folkestone and Dover up to the metropolis. In passing it would be fair comment to recall that the south London suburban electric system operated by the Southern was second to none, and this fact would, I assume, be the reason for the underground system never having spread its tentacles far south of the Thames.

The southern approaches to London encompassed some of the busiest and most densely utilised tracks in the world. The Southern's predominantly electrically operated signalling system, which incorporated most signals and many signalboxes in the close confines of the city, was particularly efficient. It was sad, however, and most unfortunate that along with the LMS and LNER, no priority was ever awarded to the installation of an ATC warning system. On the evening of 4 December 1957 a high price was to be paid yet again for its omission. Thick drifting fog had set the scene for a situation fraught with danger. On this occasion a Cannon Street-Ramsgate Express, headed by a 'Battle of Britain' Pacific over-ran signals and collided violently with the rear of a Charing Cross-Hayes electric commuter train awaiting signals at Park Bridge Junction, causing the loss of 90 lives and over 100 seriously injured. The 350-ton bridge carrying the Lewisham Loop line above collapsed onto the wrecked trains and only by luck, and the vigilance shown by the driver of a second commuter train on that particular line, was further tragedy averted. His train was halted only yards from the devastation and further havoc was, thankfully, prevented.

St John's signalbox, close to this scene of disaster and in the heart of the commuter belt, dealt with one train in every 60 seconds, an average of 1,000 trains in 24hrs. This statistic emphasises the deep concentration required to be exercised by signalmen controlling traffic in signalboxes of this standing. The tragic accident on this occasion had not been caused by a signalling mistake, but by a combination of circumstances on the narrow footplate of these specially adapted locomotives, running on a curve with signals awkwardly positioned.

Far from the concentrative nature of work in those densely populated zones, here in the spaciousness of the Vale of the White Horse, long distance trains had left the hustle and bustle of the city and its termini.

Work in a box of Shrivenham's classification where I moved on to, was indeed in marked contrast. It was the alternative to concentrated scrutiny of electrically operated diagrams. Observing their constantly flashing red lights, signifying the positions of trains as they broke, or reactivated the circuit, was a far more relaxed practice than visual sightings from the orthodox signalbox. Never could a man seated in a brick-enclosed 'panel' box have witnessed the splendour of the famous *City of Truro* locomotive passing his box following its release from York Museum, to return to its place of birth in Swindon. On a recent Sunday, this Churchward 4-4-0 had, despite all reservations, run 'light' from York without a hitch, and what a sight it presented, pounding by the box at 60mph, its huge crank a mere blur as it thrust the massive driving wheels and gave the illusion that it would sweep away the platform edge forever. This was the first locomotive in the world to tip the magical 100mph and soon it would be heading rolling stock filled with a new generation of rail enthusiasts.

A not so welcome sight was to follow early in 1958, when I signalled another locomotive through from the north. This time it was from Glasgow and fresh from the North British Locomotive works. Its passage was to herald the end of steam in Swindon, and tragically begin the decline of this prestigious works, which eventually closed in 1986. As Daniel Gooch had taken delivery of Stephenson's *North Star* from far northern lands some 120 years before, so Swindon's locomotive engineers would now receive an experimental engine from far away. This time with ominous forebodings.

The locomotive which rumbled by my box was No D600 *Active*, an ugly looking diesel-powered locomotive. Black, grimy, unattractive and distinctly unimpressive, it took a longer time to clear my section than the immaculate and powerful *City of Truro* had needed on its journey from a museum!

The diesel was a sign of things to come! Within days, tests were being held along this section of track and, subsequent to a further delivery, Swindon works rapidly had their own version on the production line. D800 was the first to be manufactured and awarded the title *Sir Brian Robertson* later that year.

Sir Brian, the Railway Executive Chairman, resided near Kemble, a small Cotswold town 18 miles north-west of Swindon on the Gloucester spur. With a hint of inborn military precision, he invariably used the late afternoon Paddington-Cheltenham for return home, this train having a Kemble stop, and with regularity we received the 'tip' whenever he was on board. The information was 'leaked' no doubt from his office, to ensure that all and sundry would be certain to keep a clear passage for this particular train. Most of us at that time hoped that one of the new D800 diesels would be up front and conveniently break down somewhere along the line. Such was the contempt in which these locomotives were held in the vicinity of Swindon in 1958.

Despite the Russian 'Sputnik' circling the earth and heralding a new space age, no Great Western man was yet in the mood to sacrifice 'Kings',

'Castles', or even the Crewe-inspired 'BR Pacifics' for Diesels. As yet, the wind of change was but a rippling breeze. Almost as a token of defiance for steam during the summer of 1958 under relatively good conditions, with a steady west wind and the sun to the rear, the up *Bristolian* was running like a demon possessed, as I had never seen it run before. On this occasion we received the 'wire' from Badminton that the *Bristolian* was up in the 90s and running almost a minute ahead of time. This information was immediately forwarded on to Didcot Junction, a further 20 miles ahead, as we were only too aware that a train travelling at this speed, one minute ahead of time, could so easily be penalised by a distant check and suffer an indignant late arrival. Through Swindon it roared as the minute hand on the huge clock which adorned the wall of East box barely tipped 5.05, 35mins from Bristol Temple Meads. Swindon West's booking lad graphically explained how it was 'tonning it' and, on receiving the 'on line' from Marston East box, I made a subconscious second glance at the signal repeater indicators to confirm all 'boards' were showing a clear aspect. Normally the 'train entering signal section' is forwarded to the box in advance as the train passes, but in a case like this I sent it several seconds beforehand in order to dash to the open window. Never in my whole lifetime, have I witnessed a more vivid illustration of pure streamlined speed coupled with the almost complete absence of locomotive sound. Piston rods and driving shafts were a complete blur and it was impossible to distinguish the name plate. Without doubt its speed was in the region of 100mph and this was on an all but level gradient. Later in the evening we were informed that the locomotive was the *Drysllwyn Castle* and that our estimates of 100mph from Shrivenham to Didcot were not far from correct.

Why this one particular passage of the *Bristolian* should have made such an impact on my mind I cannot say; I had signalled the train through a little short of a hundred times by then, along with the *Dragon*, the *Pullmans*, the *Capitals*, *Merchant Venturer*, *Pembroke* and *Cheltenham Spa Express*. Often the only time one's attention resulted in a second glance was when the gleam of the USA bell on the *King George V*, or the lines of a 'foreign' locomotive heading a train, caught your eye.

After the 100mph run came the slashing of the *Bristolian's* timings by a full five minutes. From now on it was scheduled at 100mins exactly for the 119 miles and in early 1959, with a defiant snub to the diesels and headed once more by the *Drysllwyn Castle*, the run was accomplished in just under 94mins. It was a final act of defiant pride before the curtain finally came down on steam.

Never in my railway career had the desire to become a 'relief' signalman held any particular sway. I had been happy to move among some 14 different boxes already, but the vision of not being aware today of where I would possibly be working tomorrow, or even the next week, had never offered any great appeal to me. However, a move now was becoming essential, and with railway modernisation high on the government's agenda, the manifestations were multitudinous, casting visions of a serious reduction in the amount of signalboxes, as the introduction of larger power-operated control points at strategic junctions, and automatic train control installed on the major routes, became reality. It seemed prudent to consider rapid promotion in order to combat the likelihood of potential redundancy.

The ensuing vacancy list displayed a post of 'Class 2 relief signalman' at Swindon Junction. I felt I had no alternative and my application was forwarded with a minimum amount of contemplation. The position could, I reasoned, secure me my future in any new power box that would surely appear within the next decade. The application was successful and, after a happy three-year posting at Shrivenham box, surpassing by a month or two my longest stay in one box, it was time to be on the move once more. My sad goodbyes were tempered by the thought that at least it would not be a permanent dismissal as these boxes, over a large radius of Swindon, were worked periodically by the relief staff from Swindon.

Riding home after completion of my final late shift, and a little later than usual, the down *Travelling Post Office* overtook me at speed, close to Stratton Green Bridge. So many times I had signalled this train along on the night shift, but now, passing me at rail level and travelling at some 70mph to snatch up the mail from the catching post, the train projected a much greater impression. The lone GPO man stood back to see the operation went smoothly, then as the train's tail-light faded quickly into the night mist, he returned to his empty mail-van to return to his depot. Within that unlit and grossly underpublicised train, the street lights barely illuminating the red Royal-Mail-emblazoned coaches, an incredible operation was taking place. The entire train was virtually a complete GPO sorting office on wheels. Mail for Exeter, Plymouth and the south-west of England was speedily being sorted, franked, bagged and stacked for distribution and the whole operation was exceedingly well organised.

Scores of these mail trains rolled throughout Britain through the night all over our network, and it was not surprising that the railways and postal services had for decades maintained an extremely close liaison, and it was at night-time that this spirit of teamwork was at its closest.

On the next day when I reported for my first duty as a relief man, Inspector Millsom informed me, 'First I want you to learn Highworth Junction and Goods Yard boxes, as that's where you will take your quota of Sunday duty, and next Sunday you are booked to work the Goods yard box.' It was quite a fiery start and I felt in at the deep end, as I had not worked a Class 1 box since leaving Burnley four years previously and some deep concentration would be necessary over the next few days. Sunday duty with its relatively easy workings was my good luck though the situation that faced me was not, because I would have to learn the frame and workings during the busy weekdays and no signalman, particularly in a box of this nature enjoys the company of a trainee. Nevertheless, that was the price to be paid and I learned the workings of the Goods Yard box the first week, and Highworth Junction the second.

In the course of the following three months, interposed by periods of relief work, it was necessary for me to learn, in addition, Swindon Loco box, Rodbourne Lane, Rushy Platt, Marston East and West, Swindon Town 'A' and 'B' boxes, Hay Lane, Wootton Bassett East and West, and have a knowledgeable outline of the workings of Swindon East and West boxes in order to act as a trainbooker or pilotman if the necessity arose. Along with Shrivenham there was a grand total of 13 boxes which I could be called upon to work at short notice. This concentrated period of instruction and training was intensely demanding, but by January 1959 I had settled down to the new routine. In retrospect, settling down could be a misleading phrase. The nature of my work gave profound satisfaction, but the undercurrent of dissatisfaction with working conditions at that time was festering, and the over-optimistic dreams I harboured six months ago were melting rapidly.

If 1840 witnessed the birth of railway mania, then 1959 likewise saw the birth of road mania, the threat of which caused much unease among my colleagues and myself, as we considered what effect it would have on railways. Personally I had never visualised driving, let alone possessing a car. Indeed, it was on the day of my wedding that I first actually sat inside a car! Very little time elapsed before I was actually taking delivery of my own vehicle, a Ford light goods van, although the cash required for the deposit had not come from my meagre wage. The £100 needed was contributed by my wife, who at that time was employed by a high technology company researching transistorised radio and computerisation and as she was also employed on a casual basis at the GPO over the Christmas period, her total wage amounted to a considerably higher figure than that of a railway signalman.

The railway fraternity soon learned that substantially higher wages were now earned by unskilled labour in the new pressed-steel factory producing car bodies for the Morris Motor Company. To achieve a gross income of £12 a week, a signalman would need to work, in addition to his standard 42hrs, a 12hr Sunday and several hours of overtime, whereas in this new factory, it was possible to take home £15-£20 for a 40hr week, and have immunity from either responsibility or unsociable hours.

Burrowing deep into this festering mass of disillusionment was the added fuel of doubt and fear, fed by stories of the impending closure of many lines. It was said that under newly envisaged government policy, motorways may well take priority over railways in the building of a new Britain, and soon the programme of electrification of trunk lines recently embarked upon was suspended. Finally, there rose the eternal question: when, if ever, would a pension scheme be forthcoming? Workers in all other nationalised industries held this concession, why not us? In those early months of 1959 I recall no less than six local signalmen, all possessing nothing other than railway operating experience, leaving the service voluntarily to seek new careers. Very few men considered it prudent to await possible redundancy. There were no government handouts to unfortunate employees who faithfully chose to work on and chance their destiny. For many years my eyes had remained closed to the temptation of better pay and conditions, and to abandon the magic lure of the ironroad had been unthinkable. But now the ever inescapable magnet that had gripped my passion for untold years was slowly releasing its hold.

Foremost in my mind was the revitalising and ultimate prosperity of our railways, so savagely bankrupted by war and subjected to the continual apathy expressed by politicians who now held the power to smash such a vitally important national asset. Who was I to point out to them the statistical fact that a double-track railway can carry three-and-a-half times as much traffic as a 6-lane motorway on a third of the land space, or to forecast that within 25 years the government would be awarding grants to firms to re-open sidings alongside the main lines that were now about to be erased from the map.

By Spring, the writing was clearly on the wall for a few of the lines I knew so well, namely the Hawes branch on the Midland Pennine route to Scotland, and the L&NW trail-blazer across the Gwent and Glamorgan uplands which were all on the verge of closure, perhaps for ever. This was but the start. Many more would follow and at that time no railwayman had even dreamed that a certain Doctor Beeching would, within a few years, be wielding the bloodiest hatchet that any transport system the whole world over had ever seen.

Swindon's population, now swelling at a pace to equal its expansion in the early years and augmented by the intake of London's overspill, was no longer solely reliant on the railway works as it was at the turn of the century. In 1851, 92 percent of the town's employable inhabitants were 'inside'; now, 100 years on, it was reduced to 50 percent, and a new age was dawning. Diligently turning these various facts over in my mind, I was forced to the conclusion that within 10 years time I would be either working in a panel operated control box in the Swindon of the future or, if the promotional scale deemed me unlucky, I could be redundant and searching for alternative work at the age of 50. The latter did not appeal to me in the least. It would be far better to start a new life at the tender age of 40; but doing what? As I possessed no trade or higher education qualifications it would have been a waste of time looking for work. By nature I was of an independent disposition and for most of my working life had sought to avoid any cloak of subordination. Text books had taught me bookkeeping and the rudiments of business management; I possessed a goods vehicle and driving licence and, most of all, the fascination of the unknown was an exciting challenge. That settled it, I decided. I would creep into the road transport business; joining the opposition, so to speak. 'If you can't beat them, join them' was the old adage! Indeed, the Great Western Railway did just that in the early 1900s. Ironically, that company spawned the very first timetable-operated BUS service in Britain, from Helston to The Lizard in Cornwall.

Having considered the pros and cons, I wrote out my notice of termination and on the following Monday morning dropped it into Inspector Millsom's office on the way to work. At 9.10am both Mr Millsom and his deputy, Mr Lockett, were in the box making a further effort to stem the flow of dissidents. Whilst Mr Millsom took a realistic view of the matter when he realised his pleas to withdraw my notice were doomed to rejection, Mr Lockett, on the other hand, forecast that within a very short time I would be back. Never, ever was that to happen. I knew in my heart this was the very end. The railways that my father had known all his life, and those of which I had idolised for these past 40 years, were doomed. Seven hours later, with one hell of a lump in my throat, I sadly descended the steps of the Loco Yard box, the last of some 24 signalboxes I had worked, and crossed the track, never to return as a signalman.

Easy Guide to Garden Birds
of Britain and Ireland

by Marie Louise Heffernan

Dedicated to my wonderful daughter Elva who is always asking me to go birdwatching.

Front cover: Male bullfinch (note: bright red front and black cap extending over eyes)

Inside front cover: Female bullfinch

Inside back cover: Mistle thrush

Easy Guide to Garden Birds of Britain and Ireland

Copyright © 2012 by Marie Louise Heffernan (All rights reserved)

Published by
Aster Publications
Co. Galway, Ireland

First printed in Ireland 2012
ISBN: 978-0-9574965-0-7

Photos provided by Shutterstock.com
Back cover photo: Aster by Aoife Herriott Photography
Book design by Cuán Mara Design

The birds in this book are the most commonly found garden birds in Britain and Ireland. These are the birds that you will see at your bird feeder, in your garden, in parks and hedgerows.

Usually males are more brightly coloured than the females. For example, the male and female robin look the same but the male and female chaffinch look different. In this book male and female are shown if they are different and the female is shown in a small inset picture.

Woodpigeon

Looks: Large plump bird with small head and white neck patch. Brownish-pink breast with the rest of body a blue-grey colour. Bill is short and orange.

Eats: Plants, mainly seeds and leaves.

Similar bird: The common (Feral) pigeon is similar but smaller, two black stripes on the wings and without a white neck patch.

Collared Dove

Looks: Pale coloured beige dove with thin
         black collar at neck and short
         dark bill.

Eats: Plants, mainly seeds and leaves.

Wren

Looks: Tiny brown bird with sticky-up tail and thin bill.

Eats: Insects in hedges and walls.

Dunnock

Looks: Head and breast mainly grey. The
         body is grey-brown below and the
         wings are brown with dark
         streaks. Thin dark bill.

Eats: Mainly insects on the ground.

Robin

Looks: Small roundish body. Plain brown back with orange face and breast. Large dark eye and thin bill.

Eats: Mainly insects.

Blackbird

Looks: Black with orange bill and orange
        ring around its eye.
        Females are dull brown with
        brown bill.

Eats: Berries, seeds, insects and worms.

Song Thrush

Looks: Roundish body with brown back. Sides of the face and body pale yellowish brown in colour. Front of its body spotted with arrow-shaped spots clearing to a lower white belly.

Eats: Berries, worms and snails.

Similar bird: Mistle Thrush is greyer with round-shaped spots on front including lower belly.

Blackcap

Looks: Small bird overall greyish in colour
         with black cap on head. Females
         have a brown cap. Thin bill.

Eats: Mainly insects.

Great Tit

Looks: Black head with white cheeks.
Yellow belly divided by a black
stripe. Back green.

Eats: Mainly insects in trees but also
seeds.

Blue Tit

Looks: Small bird with blue head and
white face with dark stripe
through the eyes. Yellow belly
with dark patch at the centre.
Short dark bill.

Eats: Mainly insects but also seeds.

Coal Tit

Looks: Head is black with white stripe at
back. Short tail. Dull grey with
creamy warm colours below.
Thin short bill.

Eats: Insects.

Long-tailed Tit

Looks: Small bird with a long tail — tail
         longer than it's body. White head
         with black stripe over the eye.
         Rosy-pink underneath and on
         back. Short stumpy bill.

Eats: Mainly insects but also seeds.

Magpie

Looks: Black and white large crow with a thick black bill and long tail.

Eats: Grain, fruit, eggs, small birds and other animals.

Rook

Looks: Large black crow with thick long
grey bill and black eyes.

Eats: Mainly insects and earthworms.

Jackdaw

Looks: Smallest of the black crows, grey at the nape of the neck. Black thick short bill and light blue eyes.

Eats: Many different things including insects, slugs, worms and eggs.

Starling

Looks: Black with pale tips to edges of
feathers. Overall spotty looking.
Narrow yellow bill.

Eats: Insects mainly.

House Sparrow

Looks: Small grey bird with brown dark-streaked back. Male has a chestnut-brown head with a grey crown and a black bib beneath its bill. The female is plainer with grey beige head and front; duller but similar to male.
Cone-shaped bill.

Eats: Mainly seeds.

Similar bird: The tree sparrow's head is all chestnut with white collar around neck.

Chaffinch

Looks: Grey square-shaped head. Males have orange-brown face and entire front of body. Females grey brown. Distinctive white patches on wings are visible in both males and females.

Eats: Mainly seeds on the ground.

Greenfinch

Looks: Males are bright green with yellow flash on wings. Females are similar but duller. Both have dark evil-looking eyes with a thick pale bill.

Eats: Mainly seeds.

Goldfinch

Looks: Red face, light brown back with yellow flash on wings. Long thick Pale bill.

Eats: Seeds.

Siskin

Looks: Small bright yellow and black striped bird with small cone shaped bill. The male has a dark crown. Females are duller and browner without the black crown.

Eats: Small seeds.

Redpoll

Looks: Small stripy bird. Dark-streaked back and pale underneath. Red forehead and breast. Black at base of a pale cone shaped bill. Female similar but without red breast.

Eats: Mainly seeds and some insects.

Similar birds: Linnet does not have black around bill.

Coming soon:

Easy Guide to Shore Birds of Britain and Ireland

Easy Guide to Wetland Birds of Britain and Ireland

Acknowledgements:

Thanks to Isabelle, Peter, Caroline and Jackie for their help.